Universal Design for Learning:

Teaching to **ALL** College Students

Universal Design for Learning:

Teaching to ALL College Students

Editors: Julie A. Zaloudek, Renee Chandler,
Kitrina Carlson and Renee Howarton

Copyright © 2018 by Nakatani Teaching and Learning Center

All rights reserved. No part of this publication may be reproduced, distributed, or transmitted in any form or by any means, including photocopying, recording, digital scanning, or other electronic or mechanical methods, without the prior written permission of the publisher, except in the case of brief quotations embodied in critical reviews and certain other noncommercial uses permitted by copyright law. For permission requests, please address

Nakatani Teaching and Learning Center
Robert S. Swanson Library and Learning Center
315 10th Avenue East
University of Wisconsin-Stout
Menomonie, WI 54751

Published 2018 by Nakatani Teaching and Learning Center
Printed in the United States of America

Interior design by Thomson Shore, Inc.
Cover design by Thomson Shore, Inc.

21 20 19 18   1 2 3 4

ISBN 978-1-943290-63-5
Library of Congress Control Number: 2018940318

Table of Contents

Foreword   xi
Kitrina Carlson, Ph.D. and Renee Howarton, Ph.D.

Acknowledgments   xvii

Section 1: Project Foundation

1. Understanding Universal Design for Learning   1
   *Kitrina Carlson, Ph.D., Julie A. Zaloudek,
   Ph.D. and Renee Howarton, Ph.D.*

2. Book Foundation: UDL and Conceptual Struggles   19
   *Kitrina Carlson, Ph.D., Renee Chandler, Ed.D., Julie
   A. Zaloudek, Ph.D., and Renee Howarton, Ph.D.*

3. Universal Design for Learning—Project Origins   41
   Renee D. Howarton, Ph.D.

Section 2: Classroom Application, Assessment & Outcomes

4. No Accommodations Needed: 73
   Julie A. Zaloudek, Ph.D.

5. Rethinking Environmental Education   109
   Kitrina Carlson, Ph.D.

6. Improving Access through Choice   131
   Debbie Stanislawski, Ph.D.

7. One Size Does Not Fit All   151
   Renee Chandler, Ed.D.

8. Universal Design for Learning in Group Projects   173
   Diane Olson, Ph.D.

9. Self-Reliance   201
   Monika Herrmann, Architect

10. Providing Academic Choices   215
    Glendali Rodriguez, Architect NCARB

11. Final Thoughts   239
    Renee Chandler, Ed.D.

    Index   245

Foreword

Kitrina Carlson, Ph.D.
and Renee Howarton, Ph.D.

Who are our students and how can we design and deliver an education that supports their success? For nearly two decades Beloit College (McBride, Nief, & Westerberg, n.d.) has published the popular *Mindset List* to introduce faculty to the "cultural touchstones and experiences" that have shaped that year's incoming freshman class. The list is shared broadly, including in hundreds of print publications and through millions of views online, and it is often forwarded to faculty by administrators, as it is considered a humorous but useful tool in defining and understanding the incoming cohort of college students. But how well does a list developed by private school faculty who were themselves educated at private schools address the "experiences that have shaped the worldview" of our students? Only 16% of students attend private non-profit universities and align with the expected norms of a typical college student demographic (Snyder, & Dillow, 2015). In fact, 38% of college students in the U.S. attend public 2-year institutions and are over age 29 (Snyder, & Dillow, 2015). There is no typical college student, and perpetuating the myth of the typical college student perhaps undermines the needs and visibility of actual college students. Our students may face serious challenges that affect their ability to learn in a "typical" classroom.

For example, 14% of American community college students reported being homeless and student hunger due to food insecurity is a growing problem on campuses across the country (Goldrick-Rab, Richardson, & Hernandez, 2017). We also serve students who may have significant unmet mental health needs, including 36.7% of college students who indicated they were at some point during the year "so depressed it was difficult to function" according to the American College Health Association (2016, p. 14). In addition to having their basic needs for housing, food and health met, students may face a broad array of circumstances and challenges that are too often not considered in the curricular design of the "typical" classroom. Most troubling of all, these "non-typical" students, who make up a majority of all learners, are also the least likely to graduate (Snyder, & Dillow, 2015; Freedman, 2013).

In an effort to better understand how learning occurs for all students, especially diverse, non-traditional students, research into how learning takes place in the human brain, along with how learning can be nurtured among diverse student populations, has grown significantly in recent years (Ambrose, Bridges, DiPietro, Lovett, & Norman, 2010; Steele, 2010). This has led to scientific exploration into neuroscience and brain development as well as into how the threat of stereotype affects learning. Advanced and invaluable insights have resulted from these areas of study.

> One of the clearest and most important revelations stemming from brain research is that there is no such thing as a 'regular student'.... Science shows that individual qualities or abilities are not static and fixed; rather they are continually shifting and they exist in relationship to the environment. The interaction between the individual and the environment is a dynamic and complex balancing act. In short, there is tremendous variability among individuals in how they perceive and interact with any environment, including the classroom. Variability and difference, therefore, constitute the norm from student to student—even among those who seem to share similar characteristics, such as culture, age, race, or level of success. (Hall, Meyer & Rose, 2012)

Many educators desiring to address this *variability and difference* have diligently worked to create learning environments that are supportive, inclusive and teach to the broadest array of learners. To achieve this goal, some instructors have adopted and creatively applied Universal Design for Learning (UDL) because its principles effectively embrace this variance, while providing a structure that consistently supports diverse student learning.

In this book, the authors compile a collection of personal reflections, applied classroom teaching strategies, scholarly efforts, and musings about lessons learned from a cross-disciplinary Universal Design for Learning project that they actively participated in from 2011 to 2013. In the first chapter, the editors (Carlson, Zaloudek and Howarton) summarize the history of higher education, noting that its origins were based on exclusion and elitism, affecting both those who could and could not access learning. What this disparity in education looks like in recent times is then linked to an explanation of Universal Design, and specifically Universal Design for Learning. This is followed by public policy information describing the difficult journey that teachers, families and legislators have undertaken to realize equitable educational access for children with disabilities, and what led to the eventual adoption of principles associated with Universal Design, and ultimately Universal Design for Learning. Chapter two documents the personal struggle that project participants underwent as they defined for themselves the difference between UDL and "good teaching," the grounding of content in the ADDIE Model and Scholarship of Teaching and Learning framework, and finally, examples of research that focus on student learning outcomes related to UDL-based instructional training. In the next chapter, an author describes how the project was structured, participant expectations, outcomes from an overarching study, and campus impact associated with the experience.

Chapters four through ten showcase Universal Design for Learning-based classroom projects that were conducted by faculty at University of Wisconsin-Stout. Each one contains a personalized introductory story, an honest analysis of the learning needs of their students and what they did to address those needs, the specifics of the projects they designed, developed and implemented, and their reflections on lessons learned from their efforts. The final chapter provides "pearls of wisdom" for those seeking to infuse universal design principles into their own courses, and it acknowledges that although UDL is not "universally" incorporated into higher education, its application in the college classroom has grown substantially. With future student populations becoming more diverse, the need to design learning environments that are UDL compliant is predicted to expand, thus encouraging teachers to become students of Universal Design for Learning principles and practices.

References

Ambrose, S. W., Bridges, M. W., DiPietro, M., Lovett, M. C., & Norman, M.K. (2010). *How learning works: Seven research-based principles for smart teaching.* New York: Wiley.

American College Health Association. *American College Health Association-National College Health Assessment II: Reference Group Executive Summary.* 2016, Spring. Hanover, MD: American College Health Association.

Freedman, J. (2013, September 20). *The typical college student is not a 'typical' college student (and other fun college demographics data).* Retrieved July 6, 2017, from https://www.forbes.com/sites/joshfreedman/2013/09/20/the-typical-college-student-is- not-a-typical-college-student-and-other-fun-college-demographics-data/#737483cd7c5a

Goldrick-Rab, S., Richardson, J., & Hernandez, A. (2017). *Hungry and homeless in college: Results from a national study of basic needs insecurity in higher education.* Madison, WI: Wisconsin HOPE Lab.

Hall, T. E., Meyer, A., & Rose, D. H. (2012). *Universal design for learning in the classroom.* The Guilford Press. New York: Guilford Publications, Inc.

McBride, T., Nief, R., & Westerberg, C. (n.d.). The Beloit College mindset list for the class of 2020. Retrieved July 6, 2017, from https://www.beloit.edu/mindset/2020/

Snyder, T.D., and Dillow, S.A. (2015). *Digest of Education Statistics 2013 (NCES 2015-011)*. Washington, DC: National Center for Education Statistics, Institute of Education Sciences, U.S. Department of Education.

Steele, C. (2010). *Whistling Vivaldi: How stereotypes affect us and what we can do.* New York: W.W. Norton & Company.

Acknowledgments

We are grateful for all of the accomplished, inspired teachers who initially participated in the two-year Universal Design for Learning research project co-sponsored by the Nakatani Teaching and Learning Center and the UW-Stout Online program. We are especially thankful for those who authored chapters in this book and their steadfast dedication to providing content throughout its various twists and turns and iterations. Their insights into improving their classroom teaching through the application of UDL encouraged each of us to grow and question our own understanding of what it means to develop a learning environment that reaches the broadest range of learners. We thank the authors for their honesty in expressing their concerns about UDL and especially value their willingness to keep altering and applying concepts that were initially new to many of them. The different disciplines that are represented within these chapters support the fact that UDL can be applied across the curriculum, increasing the significance of each of their contributions to this project.

The authors acknowledge with gratitude the support and funding that they received from UW-Stout Online and the Nakatani Teaching and Learning Center. That funding allowed for many faculty to experiment with applying Universal Design for Learning principles. We also recognize that we could not have accomplished the writing of this book if it were not for assistance and encouragement received from university administrators, staff and colleagues.

Rarely are tasks of magnitude created and completed in isolation. We appreciate all the help we were given.

SECTION 1

Project Foundation

1 Understanding Universal Design for Learning

Kitrina Carlson, Ph.D., Julie A. Zaloudek, Ph.D. and Renee Howarton, Ph.D.

Foundation of Exclusion in Higher Education

Plato's Academy, formed around 387 BC, is believed to be the first institute of higher learning in the Western world. It persisted in some variant for nearly 900 years and established the philosophical and pedagogical foundations of higher education in all of the West. The Academy of antiquity was primarily an exclusive and competitive club, where only those males who were recommended as academically elite, wealthy, and generally in the right social circle were admitted. In nearly a millennium of serving as a knowledge center, there are only two records of women being trained at the Academy, and one was noted as dressing in a masculine manner to hide her gender (Lynch, 1972). The exclusivity and dearth of diversity is well documented in records and academic writings of the time. Raphael's famous work, *The School of Athens* ca. 1509-1510, presents young-to-middle-aged, white, male scholars lounging and learning in the gardens of the early Academy and further exemplifies the lasting impression the early Academy has had on forming not only the academic foundations of higher education, but the social construct of higher education in the Western world as elite, exclusive and largely homogenous.

The American university has gone through many evolutions since its Harvard University origins in 1636, but despite the puritanical agenda of nearly all early American universities, the basic educational philosophy remained largely based in the classically "pagan" principles and foundations established in the Academy. These principles were later presented in a Christian atmosphere and primarily modeled after Cambridge and Oxford Universities due to "an old-boys' network" of puritan settlers who had been educated abroad and remained closely connected alumni (Marsden, 1994, p. 34-39). In fact, although it primarily served theologians and civil servants, the early American university remained largely focused in these classical pagan foundations until the Morrill Land-Grant Act of 1862 expanded the focus of a university education to include practical pursuits and de-emphasized the classical foundations of a traditional liberal education. The purpose of the Land-Grant University was:

> …to teach such branches of learning as are related to agriculture and the mechanic arts…in order to promote the liberal and practical education of the industrial classes in the several pursuits and professions in life. (Title 7, U.S. Code, n.p.)

This shift away from the classical studies as the foundation of a university education to include more practical and applied pursuits did increase attendance and broadened access to working class students (Lucas, 1994). Though access to higher education has expanded in the 20th century, university education remains inaccessible to many and highly segregated through numerous mechanisms. Through much of the 19th and 20th centuries, a majority of American universities were overtly or insidiously segregated by race, gender, and social and economic status. This segregation was largely correlated with falsely perceived academic abilities (Mays, 1949). While desegregation laws of the 1960s and 1970s did drastically shift the racial divide, a study of over 40 years of university demographics data from across the country indicates racial segregation still largely persists in most American universities (Hinrichs, 2014).

Numerous variables may restrict access to learning in higher education, even seemingly benign factors such as geography may play an important role in maintaining segregated universities and persistent "opportunity hoarding" by wealthy, urban students from elite backgrounds (Cashin, 2014). Factors like whether a student has taken the ACT or SAT will influence whether recruiters from top-tier universities will reach out. Students in the Midwest and most of the South take the ACT and also comprise a much larger proportion of low-income students. Students in wealthier regions, like the East and West Coasts are more likely to take the SAT and are the primary target of elite university recruiters (Cashin, 2014). The systemic exclusion of certain demographics from higher education as a whole, and more pointedly within various academic disciplines, is persistent and well documented. For example, the belief that certain academic fields require an innate brilliance and the stereotypical beliefs held by many that women and African Americans do not have these raw talents, may be a driving factor in the underrepresentation of women and African Americans in fields like physics, applied math and philosophy (Leslie, Cimpian, Meyer, & Freeland, 2015). There are numerous similar examples of exclusion in higher education, both socially and academically, such as exclusion of people with learning disabilities, exclusion of students who speak English as a second language, and exclusion of first-generation college students, to list just a few. In higher education, this exclusion is systemic and may occur within all aspects of a university education. More troubling for higher education is that, despite an awareness of inequitable access to higher education, academics may fail to recognize their own advantage and believe personal merits, such as superior intelligence and past work and learning experiences, are primarily responsible for their status in academia (Warikoo & Fuhr, 2013).

Promoting Diversity through Universal Design

Applying universal design (UD) to the field of education is a means of overcoming many of the factors that may restrict some students to certain institutional settings and from attaining success in college. UD may be a means to improve success of students in disciplines that are poorly diversified, and increase access to learning, particularly to those groups historically underserved in higher education or restricted to certain categories of educational opportunities.

For broad appeal and maximum relevance, we have framed our work with the concept of "academic diversity." For our purposes, we define academic diversity as *the infinite variation of human and life diversity among students in the academic setting of our classes*. We say "infinite" because, while the diversity includes those areas to which we commonly refer (e.g., culture, gender, language, social class, etc.), it also includes all human variation such as personality, learning ability, intelligence, and experience, as well as life variation such as family situation, work, and location. These factors contribute to our students' ability to learn, and Universal Design for Learning (UDL) is motivated by the desire to design courses accessible to the widest possible student audience.

Universal Design for Learning

The Center for Applied Special Technology (CAST) devised the term Universal Design for Learning (UDL); additional influence came from the 1997 reauthorization of the Individuals with Disabilities Education Act (IDEA) (Hitchcock, Meyer, Rose, & Jackson, 2002; Edyburn, 2010). UDL is a theoretical framework that describes the application of Universal Design to curriculum. Specifically, the Center for Applied Special Technology (2015) defines UDL as "a framework for designing curricula that enable all individuals to gain knowledge, skills, and enthusiasm for learning." With its "emphasis on diversity, inclusion, multimodal learning and technology, Universal Design for Learning has the potential to ameliorate some of higher education's most pressing issues, including the intractably low rates of persistence, retention, and degree of completion evident at most colleges and universities today" (Davies, Schelly, & Spooner, 2013, p. 195). The intent behind UDL is that it is designed to "tackle the limitations of a learning environment rather than address learner limitations," with many researchers suggesting that "designing 'accessible' content and delivering it in an 'accessible' learning environment can improve learning experience regardless of individual learning abilities" (Al-Azawei, Serenelli, & Lundqvist, 2016, p. 40).

The goal of UDL is to meet the needs of as many learners as possible, ultimately surpassing the limitations and minimum standards of required accommodation. In UDL the emphasis is placed not only on removing barriers to *accessing* information, but on all the facets of instruction that result in maximizing learning outcomes for all students (Rose & Meyer, 2002; Rose, Meyer, & Hitchcock, 2005).

The UDL framework is based in part on research

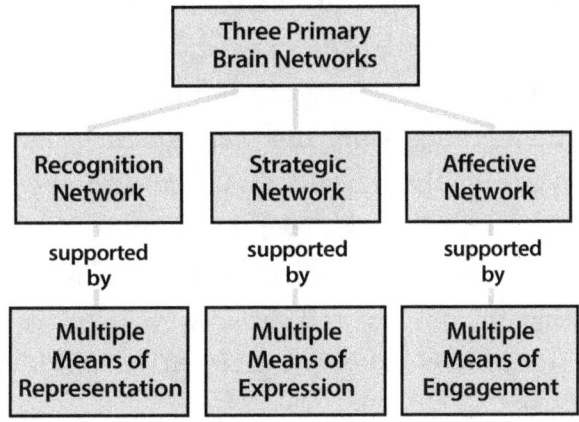

Figure 1. The primary brain networks and their alignment with CAST-developed UDL principles (Rose & Meyer, 2002)

from cognitive neuroscience that elucidates how learning occurs within the three primary brain networks, recognition, strategic and affective, each essential to learning and each functioning both individually and collectively (Fig. 1). The recognition network represents the "what" of learning; it includes how we gather and categorize information and is aligned with the UDL principle of Multiple Means of Representation. The strategic network represents the "how" of learning; it includes how we organize and express our ideas and is aligned with the UDL principle of Multiple Means of Expression. The affective network represents the "why" of learning; it includes how learners get motivated and stay motivated to learn and is aligned with the UDL principle of Multiple Means of Engagement (Rose & Meyer, 2002; Rose et al., 2005).

The neural networks and associated UDL principles correlate with prior research that proposed the prerequisites for learning include information recognition, strategic processing and learning engagement (Vygotsky, 1962). Each principle has associated guidelines and teaching strategies to assist instructors as they design courses in selecting goals, methods, assessment practices and materials that minimize barriers and increase flexibility offering all students the opportunity to participate and learn. According to Hitchcock et al. (2002), if curricula designers recognize the widely diverse learners in current classrooms and build in options to support learning differences from the beginning, the curriculum as inherently designed can work for all learners; this can help teachers maintain educational integrity and maximize consistency of instructional goals and methods, *while still individualizing learning*. One constant expressed by many UDL researchers is that despite general physiological similarities in neural networks, everyone appears to vary in the strengths and weaknesses inherent in each of their neural networks, and as such everyone will learn in complex and varied ways (Rose & Meyer, 2002).

"Learners cannot be reduced to simple categories such as disabled or bright...."

—*Rose and Meyer, 2002*

Different Names for Universal Design in the Learning Environment

Since its inclusion in education, the concept of Universal Design has been applied to teaching and the development of instructional resources, including lectures, labs, classroom discussions, group work, web-based instruction, field work, and demonstrations. It has been given different names besides Universal Design for Learning (the term used in this book due to its focus on the neurosciences and curriculum) including Universal Design for Instruction, Universal Course Design, Universal Design of Instruction, Universally Designed Instruction, and Universal Instructional Design. While each of these terms represents some adaptation of the Universal Design philosophy and principles, for educators new to the concept, Universal Design for Instruction (UDI) effectively applies UD principles to all aspects of instruction (e.g., delivery methods, physical spaces, information resources, technology, personal interactions, and assessments) (Burgstahler, 2012; The Center for Universal Design in Education [CUDE], n.d.). While the acronym UDI is sometimes used as a generic descriptor of inclusive college teaching, there is in fact a formal set of Nine Principles of UDI that are grounded in theory and research on inclusive teaching practices at the postsecondary level (Scott, McGuire, & Foley, 2003). The principles, their definitions, and examples of inclusive teaching strategies help bring clarity to instructional design and the underlying foundation of the UDI acronym (Scott, McGuire, & Shaw, 2003).

The Nine Principles of Universal Design for Instruction©

Principle	Definition	Example(s)
Principle 1: Equitable use	Instruction is designed to be useful to an accessible by people with diverse abilities. Provide the same means of use for all students; identical whenever possible, equivalent when not.	Provision of class notes online. Comprehensive notes can be accessed in the same manner by all students regardless of hearing ability, English proficiency, learning or attention disorders, or note-taking skill level. In an electronic format, students can utilize whatever individual assistive technology is needed to read, hear, or study the class notes.
Principle 2: Flexibility in use	Instruction is designed to accommodate a wide range of individual abilities. Provide choice in methods of use.	Use of varied instructional methods (lecture with a visual outline, group activities, use of stories, or web board-based discussions) to provide different ways of learning and experiencing knowledge.
Principle 3: Simple and intuitive	Instruction is designed in a straightforward and predictable manner, regardless of the student's experience, knowledge, language skills, or current concentration level. Eliminating unnecessary complexity.	Provision of a grading rubric that clearly lays out expectations for exam performance, papers, or projects; a syllabus with comprehensive and accurate information; or a handbook guiding students through difficult homework assignments.
Principle 4: Perceptible information	Instruction is designed so that necessary information is communicated effectively to the student, regardless of ambient conditions or the student's sensory abilities.	Selection of textbooks, reading material, and other instructional supports in digital format or online so students with diverse needs (e.g., vision, learning, attention, English as a Second Language) can access materials through traditional hard copy or with the use of various technological supports (e.g., screen reader, text enlarger, online dictionary).
Principle 5: Tolerance for error	Instruction anticipates variation in individual student learning pace and prerequisite skills.	Structuring a long-term course project so that students have the option of turning in individual project components separately for constructive feedback and for integration into the final product; provision of online "practice" exercises that supplement classroom instruction.

Principle 6: Low physical effort	Instruction is designed to minimize nonessential physical effort in order to allow maximum attention to learning. Note: This principle does not apply when physical effort is integral to essential requirements of a course.	Allowing students to use a word processor for writing and editing papers or essay exams. This facilitates editing of the document without the additional physical exertion of rewriting portions of the text (helpful for students with fine motor or handwriting difficulties or extreme organization weaknesses, and provides options for those who are more adept and comfortable composing on the computer).
Principle 7: Size and space for approach and use	Instruction is designed with consideration for appropriate size and space for approach, reach, manipulations, and use regardless of a student's body size, posture, mobility, and communication needs.	In small class settings, use of a circular seating arrangement to allow students to see and face speakers during discussion – important for students with attention deficit disorder or who are deaf or hard of hearing.
Principle 8: A community of learners	The instructional environment promotes interaction and communication among students and between students and faculty.	Fostering communication among students in and out of class by structuring study groups, discussion groups, e-mail lists, or chat rooms; making a personal connection with students and incorporating motivational strategies to encourage student performance through learning students' names or individually acknowledging excellent performance.
Principle 9: Instructional climate	Instruction is designed to be welcoming and inclusive. High expectations are espoused for all students.	A statement in the class syllabus affirming the need for class members to respect diversity in order to establish the expectation of tolerance as well as encourage students to discuss any special learning needs with the instructor; highlight diverse thinkers who have made significant contributions to the field or share innovative approaches developed by students in the class.

Note. From *Principles of Universal Design for Instruction* by Scott, McGuire, & Shaw, Center on Postsecondary Education and Disability, University of Connecticut. Copyright 2001. Reprinted with permission.

Public Policy and Universal Design

The incorporation of UD into public policy is largely in response to increasing inclusion of students with disabilities into mainstream classrooms. This inclusion has evolved over several decades in response to the reciprocal impacts of 1) advancement of learning technologies, 2) innovative teaching practices, 3) public policy focus on expanded access to mainstream education, and 4) challenges from parents of children with disabilities (Hehir, 2009). What is possible continues to shift as innovators use technology and teaching practices that successfully address the learning needs of students with disabilities, proving that these students can be educated in a mainstream classroom. Initiatives to advance technology and practice get incorporated into public policy which pushes educational systems to change and opens the door for parents to challenge whether a school is adequately meeting the legal requirements for inclusion (Hehir, 2009).

Background history leading to the incorporation of UDL in public policy. The first major legislation regarding inclusion was Section 504 of the Rehabilitation Act of 1973 and the Individuals with Disabilities Education Act (IDEA) of 1975, which introduced the concept of the *least restrictive environment* (Feldman & Rosenbaum, 2011; Hehir, 2009). The least restrictive environment (LRE) requires that students with disabilities be educated with nondisabled peers to the maximum extent appropriate and that segregation of students who are disabled from the mainstream classroom is only acceptable if it is not possible to educate the student there, even with supportive aids and services (Feldman & Rosenbaum, 2011). The standard of using the LRE "as much as appropriate" is a dynamic standard that has changed as technological innovations and practices have made it increasingly possible to provide education for students with disabilities in the mainstream classroom (Hehir, 2009, p. 2).

The LRE standard provided an opportunity for parents to challenge the segregation of their children with disabilities. A series of court cases in the 1980s consistently resulted in rulings that supported the requirement to provide integrated education for all students whenever possible. In 1989, a ruling in the case of Daniel RR v. State Board of Education established a two-pronged test for "appropriate placement" (Hehir, 2009). If a child could be educated in a mainstream class, even if it required supportive aids, that was considered the "appropriate placement." If a child could not be educated in the mainstream class and was segregated, the school needed to show efforts to integrate the child with nondisabled peers to the maximum extent appropriate (Hehir, 2009). In 1994, the Supreme Court allowed a ruling to stand in Sacramento City School District v. Holland, a ruling that identified a regular classroom as the LRE (Hehir, 2009). Together, these rulings set a precedent: the only way a child can legally be removed from a mainstream classroom is if the school has tried to support the child's learning in that classroom prior to removal.

In the 1990s technology innovations made it increasingly common to include children with more complex needs in the mainstream classroom. The Assistive Technology Act of 1998 ensured that states would be financially supported in providing technology needs for persons with disabilities, and the Center for Applied Special Technology (CAST) and IDEA's initiative grants focused on the development of assistive technologies (IDEA Regulations, n.d.). These technological innovations and regulatory changes had reciprocal impacts on each other that expanded inclusion and further opened the door for using UDL as a framework for meeting legal requirements for inclusive, integrated education (Hehir, 2009; IDEA Regulations, n.d.). The 1997 reauthorization of the IDEA made it clear that a need for modified curriculum was not an adequate reason to segregate a child from the classroom. This made it even more imperative that educators learn how to modify the general education curricula to make it accessible to students with disabilities. The IDEA of 1997 also focused on the inclusion of students with disabilities in the state accountability system, which raised the stakes for educating these students and questions on how to expand accessibility beyond the curriculum to assessments (Hehir, 2009; IDEA Regulations, n.d.). Incorporating UDL into policy was an idea whose time had come.

UDL and Policy. The first explicit reference to Universal Design (UD) was in the Assistive Technology Act (ATA) of 1998 that was referenced in the 2004 re-authorization of the IDEA (Assistive Technology Act, 1998; Hehir, 2009). The ATA defines UD as, a concept of philosophy for designing and delivering products and services that are usable by people with the widest possible range of functional capabilities, which include products and services that are directly accessible (without requiring assistive technologies) and products and services that are interoperable with assistive technologies." *[29 U.S.C. 3002 §3(19)]* (Sopko, 2009, p. 2).

The 2004 IDEA also referenced the National Instructional Materials Accessibility Standard (NIMAS) which required the provision of digital texts by publishers and states that they must adopt accessible print materials for persons with print disabilities in a timely way (IDEA Regulation, n.d.; Sopko, 2009). *Response to intervention* (RTI) was the second provision included in the 2004 IDEA that aligns closely with UDL principles (Hehir, 2009). RTI challenges the way that educators identify students with disabilities by viewing students on a continuum of learning and behaviors needs, requiring various intensities of interventions for success and suggesting that all students may struggle with some aspects of the curriculum and benefit from modifications (RTI Action Network, n.d.; Hehir, 2009). The assumption of the RTI concept is that all students should be supported through scaffolding and aids that will maximize learning (Hehir, 2009). The behavioral counterpart to RTI is Positive Behavioral Interventions & Supports (PBIS) which appeared in both the 1997 and 2004 re-authorizations of the IDEA (PBIS and the Law, 2015). PBIS requires schools to approach discipline with the assumption that each child has a different capacity to handle behavioral expectations, and different children need different levels of support in developing successful behavior patterns (Hehir, 2009).

While federal educational policies moved toward closer alignment with UDL principles and ushered in the first explicit reference to UDL in the 1998 ATA, which was referenced in the 2004 IDEA, some states were also explicitly implementing UDL-based initiatives. The most comprehensive and oldest UDL initiative originated in Kentucky in 2000 and focused on increased access to digital texts across the curriculum and a web-based state assessment that was more accessible to different learners (Müller & Tschantz, 2003). New York's initiative focused on developing a team of individuals to provide technical assistance and UDL training in districts across the state, disseminate UDL information through the media, and implement UDL training in the curriculum of general and special education at institutions of higher learning (Müller & Tschantz, 2003).

California was working to make statewide texts available in digital format, while Ohio cautioned against reducing UDL to digitalizing print and instead emphasized literacy and access (California, 2011; Müller & Tschantz, 2003). Michigan collaborated with CAST to incorporate UDL principles in the State Performance Plan and Annual Performance Report as well as requiring grant applicants to describe their plan for meeting the needs of the broadest range of learners (Sopko, 2009). These efforts through the mid-nineties plus those at the federal and state levels focused on K-12 education. This, however, changed with the re-authorization of the Higher Education Opportunity Act (HEOA) of 2008 (National Center on Universal Design for Learning by CAST, 2010).

The HEOA of 2008 explicitly references UDL multiple times, requiring that teaching methods be "consistent with the principles of universal design for learning…" (National Center on Universal Design for Learning by CAST, 2010, P.L. 110-315, 762(b)(2)(A)) and that a national technical assistance center be created to provide training for faculty and support students with disabilities (Sopko, 2009, p. 3). In addition to referencing the UD definition in the ATA of 1998, the HEOA defines UDL for the first time in federal legislation as "…a scientifically valid framework for guiding educational practice that provides flexibility in the ways information is presented, in the ways students respond or demonstrate knowledge and skills, and in the ways students are engaged; and reduces barriers in instruction, provides appropriate accommodations, supports, and challenges, and maintains high achievement expectations for all students, including students with disabilities and students who are limited English proficient" (National Center on Universal Design for Learning by CAST, 2010, p. 1).

The HEOA holds education accountable for evaluation of teacher preparation programs with report cards on how well each state prepares teachers to integrate assistive technology and analyze data to improve student learning that are consistent with universal design for learning (National Center on Universal Design for Learning by CAST, 2010). Although the HEOA is a higher education policy, it focuses on training K-12 teachers and administrators. Federal policy has yet to address the implementation of UDL instructive practices in colleges and universities outside of K-12 teacher training.

The HEOA addresses UDL beyond the scope of disability by explicitly including the needs of students with varied English language proficiency, but UDL continues to be largely associated with disability services. For example, the Common Core State Standards (CCSS) include a reference to UDL in the "application to students with disabilities" section (UDL and the Common Core State Standard Initiative, 2015, p. 1). The CCSS are an attempt to develop nationally consistent, evidence-based achievement standards, and were adopted by forty-six states between 2010 and 2013, though four withdrew in 2014 (Bidwell, 2014; Common Core State Standards adoption map, 2015). Advocates for UDL discuss the CCSS as the "what" in education (what we want students to achieve) and UDL as the "how" (effective framework for developing instruction that will support students in reaching the standards) (UDL & the Common Core State Standards, 2015, p. 1).

The last decade of educational policy has built on a foundation of over thirty years of increasing investment in broad student access to general education by emphasizing the importance of the UDL framework for reaching those goals. Ideas for the continued, effective integration of UDL in education through policy are discussed in the concluding chapter.

Future directions and recommendations for UDL policy. The potential of UDL for all learners has been implied in more recent legislation, but remains tightly associated with disability. It is important that UDL continue to be used to address the needs of students with disabilities, but limiting it to that unnecessarily harnesses its potential to address the varied needs of all learners. Future policies should more clearly integrate the use of UDL across the curriculum for the benefit of all students.

UDL is extremely under-utilized in higher education, and this is likely a result of higher education being absent in federal and state UDL policy initiatives, except for providing UDL training and evaluation for future K-12 educators. There is also very little research on the application of UDL in adult populations. Disparate opportunities for success in education occurs throughout the educational spectrum, and UDL is an excellent approach to making success attainable for the broadest range of learners. This justifies broadening policy initiatives to encourage the application of UDL and research on its effectiveness to higher education and non-academic educational settings (e.g., government supported community education). Schelly, Davies, and Spooner (2011, p. 18) reiterated this point when they stated that the literature about Universal Design in higher education is long on principles and "best practices," but short on empirical evidence of its benefits.

Investing in research on the effectiveness of UDL in real classroom applications and comprehensive district-wide implementation is critical (Rose & Gravel, 2010). Currently the research focuses on the effectiveness of specific technology use and practices that are consistent with UDL principles, but there is no existing research that examines the application of the UDL framework across an entire district. As UDL is a framework and not a set of specific interventions and techniques, this research is essential for moving forward with evidence-based decisions, and should be supported by policy.

Sopko (2009) summarizes high-impact policies that are easier to implement from a policy forum of diverse stakeholders in education that convened in December of 2008. One recommendation is to build a knowledge network that can influence the development and implementation of various educational standards based on UDL principles. Other high-impact recommendations include disseminating information to promote UDL among stakeholders; encouraging school boards to incorporate UDL principles into the selection of curricula; and a technical review board established by the Secretary of Education to create and publicize a set of recommendations for educators, publishers, and developers that are based on UDL principles (Sopko, 2009). Finally, creating federal grants to support UDL practices and requiring applicants of any educational grant application to include a plan for UDL application would broadly increase the intentional application of UDL across classrooms and school districts.

There has been very encouraging progress in how UDL has been incorporated into public policies and education throughout the U.S., but current policies unleash a mere fraction of the potential benefits the broad application of UDL could have on diverse learners. Public policy support of UDL research and its application to the delivery of education is the most promising way for the full benefits of UDL to be realized.

References

Al-Azawei, A., Serenelli, F., & Lundqvist, K. (2016). Universal design for learning (UDL): A content analysis of peer-reviewed journal papers from 2012 to 2015. *Journal of the Scholarship of Teaching and Learning, 16*(3), 39-56. Retrieved from http://josotl.indiana.edu/article/view/19295/28114

Assistive Technology Act of 1998, Pub. L. 105-394, S. 2432. Retrieved from https://www.congress.gov/bill/105th-congress/senate-bill/2432

Bidwell, A. (2014, February 27). A history of Common Core State Standards. *U.S. News & World Report.* Retrieved from http://www.usnews.com/news/special-reports/articles/2014/02/27/the-history-of- common-core-state-standards

Burgstahler, S. (2012). DO-IT *(Disabilities, Opportunities, Internetworking, and Technology).* University of Washington. Retrieved from http://www.washington.edu/doit/

California: Community alliance for special education and disability rights. (2011). *(SERR) Manual.* Sacramento, CA. Retrieved from http://www.disabilityrightsca.org/pubs/PublicationsSERREnglish.htm

Cashin, S. (2014). *Place, not race: A new vision of opportunity in America.* Boston: Beacon Press.

Center for Applied Special Technology (CAST). (2015). *About UDL.* Retrieved from www.cast.org/udl

Center for Universal Design in Education (CUDE). (n.d.). Seattle: University of Washington. Retrieved from http://www.washington.edu/doit/programs/center-universal-design-education/overview

Common Core State Standards adoption map. (2015). *Academic benchmarks.* Retrieved from http://academicbenchmarks.com/common-core-state-adoption-map/

Davies, P., Schelly, C., & Spooner, C. (2013). Measuring the effectiveness of universal design for learning intervention in postsecondary education. *Journal of Postsecondary Education and Disability, 26*(3), 195-220.

Edyburn, D. (2010). Would you recognize universal design for learning if you saw it? Ten propositions for new directions for the second decade of UDL. *Learning Disability Quarterly, 33,* 33-41.

Feldman, J., & Rosenbaum, S. (Ed.; 2011, September). *Special education rights and responsibilities.* Disability Rights California. Retrieved from: http://www.disabilityrightsca.org/pubs/504001Ch01.pdf

Hehir, T. (2009). *Policy foundations of universal design for learning.* Wakefield, MA: National Center on Universal Design for Learning.

Hinrichs, P. (2014). An empirical analysis of racial segregation in higher education. *Federal Reserve Bank of Cleveland Working Paper No. 14-35.* Retrieved from https://ssrn.com/abstract=2534529

Hitchcock, C., Meyer, A., Rose, D., & Jackson, R. (2002). *Providing new access to the general curriculum.* TEACHING Exceptional Children, *356*(2), 8-17.

Leslie, S., Cimpian, A., Meyer, M., & Freeland, E. (2015). Expectations of brilliance underlie gender distributions across academic disciplines. *Science, 347*(6219), 262-265. doi:10.1126/science.1261375

Lucas, C. J. (1994). *American higher education: A history.* New York: St. Martin's Press. Lynch, J. P. (1972).

Lynch, J. P. (1972). *Aristotle's school: A study of a Greek educational institution.* Berkeley: University of California Press.

Marsden, G. M. (1994). *The soul of the American university: From protestant establishment to established nonbelief.* New York: Oxford University Press.

Mays, B. E. (1949). Segregation in higher education. *Phylon (1940-1956), 10*(4), 401. doi:10.2307/272127

Müller, E., & Tschantz, J. (2003). Universal design for learning: Four state initiatives. *Project Foru*m. Alexandria, VA: National Association of State Directors of Special Education.

National Center on Universal Design for Learning by CAST. (2010). *UDL and UD provisions in the Higher Education Opportunity Act (P.L.110-315).* Retrieved from http://www.udlcenter.org/advocacy/referencestoUDL/HEOA

National Center on Universal Design for Learning by CAST. (2014). *UDL and the Common Core State Standard Initiative.* Retrieved from http://www.udlcenter.org/implementation/udl_ccss

PBIS and the Law. (2015). *Positive behavioral interventions & supports.* U.S. Office of Special Education Programs. Retrieved from https://www.pbis.org/school/pbis-and-the-law

Rose, D., & Gravel J. (2010). *Technology and learning: Meeting special student's needs.* Wakefield, MA: National Center on UDL. Retrieved from http://www.udlcenter.org/sites/udlcenter.org/files/TechnologyandLearning.pdf

Rose, D. H., & Meyer, A. (2002). *Teaching every student in the digital age: Universal Design for Learning.* Alexandria, VA: Association for Supervision and Curriculum Development.

Rose, D. H., Meyer, A., & Hitchcock, C. (2005). *The universally designed classroom: Accessible curriculum and digital technologies.* Cambridge, MA: Harvard Education Press.

RTI Action Network: National Center for Learning Disabilities. (n.d.). *What is RTI?* Retrieved from http://www.rtinetwork.org/learn/what/whatisrti

Schelly, C., Davies, P., & Spooner, C. (2011). Student perceptions of faculty implementation of universal design for learning. *Journal of Postsecondary Education and Disability, 24*(1), 17-30.

Scott, S. S., McGuire, J. M., & Shaw, S. F. (2003, November/December). Universal design for Instruction: A new paradigm for adult instruction in postsecondary education. *Remedial and Special Education, 24*(6), 369-379.

Sopko, K. M. (2009). Universal design for learning: Policy challenges and recommendations. *Project Forum.* Alexandria, VA: National Association of State Directors of Special Education.

U.S. Department of Education, Office of Special Education Programs. (n.d.). *IDEA Regulations: National Instructional Materials Accessibility Standard*

(NIMAS). Retrieved from http://www.ideapartnership.org/using-tools/topic-briefs/regulatory-provisions/1682- national-instructional-materials-accessibility-standard-nimas.html

Vygotsky, L. S. (1962). *Thought and language*. Cambridge, MA: M.I.T. Press. Institute of Technology.

Warikoo, N. K., & Fuhr, C. (2013). Legitimating status: Perceptions of meritocracy and inequality among undergraduates at an elite British university. *British Educational Research Journal, 40*(4), 699-717. doi:10.1002/berj.3108

2 Book Foundation: UDL and Conceptual Struggles

Kitrina Carlson, Ph.D., Renee Chandler, Ed.D., Julie A. Zaloudek, Ph.D., and Renee Howarton, Ph.D.

From concept to content, we grappled with how to most effectively frame the discussion and application of Universal Design for Learning principles across our campus's diverse curricula. During some of our earliest conversations, we tackled the core question, "What is the difference between UDL and good teaching?" It was through rich, robust exchange that we developed our stance on this and other issues that structure this book. We wrestled with the selection of a foundational model that could be used to consistently present information and data descriptive of our different case studies. This consistency was particularly important given the significant variation that exists among our disciplines, teaching practices, and academic threshold concepts. We finally settled on using the ADDIE model and its focus on analysis, design, development, implementation, and evaluation.

Chapter three discusses in greater detail the constructs and logistics of our cross-campus two-year UDL Communities of Practice research. However, fundamental to our usage of the Communities of Practice model was a core inclusion of the Scholarship of Teaching and Learning (SoTL) model. Our vision of the significance of aligning Universal Design for Learning and SoTL is included in this chapter.

UDL Versus Good Teaching

Some educators have argued that UDL is synonymous with "good teaching." Undoubtedly many professionals who read this book will be able to identify strategies they have used in their own teaching even though they have not purported to utilize the UDL framework. Certainly, there are highly effective teachers who have not used UDL as a framework in developing and designing their instruction but consistently create a learning environment that is accessible and supportive of the broadest range of students possible.

So, what is the relationship between good teaching and UDL implementation? UDL teaching practices and good teaching practices share many of the same strategies and often look the same. To examine the relationship between good teaching and UDL, we must first answer the question: What is good teaching? A review of the literature suggests a wide range of what constitutes good teaching. Emerging themes imply that good teaching involves a level of passion, the ability to provide students with valuable knowledge and skills, the capacity to engage students with content, and proficiency in providing students with problem-solving skills that they can generalize to a wide range of contexts (Bartram & Bailey, 2009; Leblanc, 1998; Porter & Brophy, 1988; Shulman, 2007). Although most of us believe that we recognize good teaching when we see it, it is not clearly defined in the literature and we must acknowledge that good teaching cannot be measured by a single dimension or criteria: "It is rich, nuanced, complicated, internally and longitudinally inconsistent and produces different impacts on different students and in different contexts" (Shulman, 2007, p. 6).

While UDL may sound like just good teaching practices (and may share many of the same characteristics), it actually provides a framework for making more "... explicit what good teaching is" (Rose & Meyer, 2006, p. 35). We know that traditional "good teaching" practices have left many academically diverse students marginalized (Edyburn, 2010). Good teaching includes providing individual accommodations for a few select students. If this practice was sufficient to meet the needs of all learners, we would not continue to observe a performance gap in the academic achievement of our students. We propose that UDL melds good teaching practices with emerging research in instructional design, brain imaging, and technology. As we implemented a UDL framework at UW-Stout, we discovered that UDL is really about design, not just delivery. In order for a course to truly meet the needs of a wide range of learners, the instructor must start with a sound course that is well-organized and easy to navigate and then intentionally design it so that it is accessible to all potential learners. Examples of this practice are presented throughout this book.

Application of the ADDIE Model

The **ADDIE model** is often referred to as either an approach or framework that consists of generic processes used by instructional designers, trainers and more recently, educators to guide application of effective training and performance support tools (Forest, n.d.). There are five phases associated with this model: analysis, design, development, implementation, and evaluation. The model represented in this book was originally designed for the U.S. Army in 1975 and was selected for inclusion due to its straightforward and easily understandable illustration.

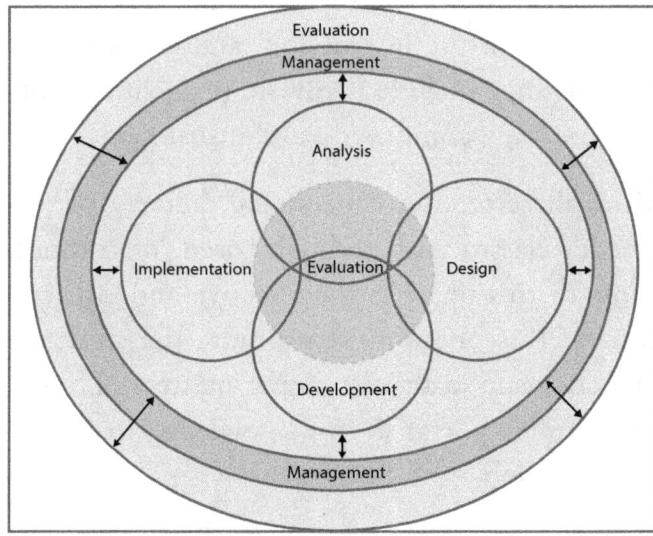

Figure 6-1. The non-linear ADDIE process

Branson, Rayner, Cox, Furman, King, & Hannum. (1975). *Interservice procedures for instructional systems development.* (Vols. 1-5) TRADOC Pam 350-30, NAVEDTRA 106A. Ft. Monroe, VA: U.S. Army Training and Doctrine Command and Florida State University for the Educational Technology Center, Tallahassee, FL. Reprinted with permission.

An expanded discussion of the ADDIE model (2011). The following information defines the five phases associated with the ADDIE Model and exemplifies how users benefit from the interactive process contained in this framework/approach.

- The **Analyze** phase is the foundation for all other phases of instructional design. During this phase, users must define the problem, identify the source of the problem and determine possible solutions. The phase may include specific research techniques such as needs analysis, job analysis and task analysis. The outputs of this phase often include the instructional goals and a list of tasks to be instructed.

- The **Design** phase involves using the outputs from the Analyze phase to plan a strategy for developing and expanding instructional goals and tasks. Some of the elements of the Design phase may include writing a target population description, conducting a learning analysis, writing objectives and test items, selecting a delivery system, and sequencing the instruction.

- The **Develop** phase builds on both the Analyze and Design phases. The purpose of this phase is to generate the lesson plans and lesson materials. During this phase, users develop the instruction, all media that will be used in the instruction, and any supporting documentation. This may include hardware (e.g., simulation equipment) and software (e.g., computer-based instruction).

- The **Implementation** phase refers to the actual delivery of the instruction, whether it's classroom-based, lab-based, or computer-based. The purpose of this phase is the effective and efficient delivery of instruction. This phase must promote the students' understanding of material, support the students' mastery of objectives, and ensure the students' transfer of knowledge from the instructional setting to the job.

- The **Evaluation** phase measures the effectiveness and efficiency of the instruction and should occur throughout the entire instructional design process. It should be done within phases, between phases, and after implementation. Evaluation practices may be formative and/or summative.

Selection of the ADDIE model necessitated that project participants frame their actual projects through its lens. Consequently, project-related chapters in the book present their research goals, design and outcomes within the context of the model's components. For example, in the **Analysis** section, instructors talked about how they typically taught their course before using the UDL framework and what student-related learning problems they encountered that intrigued or baffled them enough to study them. During the **Design** phase, they explore how they might structure their course differently and change specific assignments and assessments to infuse UDL design principles, the purpose being to more effectively meet the needs of their classroom audience and to improve overall course design. The intent of this section was to directly address concerns identified in the Analysis phase.

In the **Develop** phase, faculty discuss the specific revisions using the UDL framework that changed their course experience and content from previous semesters. For several of them, the element of choice was incorporated into class assignments, making their course more accessible and interesting to their classroom population. When creating their chapter manuscripts, many of the instructors chose to combine some or all of their Design, Develop and Implementation outcomes.

During the **Evaluation** phase, instructors discussed their project data analysis including the more formalized types of analysis such as survey results or systematic analysis of qualitative data as well as their own observations and reflections about how the design worked and improvements they might make in the future. The participants were encouraged to reflect upon the fact that their ideas for "where they would like to improve it" would move them back into the Analysis phase, which is "just right" as the ADDIE model implies an iterative process!

Commonality Between UDL and SoTL

The following sections describe the Scholarship of Teaching and Learning (SoTL) framework with the intent of showing how it was used to strengthen and support the quality and consistency of UDL scholarship conducted at UW-Stout. The alignment between UDL and SoTL enabled faculty from divergent disciplines to utilize a common project structure and speak the same research language.

What is the Scholarship of Teaching and Learning? At the core of the Scholarship of Teaching and Learning (SoTL) philosophy is an understanding that intentionally studying teaching practices and student learning outcomes is crucial for producing excellence in instruction. In 1998, the Carnegie Foundation launched Carnegie Academy for the Scholarship of Teaching and Learning (CASTL). The creation of CASTL was based on two reports by Boyer (1990; 1996), *Scholarship Reconsidered* and *Scholarship Assessed*, and the work of Illinois State University faculty and their students. When Boyer introduced the term "scholarship of teaching," it gained attention and eventual acceptance because it gave "college and university teaching a place within a broader vision of scholarship that also included the discovery, integration, and application of knowledge" (Huber, 2013, p. 1). CASTL (Carnegie Foundation, n.d.) defines scholarship of teaching and learning as a process that makes public teachers' systematic reflection on teaching and learning and its goal is to support the development of instructional scholarship that:

1. fosters significant, long-lasting learning for all students,
2. enhances the practice and profession of teaching, and
3. brings to faculty members' work as teachers the recognition and reward afforded to other forms of scholarly work.

Scholarship of Teaching and Learning Research Model. The Scholarship of Teaching and Learning (SoTL) research model includes certain practices of classroom assessment and evidence gathering; teaching that is informed not only by the latest ideas, but by current ideas about teaching generally and specifically in the field; and teaching that invites peer collaboration or review (Carnegie Academy for the Scholarship of Teaching and Learning [CASTL], 1999). This model simultaneously combines classroom inquiry, a synthesizing of ideas from different fields, and the improvement of practice (Georgia Southern University, n.d.). Traditionally, SoTL has been characterized as embodying the "work 'of the faculty, by the faculty, and for the faculty' who use its findings to improve the experience of their own students in their own settings... making this faculty-driven approach more bottom-up and close to the classroom" (Hutchings, Taylor Huber, & Ciccone, 2011, p. 69-70). SoTL researchers tend to be as passionate about actual student learning as they are about effective teaching practices. The two are intertwined for them. For teachers who are also scholars, good teaching "means not only transmitting knowledge, but *transforming* and *extending* it as well" (Boyer, 1990, p. 24); the pursuit of SoTL supports this extension of instruction.

A list of components comprising the Scholarship of Teaching and Learning Research Model (Vanderbilt University Center for Teaching, 2010-11) includes:

1. Ask learner-centered questions,
2. Build on the works of others,
3. Determine the method you will use to gather data,
4. Analyze the evidence,
5. Disseminate the results, and
6. Reflect and apply.

These criteria were inspired by a speech given by Karen Richardson, Office of Teaching and Learning Fellow, at Bridgewater State University, in September 2011. The talk was entitled, "Getting Started on the Scholarship of Teaching and Learning." The ideas are also based on information that was housed on the Office of Professional and Instructional Development website (2014), University of Wisconsin System, Madison, Wisconsin.

Scholarship of Teaching and Learning Research Model components. Those who actively apply the Scholarship of Teaching and Learning research model find that it is very similar to more traditional research frameworks, with the exception that it emphasizes the importance of disseminating project outcomes to wider audiences. This is significant because SoTL oriented conferences and publications support the reporting out of classroom scholarship regardless of whether or not the results are successful or disappointing. This provides freedom and encouragement to the potential scholar. The model is comprised of five phases:

- **Ask learner-centered questions**—All meaningful investigative work begins with the asking of important, relevant, and significant questions. In Approaching the Scholarship of Teaching and Learning, Pat Hutchings (2000, p. 3) stated that the "shaping of a good question for the scholarship of teaching and learning is not only a practical and intellectual task but often a moral and ethical one as well." Hutchings (2000) is well-known for encouraging researchers to ask such questions about their student learning environment as "What is?," "What works?," "What is possible?," as well as to explore "theory building"-related questions.

- **Build on the work of others**—Although researchers are trained in conducting literature reviews, this model encourages educators to not only study a topic, but to also explore their misperceptions of it. It specifically supports the investigation of others' work on student learning in the classroom or digital learning environments, fostering creative ways of enabling teachers to answer the age-old question, "Are my students really learning what I want or need them to learn?"

- **Determine the method you will use to gather data and analyze the evidence**—Research methods in SOTL include reflection and analysis, interviews and focus groups, questionnaires, content analysis of text, secondary analysis of existing data, quasi-experiments (comparison of two sections of the same course), observational research, and case studies, among others. This framework supports the usage and application of multiple methods often weaving together quantitative and qualitative assessment practices.

- **Disseminate results**—One of the unique aspects of SoTL is its emphasis on public dissemination of teaching and learning research outcomes. Educators are encouraged to share their results in local, regional, national and international venues to expand recognition and acceptance of teaching and student-based research within and across disciplines.

- **Reflect and apply**—Perhaps the most valuable contribution associated with the Scholarship of Teaching and Learning model is the application of research to improving classroom instruction. SOTL doesn't end with the public sharing of one's findings, but rather it involves an ongoing application and tweaking of teaching attitudes and activities.

Alignment between the Scholarship of Teaching and Learning and UDL frameworks. During the two-year UDL project at UW-Stout, the SoTL Research Model was intentionally applied to the design, implementation and assessment of faculty projects within the classroom. As discussed in Chapter 3, implementation of the model provided standardization of quality inquiry and research guidance for those with either extensive or limited scholarly experience. In addition, it provided a research structure that supported faculty as they dared to question their teaching practices. As Randy Bass (1999, n.p.) noted, "changing the status of the *problem* in teaching from terminal remediation to ongoing investigation is precisely what the movement for a scholarship of teaching is all about." Given that UDL project participants intentionally questioned how to make learning in their courses accessible to the broadest range of students, the application of the SoTL research model appeared to be a natural fit because of how well both frameworks complement and align with one another. Upon reflection, <u>both</u> frameworks possess the following supportive characteristics:

1. They each seek to improve teaching and learning and are learner-centered; they are both concerned about student learning outcomes.

2. They elicit self-reflection from educators, encouraging them to evaluate their teaching practices in an ongoing, consistent process.

3. They focus on identifying teaching questions or classroom dilemmas that challenge effective instruction and student learning.

4. They can be applied to diverse curricula housed in vastly different disciplines, used in small or large classrooms, and within public or private institutional settings.

5. They encourage the evaluation of teaching practices with the intent of revising them to improve their efficacy and ultimately enhance learning for the broadest number of students. CASTL (1999, n.p.) publicly supports "significant long-lasting learning for all students."

6. They enable students to become co-inquirers in the classroom as oppose to just objects of the teacher's research inquiry.

7. They incorporate the use of quantitative and qualitative research methodologies and assessment practices.

8. They can lead to significant transformation and beneficial change in teaching and learning practices and an improved learning environment.

9. They embrace a sense of intentionality in their design, implementation and assessment processes.

According to CASTL, "if Scholarship of Teaching and Learning is to have a lasting place—and make an enduring difference—in academic life and work, it must connect to other institutional agendas, including those that matter to the public and to policymakers..." (Hutchings et al., 2011, p. 82). Universal Design and its application to education is one such institutional agenda that is becoming increasingly more important due to increasing diversity of learners filling our nation's classrooms.

UDL Instructor Training Research

Research exploring the impact of UDL on student learning outcomes is sparse, especially within higher education; most of it has been conducted in K-12 settings (Davies, Schelly, & Spooner, 2013). Many of the literature reviews and actual studies done at the university level tend to focus on students with disabilities (Schelly, Davies, & Spooner, 2011). Since students with disabilities are less likely to complete college than their nondisabled peers, Schelly et al. (2011) suggest that applying the UDL framework to students with disabilities can create opportunities for engagement, expression and enhanced academic performance, ultimately resulting in greater academic performance, persistence and retention. While the number of students with mobility or orthopedic disabilities has declined in recent years, the number of students with non-apparent disabilities such as attention deficit disorder (ADD) and specific learning disabilities has grown, bringing challenges to instructors, many of whom are not skilled in properly handling these learning needs (Vreeburg Izzo, Murray, & Novak, 2008). In addition, with increasing numbers of wounded veterans, and educationally ill-prepared low-income and minority students attending college, application of the UDL framework to design and maintain supportive, favorable learning environments is wise and essential. According to Vreeburg Izzo et al. (2008, p. 60), "students who were once considered 'nontraditional' are now the norm, as sociological factors have significantly altered the student constituency and thus are pushing at the doors of 'tried and true' instructional practices that have been the bedrock of educational delivery for years."

In recent years, some UDL researchers have begun to explore the efficacy of UDL training for instructors and its potential to improve student learning. Much of this research is of a descriptive nature or focused on the application of universal design principles (Center for Universal Design, 2008; Smith, 2012).

Universal Design for Learning (UDL): A content analysis of peer reviewed journal papers from 2012 to 2015. In an analysis of twelve journal articles, Al-Azawei, Serenelli and Lundqvist (2016) reviewed scholarly papers that satisfied four criteria: the papers had to be peer-reviewed, possess empirical results, use the UDL framework, and be published between 2012 and 2015. According to these authors, "this study sought to verify the UDL implications on user experience, academic performance, and educational contexts," as well as to "identify research gaps in the current UDL implementation" (Al-Azawei et al., 2016, p. 44).

Improved lesson planning with Universal Design for Learning (UDL). Of particular relevance to this book, Al-Azawei et al. (2016) reviewed the research work of Courey, Tappe, Siker and LePage (2012) and McGhie-Richmond and Sung (2012), both of which focused on how training can affect the application of UDL. In the first article, Courey et al. (2012) reported studying 45 graduate students in two sections of the same course, *Introduction to Mild/Moderate Disabilities*, who were working on their special education certification. They required participants to write three lesson plans, one at the beginning of the semester and prior to receiving UDL training, one directly after receiving a three-hour UDL training, and one at the end of the semester. Completion of the first two lesson plans, necessitated that students respond to case study scenarios descriptive of a general education classroom that included students with learning disabilities. The graduate students were directed to use a lesson plan template for all three case studies with the intent being to document and determine what they knew about incorporating UDL principles and differentiating instruction before and after receiving specialized UDL training. The UDL training was disseminated in multiple ways including a web-based module (IRIS Center for Training Enhancements, 2016) and researcher-delivered content. In both modalities, content and corresponding materials modeled UDL principles and practices. For the third case study, students created their own scenario for a general education setting that included hypothetical students in special education and complied with authentic state education regulations.

The findings from this study showed that after receiving the UDL training, "teachers incorporated more differentiated options and varied teacher strategies based on UDL principles into their lesson plans, so that content was more accessible to all students" (Courey et al., 2012, p. 7).

For the researchers, successful application of UDL principles meant "that they (students) included at least one novel manner to deliver content, engage students, and assess student learning in ways that may overcome barriers inherent in more traditional forms of teaching" (Courey et al., 2012, p. 16). However, they also acknowledged that although their students' understanding of UDL principles was elevated after the training, more actual hands-on practice was needed to become competent at applying UDL strategies in an actual classroom setting.

Applying Universal Design for Learning to instructional planning. In the study conducted by McGhie-Richmond and Sung (2012) at a Canadian university, they researched 16 preservice as well as 10 practicing teachers. The preservice teachers were in a course focusing on applied assistive technologies that support diverse and inclusive classrooms, while the latter group was enrolled in the first of a four-course post-degree Special Education program. After receiving an introduction to UDL principles, research participants were asked to a) review and modify a previously taught lesson plan through a UDL mindset and to reflect on the diverse learning needs of their students, b) watch a YouTube video that discussed UDL principles, and c) explore the website for the National Center on Universal Design for Learning (http://www.udlcenter.org/implementation/examples, 2014) for examples of lesson plans. According to the researchers (McGhie-Richmond & Sung, 2012, p. 46), "the assignment supported several course learning outcomes: (1) recognizing diversity in the classroom, (2) understanding barriers that are experienced by students who have learning differences and needs, and (3) addressing barriers to student participation by applying Universal Design for Learning principles to instructional planning."

The results of this study were directly linked to the three UDL principles. Although both student groups made changes to their lesson plans relative to Multiple Means of Expression (specifically in the areas of perception, expression and comprehension), the preservice teachers made noticeably more revisions than did the practicing instructors. However, just the opposite occurred for the other two principles, with practicing teachers consistently modifying their lesson plans more than the other students for the Multiple Means of Representation and Engagement principles. The study also utilized thematic analysis to identify two themes, *learning for all* and *transformative practice*, that captured teacher reflections of the assignment that they completed. For the *learning for all* theme, both the practicing and preservice students increased their understanding and acceptance that UDL has the potential to expand learning for the "full range of student diversity in the classroom" by reducing "barriers, focus(ing) on strengths, and consider(ing) learner preferences/characteristics" (McGhie-Richmond & Sung, 2012, p. 49). Both student groups were particularly impressed with the inclusiveness of UDL and its application to more than just students with special needs.

In the *transformative practice* theme, students from both groups described how the application of UDL principles could help improve their professional practice as teachers. The researchers found that from the students' perspective, "adoption of Universal Design for Learning challenges prior teaching and learning assumptions" and as a *transformative* practice, it could be "understood as a *way of thinking about teaching and learning* rather than a set of specific instructional strategies that, if followed correctly, would establish an inclusive classroom" (McGhie-Richmond & Sung, 2012, p. 50-51).

According to McGhie-Richmond and Sung (2012), one limitation to their research was that application of UDL only occurred as part of an assignment and not in an actual classroom setting. Similar to Courey et al. (2012), they acknowledged the need for students to get the hands-on experience of implementing the UDL framework. They also questioned the potential impact of applying UDL principles throughout curriculum and instruction courses, and whether the transformative practice associated with their UDL intervention would continue over time.

Measuring the effectiveness of Universal Design for Learning intervention in postsecondary education. Davies et al. (2013) reviewed journal articles and found three that specifically studied the potential beneficial impact of training instructors on UDL principles and strategies to improve student learning. In the first article, "The Faculty Perspective on Universal Design for Learning," Vreeburg Izzo et al. (2008) discussed two research studies, the first occurring from 1999-2002, while the second was conducted from 2003-2006. The intent of the former study was to gather and assess information that would be used to design faculty development opportunities and products for the training of instructors involved in teaching students with disabilities. This pilot study was implemented across seven diverse academic units, including both university and community college participants. Faculty and teaching associates (TAs) were surveyed, while focus groups comprised of instructors, TAs, and students with and without disabilities were used to gain more in-depth information.

Relative to faculty perceptions, the questionnaire collected information on "preferred training topics and means of delivery, perceptions of teaching students with disabilities, and instructional methods used by respondents in the classrooms" (Vreeburg Izzo et al., 2008, p. 62). Twenty-two of the survey questions pertained to faculty and TAs and of the 271 surveys that were returned (1,150 surveys distributed/24% response rate), 27% of respondents desired UDL training, 15% wanted web accessibility training, and 11% requested distance education training. A smaller response was received regarding instructor training needs for technologies and disabilities related policies. Questionnaire results regarding means of delivery showed that the teachers (35%) wanted access to web-based technical assistance whenever they needed it, with 30% desiring a workshop format.

Although five themes were identified from the focus group sessions that directly dealt with making university experiences more accessible and successful for students with disabilities, the fifth theme was specifically aligned with UDL. It identified the need to design instructional practices that meet the diverse learning needs of *all* students, it was further broken down into subcategories that included "(a) perceived uncertainty about how to meet the learning needs of an increasingly diverse and technologically expectant student demographic, (b) instructional strategies used to support student learning, and (c) the need for training and technical assistance on promoting education access" (Vreeburg Izzo et al., 2008, p. 64). The focus groups were comprised of 57 faculty members and 35 TAs and they were asked to discuss 12 open-ended questions.

The second study that occurred from 2003-2006 was created in response to faculty needs identified in the first study. Within its design were incorporated Level I (formative) and Level II (summative) research phases. To assist in the systematic gathering of information, a FAME curriculum was developed. It consisted of the following instructional modules: "a) Rights and Responsibilities in the Accommodation Process, b) Universal Design for Learning, c) Web Accessibility, d) College Writing, and e) Climate Assessment" (Vreeburg Izzo et al., 2008, p. 65). The dissemination of FAME was done in a way that modeled UDL practices and utilized multimedia representations and throughout the research it was referred to as the UDL module.

As part of the Level I study, Disability Services administrators helped recruit 63 instructors and administrators from five universities and community colleges. They were asked to review an online UDL module and assess the functionality of the website navigation. Their perceptions and opinions were captured in a 48 question Likert-scale survey, with additional open-ended questions being included. Survey responses were evaluated relative to "ease of navigation, skill level of module content, pre- and post-test content, design of the computer interface, system reliability, and campus technology access and configuration" (Vreeburg Izzo et al., 2008, p. 66).

During the Level II phase, 35 faculty and administrators representing 23 universities and colleges piloted and evaluated the UDL module that was part of the FAME curriculum over a 3- month period. Their thoughts were captured via open-ended questions and a Likert-scale survey containing 12 questions.

Results from the pilot study showed that participants strongly agreed or agreed that they now felt more comfortable meeting the needs of students with disabilities and most interestingly, while only 31% initially possessed knowledge of UDL practices, the post-survey revealed that 83% felt knowledgeable after completing the training. Similar changes in perceptions were evident in the Level II study, with the response rate going from 29% of participants feeling knowledgeable to 94% gaining confidence and information after completing the module.

Student perceptions of faculty implementation of Universal Design for Learning. In the second article that was reviewed, Schelly, Davies, and Spooner (2011) measured student perceptions of teachers before and after the faculty had received UDL training. Although these researchers focused on gathering data pertaining to students with disabilities, the overall intent was to improve learning experiences for *all* students. A questionnaire based on the three UDL principles (Representation, Expression and Engagement) was created, with initial pre-survey results (n = 1,362) being used to direct instructor training prior to the implementation of the post-survey. The questionnaire's content concentrated on classroom instruction and course materials within nine large "gateway" psychology courses. In between the pre- and post-surveys, instructors were mentored in weekly meetings on UDL principles; the actual training curriculum was modified based on the pre-survey findings. In addition, they accessed tutorials on effectively employing assistive technologies and developing "universally designed" course materials. Results from the first survey indicated that students wanted instructors to more effectively summarize course content at critical points during each class period, provide more content in electronic formats, and make course content accessible in multiple venues. Training was provided addressing these findings. The final survey outcomes (n = 1,223) indicated that for 6 of the 24 survey questions, students perceived a noticeable improvement in their instructors after the UDL mentoring. Although this study did not include a control group comparison, the findings showed that the teachers improved their 1) use of multiple formats to present course content, 2) regularly provided electronic versions of course materials, 3) put more reading assignments online, 4) emphasized key points in videos, 5) gave more constructive and prompt assignment feedback, and 6) supplemented reading and lecture materials with supportive visuals. Finally, this study also found that only a fraction of students with disabilities self-report to campus authorities and Schelly et al. (2011) recommended that the application of UDL strategies become a standard in postsecondary education.

Analyzing a College Course that Adheres to the Universal Design for Learning (UDL) Framework. Smith (2012) describes one instructor's efforts to apply the UDL framework to two sections of an introductory graduate-level research methods course. The study was conducted over four semesters from 2010 to 2011 and included a total of eighty graduate students enrolled as education majors. During 2011, an additional instructor joined the research team, and having received an orientation to UDL, he applied the framework to his section of the same course. He only participated in the survey portion of the study.

The main researcher was extensively trained in applying UDL practices in the classroom, allowing her to provide students with an introductory overview of UDL principles during each semester. To address the UDL principles of recognition, strategic, and affective learning, she intentionally presented course information in a variety of formats including "class notes, PowerPoint presentations, links to audio, video and text files, and course readings" (Smith, 2012, 43). This resulted in students having access to multiple representations of content and opportunities for learning to be reinforced. In addition, she provided timely feedback on assignments and gave students numerous opportunities to demonstrate their learning, including participating in "cocktail party reviews" in which they portrayed their favorite researcher and briefly summarized his or her scholarly findings. To support affective learning, the researcher identified student interests through a multiple intelligences inventory (McKenzie, 2002; Smith, 2012) and then selected readings and instructional approaches that were reflective of their background interests.

Using a reflective and instructional responsive practice, the researcher and instructor studied "(A) student perceptions of faculty use of UDL in the courses, (B) student engagement related to the infusion of these practices, and (C) the relationship between the use of UDL approaches and student engagement" (Smith, 2012, p. 38). Students were given a 33-item UDL-based survey and asked to complete the Utrecht Work Engagement Scale for Students (Schaufeli & Bakker, 2003). Numerous investigative conversations also occurred between the main researcher and additional instructor, with the information being used to intentionally revise courses scheduled for the next semester. According to Smith (2012, p. 50-51), the value of this longitudinal study is threefold: 1) it provides a survey tool "that begins to discern which UDL variables are perceived to have a relationship with student interest and engagement, 2) offer(s) data (statistically significant for several of the survey questions) that support(s) the relationship of UDL strategies and technologies on student interest and engagement, and 3) provide(s) a detailed look at how a faculty redesigned a traditional graduate course through a UDL lens in college classrooms."

Concluding comments. Each of these UDL research studies was chosen because a major component of our two-year project was the intentional inclusion of faculty training prior to the application and assessment of classroom practices. While our study produced a variety of outcomes that are discussed throughout the book, the model used did attempt to provide consistent, supportive training throughout the experience. We felt that UDL-related training was essential in producing knowledgeable, skilled and confident faculty. We provided training opportunities in multiple venues as discussed in Chapter 3.

References

Al-Azawei, A., Serenelli, F., & Lundqvist, K. (2016). Universal design for learning (UDL): A content analysis of peer-reviewed journal papers from 2012 to 2015. *Journal of Scholarship of Teaching and Learning, 16*(3), 39-56.

Bartram, B., & Bailey, C. (2009). Different students same difference? A comparison of UK and international students' understandings of 'effective teaching'. *Active Learning in Higher Education, 10*(2), 172-184.

Bass, R. (1999). The scholarship of teaching: What's the problem? Creative thinking about learning and teaching. *The Carnegie Foundation for the Advancement of Teaching, 1*(1), n.p.

Boyer, E. (1996). *From scholarship reconsidered to scholarship assessed.* Presentation at 1995 National Association for Physical Education in Higher Education. Retrieved from http://boyerarchives.messiah.edu/files/Documents4/1000%200001%206487ocr.pdf

Boyer, E. (1990). *Scholarship reconsidered: Priorities of the professoriate.* San Francisco, CA: Jossey-Bass.

Branson, R.K., Rayner, G. T., Cox, J. L., Furman, J. P., King, F. J., & Hannum, W. H. (1975). *Interservice procedures for instructional systems development* (Vols. 1- 5). TRADOC Pam 350-30, NAVEDTRA 106A. Ft. Monroe, VA: U.S. Army Training and Doctrine Command.

Carnegie Academy for the Scholarship of Teaching and Learning (CASTL). (1999). *Informational program booklet.* Menlo Park, CA: The Carnegie Foundation for the Advancement of Teaching.

Carnegie Foundation for the Advancement of Teaching (n.d.). *Carnegie Academy for the Scholarship of Teaching and Learning.* Retrieved from http://carnegiefoundation.org/scholarship-teaching-learning

Center for Universal Design. (2008). *About UD: Universal design principles.* Raleigh, NC: Carolina State University. Retrieved from http://www.ncsu.edu/ncsu/design/cud/about_ud/udprinciples.htm

Courey, S. J., Tappe, P., Siker, J., & LePage, P. (2012). Improved lesson planning with universal design for earning (UDL). *Teacher Education and Special Education, 36*(1), 7-27.

Davies, P., Schelly, C., & Spooner, C. (2013). Measuring the effectiveness of universal design for learning intervention in postsecondary education. *Journal of Postsecondary Education and Disability, 26*(3), 195-220.

Edyburn, D. (2010). Would you recognize universal design for learning if you saw it? Ten propositions for new directions for the second decade of UDL. *Learning Disability Quarterly, 33*, 33-41.

Florida State University. (n.d.). *ADDIE Model diagram.* Tallahassee, FL: Center for Educational Technology.

Forest, E. (n.d.). Framework and Theories/ Addie Model Instructional Design. Retrieved from http://educationaltechnology.net/the-addie-model-instructional-design/

Georgia Southern University. (n.d.). Thoughts on SoTL. *International Journal of Scholarship of Teaching and Learning.* Retrieved from http://digitalcommons.georgiasouthern.edu/ij-sotl/scholarship.html

Huber, M. (2013, April 26). What is the scholarship of teaching and learning? Retrieved from https://teachingcommons.stanford.edu/teaching-talk/what-scholarship-teaching-and-learning-mary-huber

Hutchings, P. (2000). Introduction. *Opening lines: Approaches to the scholarship of teaching and learning.* San Francisco: Jossey-Bass.

Hutchings, P., Taylor Huber, M., & Ciccone, A. (2011). *The scholarship of teaching and learning reconsidered: Institutional integration and impact.* San Francisco, CA: Jossey-Bass.

The IRIS Center for Training Enhancements. (2016). *Universal design for learning: Creating a learning environment that challenges and engages all students.* Retrieved from https://iris.peabody.vanderbilt.edu/wp-content/uploads/pdf_module_outlines/udl.pdf

Leblanc, R. (1998, October 8). Good teaching: The top ten requirements. *The Teaching Professor.* Retrieved from http://www.appleseeds.org/good-teach.htm

McGhie-Richmond, D., & Sung, A. (2012). Applying universal design for learning to instructional lesson planning. *International Journal of Whole Schooling, 9*(1), 43-59.

McKenzie, W. (2002). *Multiple intelligences and instructional technology: A manual for every mind.* Eugene, OR: International Society for Technology in Education.

Office of Professional and Instructional Development. (2014). *UW-System's SoTL Leadership Site.* Retrieved from https://www.wisconsin.edu/faculty-development/

Porter, A., & Brophy, J. (1988, May). Synthesis of research on good teaching Insights from the work of the Institute for Research on Teaching. *Educational Leadership, 45*(8), 74-85.

Richardson, K. (2011). Getting started on the scholarship of teaching and learning [paper]. Bridgewater, MA: Bridgewater State University.

Rose, D. H., & Meyer, A., (Eds.; 2006). *A practical reading in universal design for learning.* Cambridge, MA: Harvard Education Press.

Schaufeli, W., & Bakker, A. (2003). *Utrecht work engagement scale. Preliminary manual.* Utrecht, Netherlands: Occupational Health Psychology Unit, Utrecht University.

Schelly, C., Davies, P., & Spooner, C. (2011). Student perceptions of faculty implementation of universal design for learning. *Journal of Postsecondary Education and Disability, 24*(1), 17-30.

Shulman, L. S. (2007). "Good teaching." Box content in Loeb, S., Rouse, C., & Shorris, A., "Introducing the Issue," in *The Future of Children, 17*(1), 6-7.

Smith, F. (2012). Analyzing a college course that adheres to the universal design for learning (UDL) framework. *Journal of the Scholarship of Teaching and Learning, 12*(3), 31-61.

Vanderbilt University Center for Teaching. (2010-2011). *Getting started*. Nashville, TN: Vanderbilt University. Retrieved from https://my.vanderbilt.edu/sotl/doing-sotl/getting-started/

Vreeburg Izzo, M., Murray, A., & Novak, J. (2008). The faculty perspective on universal design for learning. *Journal of Postsecondary Education and Disability, 21*(2), 60-72.

3 Universal Design for Learning—Project Origins

Renee D. Howarton, Ph.D.

At UW-Stout, Universal Design (UD) concepts have been present throughout the campus for many years as a result of mandated institutional policy requirements and specific academic programs that have incorporated them. Such disciplines as Rehabilitation and Counseling, Interior Design, Special Education, and Communication Technology have historically grounded UD concepts within their curriculum in an effort to assist students in designing physical and technical environments that are barrier-free. However, an effort to infuse these principles within a broader range of disciplines is a more recent application and has prompted the design and implementation of the Universal Design for Learning (UDL) yearlong programs described in this chapter.

Beginnings of the UDL Project at UW-Stout

Every once in a while a topic comes along that has the potential to affect the lives of most, if not all, individuals. For me, that topic was Universal Design for Learning. In my position as director of the Nakatani Teaching and Learning Center (NTLC), the staff develop and facilitate programs that creatively and intentionally value and support excellence in teaching and learning. Our Center works to nurture a climate of scholarship, understanding, and celebration of effective teaching practices through workshops, speakers, conference attendance, and short- and long-term program offerings.

Although efforts to advance the quality of teaching and learning on our campus have been intentionally pursued for many years, the Nakatani Teaching and Learning Center has officially existed as a Center since 2008. The programs offered by the Center are supported with funds from the Nakatani Endowment, as well as outside faculty development grants. The endowment was created by a bequest established in 1993 and the NTLC continues to carry out its goal: *to create and apply technology and research to promote the art and science of teaching.*

Inspiration for many of the Center's yearlong projects and programs is often generated from discussions associated with University of Wisconsin System Initiatives, conference themes, and academic issues. The 2008 UW System Inclusive Excellence Initiative was one of the catalysts that encouraged initial conversations about UDL and its potential application across the curriculum. Several of its premises, "creating learning environments in which students of all backgrounds can thrive," "requiring a more comprehensive, widespread level of engagement and commitment ensuring that every student fulfills their educational potential;" and "[developing] a close attentiveness to the student experience itself, including the impact of race and ethnicity, and the influence of physical ability, sexual orientation, gender expression, socioeconomic background, and first-generation status on their learning experiences" (UW System, 2013) sparked early brainstorming and exploration of possible UDL applications.

At UW-Stout, the director of UW-Stout Online, our distance education program, was seeking ways to meaningfully support online training of faculty who were or could potentially teach courses for this program. UW-Stout first began offering online courses in 1996 and has since expanded its online and distance education programs to include 13 undergraduate, 15 graduate and 24 certificates and certifications (UW-Stout Online, 2014). The course offerings include discipline-specific, customized general education courses, and School of Education professional development courses that target a range of topics from assessment to writing competencies. Many of the certifications satisfy the state's licensure requirements. UW-Stout was the first university in Wisconsin to be USDLA Quality Certified for excellence in distance education practices (UW-Stout Online, 2014).

How the UDL Project Was Structured

A cross-campus call for faculty applications was issued during spring 2011 and eleven were submitted. In addition to basic questions regarding their ability to commit to a yearlong project and courses they would be teaching in spring 2012, the application also asked for detailed paragraphs describing why they wanted to participate in the Universal Design for Learning program and how they believed this experience would benefit them as educators and enhance student learning in their particular course(s). All of the applications contained strong, thoughtful responses which resulted in all eleven faculty members being invited to participate in the program. However, as the year progressed, one person left the program due to other professional commitments.

It was always the intent of the UDL program advertisement to attract faculty participants from the widest range of disciplines possible. The objective was to encourage involvement and commitment from instructors whose disciplines had not historically applied UDL to their curricula. Those of us facilitating this yearlong, multiphase research program wanted to expand and apply UDL beyond traditional thinking. The ten faculty members who ultimately completed the program came from disciplines including Communications Technology, Construction, Business, Human Development and Family Studies, Operations and Management, Chemistry, Biology, and Education, with the majority of the participants being drawn to the in-depth project because of their desire to enhance their students' learning by making it *accessible to the broadest audience possible.*

> Once selected for the program, participants fulfilled the following requirements:
>
> - Read the book, *Universal Design in Higher Education: From Principles to Practice* (Burgstahler & Cory, 2010), as a pre-requisite for attending a two-half-day Universal Design Summer Institute workshop in August 2011.

Participants attended a workshop

- The workshop facilitator was the nationally recognized expert in Universal Design, Dr. Dave Edyburn (2016). His research investigates the use of technology for enhancing teaching, learning and performance especially in special education.

- Faculty members learned about factors affecting today's teaching environment, received an introduction to Universal Design both from a historical as well as a conceptual-based understanding, learned how to dissect course content for the purpose of meaningfully infusing UD principles and how to assess the effectiveness of UD course assignments, and were given examples of UD classroom applications.

- Participants grappled with what could best be summarized as a new way of thinking about teaching and presenting content to students. In fact, many of the participants struggled with such questions as:
    - How does the application of Universal Design principles significantly differ from "good teaching" in the classroom and across the curriculum? How could specific assignment design be utilized to enhance accessibility and improve student learning?
    - What would different UDL-based course assignments look like coming from diverse disciplines?
    - How can UDL be applied and assessed in ways that positively impact student learning and enhance the quality of the teaching environment for both students and faculty?

Following the workshop experience, project participants:

- Met twice a month during fall to discuss, plan and develop UDL teaching and learning activities that they would later implement and assess in spring semester 2012 courses. Each faculty member selected at least one course to insert one or several

UDL-oriented assignments/projects into. It was during these meetings and dialogue opportunities that instructors learned more about the UDL framework and reflected on how those principles could be applied to their disciplines and specifically, their course assignments. For guidance purposes, group members used definitions and examples derived from the *Principles of Universal Design for Instruction* (Scott, McGuire, & Shaw, 2003). They also read articles and continued referencing Burgstahler and Cory's book. While every meeting was organized by desired outcomes, the discussion and insights that occurred were organic and reflective of the various disciplines being represented.

- Interacted with Dr. Edyburn in December 2011 through Skype.

  - A wealth of ideas flowed from this synchronized conversation including the realization that a definition of UDL as it pertained to teaching in the classroom was lacking. As a result, participants suggested that it be defined as *the intentional effort to improve one's course or assignment design in an effort to make learning more effective and accessible to those who have a learning challenge while at the same time making it more accessible to everyone.*

  - They further agreed that instructors who wanted to practice effective UDL needed to incorporate multiple means of representation, multiple means of expression, and multiple means of student engagement (CAST, 2011).

  - In addition, faculty members felt that it was essential that effective universal design applications be based on a deep understanding of who one's students are before attempting to infuse UDL concepts into the classroom. They discussed the need to identify who teachers want to reach, which particular students are being targeted, and what are the most descriptive students' characteristics, including physical, mental and emotional abilities. They acknowledged the challenge of gathering this information since most faculty members develop their assignments and course strategies prior to actually meeting their students on the first day of class. However, an understanding of previously collected university data, conversations with a sampling of students enrolled in an upcoming course, and dialogue with colleagues, particularly those involved in disabilities services, could help to create a meaningful, beneficial student profile.

A discussion of "who" is in the classroom is becoming increasingly important as the number of traditional-aged college students is decreasing both within Wisconsin and throughout the nation. In an effort to maintain enrollment, more effort is being done to recruit non-traditional students such as returning veterans, professionals seeking advanced certifications and degree-completion, transfer students, and older individuals looking to take courses for personal enhancement. Thirty-eight percent of those enrolled in higher education are over the age of 25 and one-fourth are over the age of 30, with the share of all students over age 25 projected to increase another twenty-three percent by 2019 (Hess, 2011). However, regardless of traditional or non-traditional labels, the UW System works tirelessly to attract as diverse a student body as possible. As a result, the classroom can become a tapestry of different learning needs and for effective teaching and student learning to occur, a better understanding of those enrolled in courses is warranted.

- Participants also discussed that in order for the implementation of UDL to be effective, course tools and assignments had to be developed that encourage and produce student engagement, and that students needed different options and techniques for accessing information. In other words, project/assignment diversity and accessibility are prerequisites for student engagement. Faculty agreed that an ongoing challenge exists regarding how to offer students different options (choice) (CAST, 2011) for demonstrating their comprehension of course content while still creating meaningful challenge (academic rigor) in the course. Identifying a variety of ways that students can show teachers what they know and how well they understand the course content serves as the impetus for putting forth the effort to develop and offer students different options (choice) for course projects/assignments; however, participants acknowledged that offering more options often equates to increased workload. Therefore, for faculty wellbeing, participants discussed strategies for addressing the manageability and sustainability of expanding the number of UDL-based learning options they were planning on offering, agreeing that all faculty need to consider this before embracing this aspect of UDL.

- Dr. Edyburn encouraged instructors to begin their fall assignment/project development by only *targeting smaller units* that would be incorporated within their spring courses. The purpose of this request was to lessen the likelihood of instructors becoming overwhelmed by projects that were too complex, to increase the assessment and effectiveness of applied UDL tools, and to maintain commitment throughout the duration of the yearlong program. Dr. Edyburn was intentionally trying to help the group avoid faculty burnout.

- Submitted Institutional Review Board (IRB) protocols seeking approval for individual UDL research projects.
  - Specifically, the IRB forms asked that faculty be allowed to implement individualized, discipline-based assignments and assessment tools that they developed. This approval comes from our campus' Human Subjects area, housed under UW-Stout's Office of Research and Sponsored Programs, and is necessary for instructors desiring to publish or present faculty and student-related research. Our instructors did receive IRB approval for their proposed projects. As the program's

Primary Investigator, I also received IRB approval for the overarching pre- and post-surveys that were distributed to all participant courses during spring 2012.

- Implemented individualized UDL assignment projects into spring (2012) semester courses.

- Met with Dr. Edyburn in May 2012, the purpose of which was to meet in a small group setting for face-to-face conversations regarding what each faculty member did within his or her course, how their projects went, what assessment tools were used, their student learning outcomes, and their perceptions of the overall experience. He also shared his overarching perceptions of the project experience and suggested ideas for future directions.

- Completed yearlong program commitments by June 2012, including submitting a final report. The UDL report guidelines required that they answer the following questions:

1. What did you do this semester? Please describe your project/assignment.

2. How did you do that project and how did you document and assess what your students learned?

    - How did you implement your UD-oriented activities, projects or policies into your course? What steps or procedures did you take?

    - Describe the assessment tools you used in your course to document student learning. Was it one thing or a series of actions that were implemented?

    - Please attach physical examples of assignments, assessment tools and learning outcomes that you produced and collected.

3. What did you and your students learn from the experience?

- How did you capture their reflections of the experience?
- How did you document your own perceptions of how the UD project went for you and your students? Please include examples of your findings.
- What long-term lessons were learned from your experience? How do you plan to apply what you learned to future courses?

4. What are some "words of wisdom" or best practices that you would suggest that future instructors consider if implanting Universal Design for Learning concepts into one of their courses?

A collection of reflective responses capturing faculty perceptions of the experience:

As an instructor, I felt this activity was highly rewarding. I realized during this process that my biggest goal as an instructor of this course is that I want students to leave with a greater understanding of their relationship to the natural world and begin to define for themselves ethical standards for interactions with the environment. Without taking the time to thoughtfully process what I perceived the barriers to achieving this in the class room to be, I don't think I would have found this activity or this semester very rewarding. Instead, because I really processed the "what/why/how" of achieving this outcome in the classroom and the barriers students may encounter along the way, I believe I'm much better prepared to support students in the process of understanding their own relationship and connection to the natural world in all of my future courses.

K. Carlson

As a special education teacher, I was familiar with the concept of Universal Design prior to my participation in this project. Participating in this project, however, gave me a much deeper understanding of the concept of Universal Design and how it surpasses what is commonly thought of as "just good teaching." Reading the common text was a good starting point, followed by the conversations with Dr. Dave Edyburn. UDL truly came to life as I began designing and teaching my own course with UDL as a guiding construct. Working with colleagues and peers, in my own department and college as well as those from other disciplines provided a rich opportunity to discover just how powerful UDL can be in various higher education classrooms.

R. Chandler

As an instructor teaching quality control and production operations management courses, I encounter students who have difficulty understanding industrial operations because they have very limited working experience. Creative UDL approaches are needed to enhance students' awareness of the operations systems which will improve their learning outcome, encourage their use of critical thinking and strengthen their ability to identify and solve problems. Virtual modeling which virtually illustrates the operations systems, will give students an opportunity to do that.

D. Ding

What I learned was there is a better way to create or recreate assignments and other learning outcome tasks which can and for me, did show an improvement in student learning outcomes. The UDL project for me has already started to have a longer term impact. As the Business Administration Program Director, I have been working on how I teach the Introduction to Business course. This is not a challenging course, but I believe students need to have a better understanding of how to use their program plan and how advisement past the first-year works. I have a working advisement document I send to program faculty and make it available to students. Now I am going to incorporate Universal Design into this and maybe it will have more of an impact and my students and fellow colleagues will pick up on the UDL concepts.

M. Fenton

UDL has provided me with a different, more critical lens at curriculum development and pedagogy, with a goal to improve student learning at varying levels. At first, I was skeptical about going through extra steps to provide choices for the students, since the "real world" may not be so accommodating. My goal is to prepare students for their next professional experience, and I didn't want to compromise this. However, through this journey, I have learned that a student who is passionate about learning (regardless of their style), benefits from choices for engagement and expression and still delivers a quality product.

G. Rodriguez

Choice in accessing learning materials and demonstrating learning is not something all college students are accustomed to; yet, examining choices and making choices can be a motivator for learning. I learned that the choices given are important in terms of what students will choose to complete. They need to be perceived as equitable in work and in learning opportunities by students. Students' comments on surveys about the choices they made clearly indicated that the "weight" I put on certain choices or their perceptions of the easiness or quality of the choice impacted their decision about choice. "For years, researchers have studied ways to improve such student assignments by making them more interesting, applicable, and valuable to the student with a goal of improving learning outcomes by increasing student appeal. One often studied way to improve the learning outcomes is by allowing students a choice in assignments" (Fulton & Schweitzer, 2011 p. 1,). I learned that choice can be successfully implemented.

D. Stanislawski

Future cohorts need to understand that there is a significant time factor related to doing Universal Design for Learning, that there are not always clear answers or even questions, but that the time dedicated to inquiry in this area will benefit their students, and will aid them in improving their ability to reach some students who they may have had trouble reaching before and not known why. Ultimately, it is this type of activity dedicated to improving my ability to help students learn that will make me a better teacher. It has been well worth the time that I have put into this challenge.

K. Tharp

One of the most significant things I learned from this experience is that meeting the needs of all learners is a daunting task. My project was a small component of what Universal Design is. The videos that we created did not meet the needs of all learners. There are still numerous things I can do in the general chemistry course to make it a true UDL course. In order to accomplish these, we need support from the administrators which include financial support to hire students or professionals to assist the faculty member. The videos that we created are now being used in my general chemistry course for summer (2012). I am also creating more videos that I will use in this course and I will continue to assess if these videos will improve learning outcome in the online version of general chemistry.

A. Vande Linde

Reflecting on the year-long project, the concept that will have the most effect on future instruction is that content can be delivered many ways and learners are diverse. Delivering content in more than one way will likely improve learning. For future students of Universal Design, I would advise that UDL is not a method of teaching; it is more of a philosophy. Since the instruction and subjects taught at the university level are diverse, so are the applications of UDL.

D. Wirtanen

The most important thing I gained from this experience is a new lens through which to view my own course designs and the delivery of education. There are many things about UDL that I do not know yet and many other ways of making education more accessible for all that I have not heard of, but I "see" education in a new way—especially in course design. This new lens allows me to see opportunities to design and deliver my course differently. For example, I see "new opportunities" to utilize software, applications, learning activities, and course organizational tools that will make education more accessible. I am also developing a new orientation to students as collaborators in education because they are the only ones who can say what is needed, what is working, and what is not.

J. Zaloudek

Overarching UDL Research Study

During the spring semester, the program received additional funding to launch a comprehensive pre- and post-survey. With assistance from UW-Stout's Applied Research Center (ARC), the questionnaires were electronically distributed. The pre-survey consisted of 15 questions that assessed students' perceptions of how effectively previous instructors accommodated their sensory, learning, and communication needs in previous courses, as well as collected basic demographic data. A post-survey comprised of ten questions was administered to the same students to assess how well faculty participants in the current Universal Design for Learning research project satisfactorily met their educational needs and how accessible the course was to the broadest range of students. Students' attitudes regarding their learning environments were measured using a Likert-scale. One open-ended question was included in each of the surveys in order to allow respondents to voice additional comments. Survey findings were analyzed using descriptive statistics, a t-test and chi-square analysis. Individual faculty participants chose to report findings from the overall study as it personally applied to their particular course(s). Discussion of these research outcomes are referenced in several of the book's chapters.

- Courses in which the pre- and post-surveys were implemented included: AEC 191: The Built Environment, AEC 458: Structural Systems: Wood and Steel, BIO 141: Plants and People, BUINB 260: Introduction To International Business, CHEM 115: General Chemistry, EDUC 210: Impacts of Technology on Learning, EDUC 745: Assessment for Learning, HDFS 101: Introduction To Human Development And Family Studies, ICT 375/575: Web Production and Distribution, and INMGT 325/525: Quality Management.

- The pre-survey was administered in February 2012 to 320 students with a 69% (221) return, while the post-survey was sent in May 2012 to 305 students with a 71% return rate (217). One hundred eighty students completed both surveys.

- More females (104) than males (71) answered the survey, with 5 not reporting gender. The majority of respondents were between the ages of 17 and 20 years old (67), while 58 were 21 to 25. The remainder were older.

- One of the demographic questions asked students: *How do you most prefer to learn information?* Responses indicated that 115 preferred hands-on (doing); 53 preferred visual (seeing) and 9 preferred auditory (listening); 3 did not respond.

- Findings from the overarching survey were thematically categorized according to 1) Teaching Methods, 2) Sensory Abilities, 3) Practical Assignments and Feedback, 4) Use of Technology, 5) Environment Accommodating to Differences, 6) Environment Promoting Interaction, 7) Welcoming Environment, 8) Individual Learning Needs Met, and 9) Additional Comments. Summary of survey results:

	2012 Overarching UDL Course Pre-and Post- Survey Results
Thematic category	**Respondents were asked . . .**
Teaching Methods	*. . . about the teaching methods used in class and whether or not they accommodated a wide range of needs.* The mean difference (.37) between the pre- and post-survey was statistically significant, but the effect size indicated no practical significance (d .33). However, three courses, BIO 141 (d .93), HDFS 101 (d 1.24), and EDUC-210 (d .69) produced statistically higher mean ratings than the other courses, exemplifying effect sizes indicating practical significance. One of our Chemistry courses received statistically lower mean ratings with an effect size indicating practical significance (d 1.10).
Instructor Expectations	*. . . whether or not past instructors laid out their course expectations for exam performance, papers, or projects in a straightforward, clearly understandable and predictable manner.* Overall, the mean difference (.37) between the pre- and post-surveys was statistically significant, but the effect size indicated no practical significance (d .33). However, EDUC-745 indicated an effect size of d .69.

Sensory Abilities	*... whether or not the course instruction accommodated people with various different sensory abilities.* Overall, the mean difference (.54) between the pre- and post-surveys was statistically significant and had an effect size indicating practical significance (d .51). Six of the nine individual courses produced statistical differences in mean ratings and each had an effect size indicating practical significance. Those courses included: AEC-191 (d .71), AEC-458 (d .88), BIO-141 (d .57), BUINB-260 (d .73), EDUC-745 (d .76), and HDFS-101 (d 1.08).
Practical Assignments and Feedback	*... about the nature of assignments and the quality of feedback given.* Overall, the mean difference (.67) between the pre- and post-surveys was statistically significant and had an effect size indicating practical significance (d .57). Seven of the nine individual classes produced statistical differences in mean ratings and each had an effect size indicating practical significance. These courses included: AEC-191 (d .56), AEC-458 (d .90), BIO-141 (d .69), BUINB-260 (d .69), EDUC-210 (d .93), HDFS-101 (d 1.08) and ICT 375/575 (d .58).
Use of Technology	*... about the use of technology in the classroom and whether or not it helped focus the attention on learning.* Overall, the mean difference (.53) between the pre- and post-surveys was statistically significant and had an effect size indicating practical significance (d .50). Five of the nine individual classes produced statistical differences in mean ratings and each had an effect size indicating practical significance. These courses were AEC-191 (d .61), BIO-141 (d .78), BUINB-260 (d .69), EDUC-210 (d 1.30), and HDFS-101 (d .88).
Environment Accommodating to Differences	*... whether they thought the classroom environment was accommodating to differences in students' physical, intellectual and communication needs.* Overall, the mean difference (.61) between the pre- and post-surveys was statistically significant and had an effect size that indicated practical significance (d .57). Five of the nine individual classes produced statistical differences in mean ratings and each had an effect size indicating practical significance. These courses were AEC-458 (d .74), BIO-141 (d .74), EDUC-210 (d .73), HDFS-101 (d 1.22) and ICT-375/575 (d .81).
Environment Promoting Interaction	*... whether they thought the instructor created an environment that promoted interaction.* Overall, the mean difference (.32) between the pre- and post-surveys was statistically significant, but the effect size indicated no practical significance (d .29). By course, three of the nine individual classes produced statistical differences in mean ratings and each had an effect size indicating practical significance. These courses were AEC-191 (d .68), BIO-141 (d .74), and HDFS-101 (d 1.00).

Welcoming Environment	*. . . whether they thought the instructor created a welcoming environment in the classroom through a discussion of student needs.* Overall, the mean difference (.43) between the pre- and post-surveys was statistically significant, but the effect size indicated no practical significance (*d* .40). By course, AEC-191 (*d* .65), BIO-141 (*d* .78), BUINB-260 (*d* .47) and ICT-375/575 (*d* .53) produced statistically higher mean ratings and the effect sizes indicated practical significance. CHEM-115 had statistically lower mean ratings and the effect size indicated practical significance (*d* .88).
Individual Learning Needs Met	*. . . whether the class environment and materials met their individual learning needs.* Overall, the mean difference (.52) between the pre- and post-surveys was statistically significant and had an effect size indicating practical significance (*d* .48). Four of the nine individual classes produced statistical differences in mean ratings and each had an effect size indicating practical significance. These courses were AEC-191 (*d* .67), BIO-141 (*d* .86), BUINB-260 (*d* .54), and HDFS-101 (*d* .96).
Additional pre- and-post survey comments	*. . . whether they had any additional comments they wished to share.* The most common theme across both surveys related to the overall quality of the experience with either the instructor or the class itself. Comments for the pre-survey were coded into one of seven themes or subthemes. The most frequent theme cited by respondents pertained to comments about the individual *Instructor or Course* (17 comments). These comments were further broken into subthemes with an equal number of comments pertaining to a *Good Instructor or Course Experience* (3%) and *Bad Instructor or Course Experience* (3%). Comments that referred to good experiences mentioned that instructors were helpful, accommodating and knowledgeable and that they provided hands-on learning. Comments that referred to bad experiences mentioned instructors that were not helpful and did not provide feedback to students. Comments from the post-survey were coded into one of ten themes or subthemes. The most frequent theme cited by respondents pertained to respondents having a *Good Experience* (40 comments). These comments were further broken into two subthemes. The first subtheme pertained specifically to the *Instructor* (12%); comments in this theme referred to the instructor being accessible, accommodating and giving timely feedback. The second subtheme pertained specifically to the *Course* (7%); comments in this theme referred to the overall enjoyment of the course and the course being well-designed.
	Note: ** *statistical significance at the .01 level;* *statistical significance at the .05 level; and a practical significance of a minimum d of 0.41 (Ferguson, 2009).*

These survey outcomes suggest that for specific courses, the project participants were very effective in infusing UDL-based assignments and activities that made their classes feel accessible to their students. The results, however, also highlight the fact that incorporating UDL principles is complex and is dependent on many factors including: the teaching methods being used, available classroom technologies, course content, attitudes toward faculty-student engagement, quantity and quality of feedback given to students, and time and skill-related issues. This data certainly warrants future study but does provide evidence supportive of the intentionality of many of the faculty to create a better learning environment for our UW-Stout students.

Sharing Project Outcomes with Others

Since completing the 2011-12 UDL program, several of the faculty disseminated their individualized course project outcomes in a variety of scholarly venues including presentations at the Association for Environmental Studies and Sciences Conference in Santa Clara, California, June 2012; Applied Universal Design for Learning in STEM Education Conference held at UW-Stout, July 2012; International Society for the Scholarship of Teaching and Learning in Hamilton, Canada, October 2012; and National Council of Family Relations in Phoenix, Arizona, November 2012. Many of the participants also shared their outcomes in departmental gatherings and events sponsored by the Nakatani Teaching and Learning Center.

Next Phase of the UDL Program

By spring 2012, plans were underway for identifying a new cohort to further extend the infusion of Universal Design for Learning concepts into more UW-Stout classrooms. Five faculty members were accepted into the program and their disciplines included: English and Philosophy, Human Development and Family Studies, Operations Management, and Technology. Once again, the new cycle was kicked off with a summer workshop. However, instead of bringing in Dr. Edyburn for the workshop, an invitation was extended to former participants to present during a full one-day event. Three of the previous group members joined me in facilitating the workshop. One of them initiated the event with a description of Universal Design concepts that provided a greater understanding of the basics of UDL. During her presentation, she demonstrated the CAST UDL Studio website http://udlstudio.cast.org/ as well as UDL Connect http://community.udlcenter.org/. She also shared ideas for designing assessment-based learning outcomes and encouraged the new cohort to start from where they were comfortable because she had observed that it was easy to lose sight of the bigger picture if attempting a UDL project that was too overwhelming. The two other facilitators shared personal stories regarding the UDL projects they had implemented, the assessment tools they used, their student learning outcomes, and the overall lessons learned and insights gained from having participated in the yearlong program. Between speakers, the new participants discussed their personal perceptions of Universal Design compared to what was shared by the speakers. They also talked about what they had previously observed in their courses regarding student learning issues that might be UDL-related and brainstormed ways they could make learning discipline-based subjects more accessible for the broadest number of their students.

In fall, members of the new cohort met on a bi-weekly basis to develop assignments/projects as well as assessment tools that they implemented in spring 2013. In other words, they replicated activities that characterized the pilot program with a few modifications.

- Instead of reading the book, *Universal Design in Higher Education: From Principles to Practice*, prior to attending the August workshop, they read and discussed it throughout the year.

- Former participants periodically joined the group to discuss their UDL assignments/projects in greater detail and several administrators representing key areas on campus that were directly linked to Universal Design issues were invited to dialogue about the services their Centers offer. For example, our director of Disability Services helped participants better understand the process and options available for accommodating students with disabilities on our campus, and her information sparked a discussion regarding what is expected of teachers relative to meeting specialized student needs versus an ethical obligation to provide quality, equitable educational experiences for everyone. The director of Counseling Services was instrumental in helping the faculty better understand changes in student behaviors that we are seeing today that affect classroom environments. The intent behind these visits was to assist faculty in better understanding the students they would be designing UDL projects and assignments for in their courses.

- During each group meeting, faculty provided an update of how their assignments/projects and assessment tools were coming, both from developmental and implementation perspectives. At one point in the semester, they brought in outside articles that exemplified ideas for applying UDL to their discipline areas, and as a group, they also explored avenues for disseminating their project outcomes, including contributing to the writing of this book.

Simultaneously, another more advanced yearlong program was formed that consisted of three of the first year's cohort members committing to continue their Universal Design research. They agreed to meet bi-weekly to discuss how they would enhance and expand previous UDL projects, assist in identifying future grant options that could possibly be used to create more Universal Design-related faculty development opportunities, serve in a variety of mentorship roles for the new UDL cohort, and participate in the writing of a book that would showcase what was achieved with the current and former UDL program participants. They also played an important role in bringing Dr. Edyburn back to UW-Stout to work with them and the new cohort members. To assist them in developing their advanced UD projects/program, participants were asked the following questions:

1. Now that you have had some time to reflect on last year's UD program experience and accomplishments, what do you personally want to work on and achieve in a more advanced program?

2. What resources do you think that you will need to accomplish your goals?
3. Are you willing to play a role in helping the new cohort group develop their projects throughout the coming year? What might your involvement look like?
4. What should we do with the artifacts of last year's UD project? Final reports? Overarching survey outcomes?

Funding for UDL Program

UW-Stout Online provided funding for both the 2011-2012 and 2012-2013 versions of this research project as well as for the Advanced UDL program. That funding supported services and supplies allocations for all program participants, covered speaker fees, paid for services provided by our on-campus Applied Research Services office that handled the distribution and analysis of survey data, and funded workshop expenses. Faculty participants were deeply grateful for the generous and ongoing financial support that they received.

The UW-Stout Online director agreed to fund these programs because of his sincere interest in identifying ways to continually improve online course instruction and to make learning as accessible to the broadest range of students, many of which are non-traditional students. Readers will notice as they peruse the remaining chapters that not every course that was involved in this research program turned out to be an online class. Educators are well aware that course schedules that are planned a year in advance can and often do change. Understanding this reality of academia, the UW-Stout Online director embraced the value of different research outcomes being produced from both learning environments, believing that this was a productive use of funding.

Additional Project Reflections

Although I have attempted to accurately describe the UDL program as it was implemented at UW-Stout, I encourage readers to realize that funding on their campus for a project of this nature might come from other sources including working with the Provost's Office and/or tapping into financial support administered by deans and department chairs. Financial support connected with specific campus Centers such as those related to vocational rehabilitation, disabilities, special education and design may be excellent sources to pursue.

Applying to granting agencies should also be considered since this is a very timely and significant topic in the field of education. Finally, industries may be open to financing this type of research especially if instructors are willing to design UDL projects/assignments that are related to their professional interests. A successful working partnership is possible provided that these companies recognize and value the need for educating/training the broadest range of learners/employees.

2011-2012 UDL Cohort Project Timeline		
Met with UW-Stout Online	Secured funding commitment	November/December 2010
Identified D. Edyburn as a potential workshop facilitator	Began arranging August workshop logistics	February 2011
Created UDL program advertisements	Distributed across campus	March 2011
Received faculty applications	Selection of applicants & notification of yearlong project expectations	April 2011
Faculty workshop preparation	Books for August workshop were distributed to participants	May 2011
NTLC & UW-Stout Online hosted UDL workshop	10 faculty participants met for UDL Workshop	August 8-9, 2011
Fall bi-weekly meetings	Participants met to learn more about UDL & to develop assignments/ projects & assessment tools; 2 groups instead of 1 large one were formed due to conflicting work schedules	September to December 2011
IRB program submission	NTLC submitted IRB form for overarching program; UDL participants submitted their IRBs shortly thereafter	November/December 2011
Synchronized distance education conference with D. Edyburn	Project updates were shared & UDL questions were discussed	December 19, 2011
Spring bi-weekly meetings	Faculty implemented their projects, shared updates, & explored dissemination opportunities	January to May 2012

Overarching UDL questionnaires	Disseminated pre-surveys	February 2012
Overarching UDL questionnaires	Disseminated post-surveys	April/May 2012
D. Edyburn returns to UW-Stout	On-campus individual & group meetings	May 9, 2012
NTLC's MayDay Event	First UDL participant presentation of projects	May 21, 2012
Applied Research Services	NTLC received UDL overarching survey results	June 2012
UDL project reports	Final reports summarizing individual projects & outcomes due	June 30, 2012
UDL faculty presentations	Several on-campus & off-campus professional presentations	July to October 2012
2012-2013 UDL Cohort		
Replication of UDL yearlong program	Most of the previous program activities were duplicated; a mentoring component was added	April 2012 to June 2013
2012-2013 Advanced UDL Cohort		
Previous UDL participants – advanced program	Met bi-weekly to discuss expansion of last year's UDL projects & new responsibilities (book facilitation, mentoring, etc.)	April 2012 to 2014

The project participants, with their diverse background of disciplines and different approaches to teaching, have made valuable inroads into moving beyond the traditional disabilities model of simply accommodating students with self-proclaimed learning challenges that limit course access to becoming instructors who preemptively present course content in ways that address and account for defined and/or undefined accessibility challenges. This transition in understanding and application, however, did not come easily nor was the cognitive process identical for every participant. Changes in the way that our faculty came to view UDL fell along a continuum, ranging from a "greater awareness of UDL" to a "genuine paradigm shift." For some, project participants were content to learn more about UDL and apply it on a limited basis, whereas others initiated extensive revision of course content and have since continued to study UDL, modify their curriculum, and espouse the value of Universal Design for Learning to others.

Ongoing Impact of the UDL Program

At the start of this chapter it was mentioned that several of our campus disciplines incorporate Universal Design concepts within their curriculum in an effort to meaningfully imbue our graduates with an understanding of how to design processes and products that are accessible for the broadest range of students possible. Knowing that such application of UD concepts already exists warrants intentional reflection on what real impact and value our two faculty research studies had at UW-Stout. While the specific UDL research program has yielded a plethora of individual course and overarching project data, examples of campus-wide influence and impact have often been anecdotal, but no less important.

From discussions with colleagues at every level of the university, the significance and impact of the project appears to be multifold:

- Faculty who were not necessarily in UD related fields have learned and applied these principles to their curriculum, with 15 cohort members completing the 2011-2012 and 2012-2013 programs. As a result of the assignments and activities they wove into their courses, 510 students were provided more "choice" and ways to "express" what they learned, and with assessment being a required component of the yearlong project, a large body of documentation now exists for future instructors to utilize. Many of those findings are discussed within this book.

- Inspired project participants have shared with colleagues and administrators alike what they learned about UDL, along with their project outcomes. These conversations have often been relayed back to NTLC. With an increased understanding of UDL and its importance in making classroom learning more accessible to current and potential students, many administrators have become more supportive of their colleagues' involvement in the UDL projects. In some cases, they have even provided follow-up support for the creation of additional UDL course offerings. Again, 10 different disciplines were represented within our two-year research project, with many of the participants also being involved in professional activities and serving on committees where this topic was discussed.

- In general, the use of UD terminology and the intentional inclusion of it as talking points has increased and is more commonly heard throughout our campus, especially in disciplines where it was previously nonexistent. This is a considerable change from years past and we believe that our UDL projects and efforts to disseminate our outcomes have aided in supporting this greater awareness and acceptance.

- As a result of this project, the NTLC staff now intentionally references it in a variety of its programming including its application and relevance to:

  - New Instructor Workshop, a four-day program designed to orient new hires about the teaching, research and service expectations characteristic of our campus culture.

  - Infusing Diversity across the Curriculum five-year research project which has now included 40 faculty members and over 500 students.

  - Faculty Sharing Communities such as our Online Pedagogy in Higher Education in which 8 to10 faculty gather on an ongoing basis to discuss how to utilize our extensive campus technology in ways that enhance learning for students taking online courses.

  - Scholarship of Teaching and Learning (SoTL) program offerings that intentionally promote research in the classroom in an effort to improve instruction and learning outcomes. These UDL projects were an excellent example of SoTL research in action.

  - Cross-campus involvement in the expansion of Credit for Prior Learning and assessment components intended to make our curricula more accessible to returning and nontraditional students.

- For several of the participants, project involvement encouraged them to learn and apply new technologies to their course(s) including the application of Canvas, a software editing program that enables students to create original art work and Web graphics, along with modifying existing visuals and documents. Some of them introduced discipline-based technologies into their course(s) such as in the area of Communication Technology, while many of them also explored ways to more effectively utilize our Communication Management Service (CMS), better known as Learn@UW-Stout, for making course content more UDL-friendly via increased organization and greater accessibility. They did this in an effort to enhance learning, lessen student frustration, and encourage retention of course content.

- Some of the participants created UDL experiential learning opportunities for students outside the classroom. In one particular case, a student was hired to analyze extensive data from individual faculty project assessments. By participating in this research, she developed a greater understanding of UDL and how it could be applied to a discipline-specific study, while simultaneously assisting her faculty mentors with their research needs. Additional students were exposed to UDL as faculty assistants, helping to prepare and assess UDL-based classroom assignments and activities.

- Involvement in this project has led to the design of new courses and the revision of existing ones. When asked, former participants refer to the following course modifications as "UDL informed." In other words, they were inspired to apply what they learned from their participation in our UDL projects. For example, some "informed" courses include:
    - HDFS 101: Introduction to Human Development and Family Studies (1 credit—online); HDFS 215: Family Dynamics (3 credits—online); HDFS 365: Family Resource Management (3 credits—online); HDFS 450: Family Policy (3 credits—online and f2f); HDFS 490: Professional Issues (2 credits—online); HDFS 330: Human Development—Middle

Adulthood (3 credits—online); and HDFS 420: Research Methods (3 credits—online).

- In the area of Special Education, a project member implemented UDL practices into her EDUC-745 Assessment for Learning course and has helped develop curriculum for EDUC-643 Differentiated Instruction. This particular program also offers EDUC-652 Universal Design for Learning, http://www.uwstout.edu/soe/profdev/universal-design.cfm.

- As noted earlier in the chapter, numerous local, national and international presentations by members of our two UDL cohorts have resulted in the sharing of stories and project outcomes with wider audiences.

Preparation for Writing this Book

For those who authored chapters for this book, the learning curve has been high. The team consisting of Drs. Carlson, Chandler, Zaloudek and myself have continually accessed information and expertise for the purpose of informing and training fellow colleagues along the way. These efforts have included learning from those who have successfully published UDL books to actually contacting book publishers and learning from their critiques. Each insight has resulted in personal reflection and often the revision of existing manuscripts. For example, focusing the book's content within "academic diversity" and applying the ADDIE model to present project content in a more understandable and interesting manner were the rich outcomes of conversations sparked by comments and questions from others. Through the use of e-mail communication, face-to-face meetings, and personalized manuscript feedback, the team endeavored to be transparent throughout the process, serve as problem-solvers, be cheerleaders when necessary, and never ever give up on moving forward with the writing of this book.

Final Thoughts

This chapter describes the journey that my colleagues have taken from idea conception to implementation, evaluation and ongoing course modification. All along the way, friendships have been forged and numerous UDL lessons learned. Perhaps the most valuable lesson for our campus is the growing acceptance and realization that creating courses that are accessible to the broadest range of students is not an option, but rather it is essential for reaching tomorrow's student, and it is inherent in achieving equitable, quality education in the classroom.

About the Author

Dr. Renee Howarton is a full professor currently serving as director of the Nakatani Teaching and Learning Center (NTLC) at UW-Stout. For most of her 30-year career in academia, she taught retail-related courses, both face-to-face and online. Her research interests have included studying how to teach appearance-based and minority and aging related consumer marketing issues in ways that support deeper student learning. In recent years, she has designed and assessed faculty development opportunities that bring instructors and funding together to enhance learning and classroom scholarship, while improving teaching practices across the curriculum.

References

Burgstahler, S., & Cory, R. (2010). *Universal design in higher education: From principles to practice*, Cambridge, MA: Harvard Education Press.

Center for Applied Special Technology (CAST). (2011). *About CAST*. Retrieved from http://www.cast.org/

Edyburn, D. (2016). *University of Central Florida* [website]. Retrieved from http://education.ucf.edu/faculty_detail.cfm?id=1022&pid=fd&cat=1

Ferguson, C. (2009). An effect size primer: A guide for clinicians and researchers. *Professional Psychology: Research and Practice*, p. 1-2.

Fulton, S., & Schweitzer, D. (2011). Impact of giving students a choice of homework assignments in an introductory computer science class. *International Journal for the Scholarship of Teaching & Learning, 5*(1), 1-12.

Hess, F. (2011, September). Old school: College's most important trend is the rise of the adult student. *The Atlantic.* Retrieved from https://www.theatlantic.com/business/archive/2011/09/old-school-colleges-most-important-trend-is-the-rise-of-the-adult-student/245823/

Scott, S. S., McGuire, J. M. and Shaw, S. F. (2003, November/December). Universal design for Instruction: A new paradigm for adult instruction in postsecondary education. *Remedial and Special Education, 24*(6), 369-379.

UW-Stout Online. (2014). *Online and distance education programs and degrees* [website]. Retrieved from http://www.uwstout.edu/de/deo.cfm

University of Wisconsin System. (2013). *Academic and student affairs inclusive excellence* [website]. Retrieved from https://www.wisconsin.edu/inclusive-excellence/

Acknowledgements

John Achter, director of Counseling Services at UW-Stout. The Center provides free, confidential counseling to currently enrolled students, offering such services as group counseling as well as individual or couples counseling.

Dave Edyburn, UW-Milwaukee, has authored over 150 articles and book chapters on the use of technology in special education. Also as the co-principal investigator for the Universal Design Infusion of Technology and Evaluation for Accessible Campuses of Higher Education (UDITEACH) Project, he has been participating in the development of the federally-funded model demonstration project that seeks to infuse universal design across college campuses (Edyburn, UW-Milwaukee website, 2011).

Kara James, director of Disability Services at UW-Stout. Once admitted to the university, this office works with students to ensure that they receive academic accommodations (extended time on tests, interpreting, braille, audio textbooks, etc.), if needed.

Kiyo Nakatani, in memory of her late son, Arthur M. Nakatani, a UW-Stout alumnus, established a bequest in 1993; the Nakatani Teaching and Learning Center continues to receive funding from this endowment.

Dan Riordan championed the pursuit of quality teaching and learning at UW-Stout for over twelve years, establishing the Nakatani Teaching and Learning Center in 2008. He served as NTLC Director from 2008 to 2010.

Doug Stevens, director of UW-Stout Online, our customized tuition program, provided funding and essential support throughout all of the Universal Design projects. It has been a pleasure and a privilege to work with him throughout the duration of the different UDL research programs.

Section 2

Classroom Application, Assessment & Outcomes

4 No Accommodations Needed: Designing by and for the Students

Julie A. Zaloudek, Ph.D.

Course Design by and for the Students

"Your ego is a bad designer" (Butler, 2012). This is the title of an article I read about designing websites when I was working on a volunteer project. But I am not a web designer. I am a teacher. I design curricula, courses, spaces for learning, and specific learning opportunities. Still, I am convinced that my ego IS a bad designer. I am also quite sure that my ego is a bit fragile sometimes. There have been times when I reacted to criticisms of my courses with defensiveness, hurt feelings, or even anger. All of these emotional reactions tempt me to dismiss the criticisms and the students who make them. After all, I work very hard on my courses. I am trained in teaching and learning. I am competent. I know how to do my job better than the student. I am the expert!

If I fail my students, it is not for lack of expertise or competency: it is for a lack of humility and insight. Butler (2012) says that good leaders know that they may be their own worst enemies, that leaders must value progress more than their egos. I am trying to value student learning more than my own ego-driven preferences for teaching, and it is not easy. Letting go of my ego does not mean doing whatever the students want, and that is the tricky part: I must have the patience to listen to my students, the insight to interpret their comments and accurately infer learning needs they may not fully know themselves, the creativity to martial my knowledge and skills to envision a course design responsive to student needs, and the courage to act on that design idea. Tall order. That was the goal of the pilot project that I will describe in this chapter. I will attempt to describe it honestly—from brilliant successes to dismal failures—with a transparency that I hope will allow the reader to "follow along" and use what is helpful.

Analysis: Why I Needed to Change my Course to "Student Designed"

"You don't find out anything until you start showing it to people" (Kelly as qtd. in Butler, 2009, para. 2). How many times have I designed a well-organized, engaging, appropriately paced course with crystal-clear explanations that is perfectly suited to the level and abilities of my incoming students and then found out that, well, it wasn't? The answer is, every time I design a new course. How many times have I complained about students not getting it? A lot. And when I began teaching fully online courses in 2010, I discovered very quickly that if I didn't change how I designed courses to better suit students, I would have to forgo leisurely evenings, weekends, and lunch breaks to deal with the deluge of emails, instant messages, and calls from students asking for clarifications. And I began to wonder, if it is unclear to students how to format their current event logs or use the course website, how could I assume that the content I was delivering and learning exercises I was assigning were effective in facilitating student learning? I couldn't.

How I Taught Before Using the Universal Design for Learning Framework (UDL).

Before using UDL as a design framework, my courses were tightly designed with a logical sequence and assignments that fit the learning objectives. Students and colleagues highly evaluated my course designs and teaching. The approach was also very instructor driven with a specific plan for learning, sequence, path to completing coursework, and tools to aid students in doing so. For example, the syllabus would say EXACTLY what students should do, how they should do it, in what order they should do it, where they could find supportive tools (e.g., technology, tutorials, writing center), when and where they should turn in work, and the criteria that I set for evaluating their work. Deviations in this specific plan generally meant that students would not do as well in the class as if they fully conformed to my conception of their learning. In short, my classes were considered to be very well designed and executed without major flaws. If students struggled to understand my expectations or grasp instructions, my "go-to line" was, "Read the syllabus!"

Learning Needs. Despite good designs, my students continued to struggle with two main problems. **First, students struggled to adequately track the expectations of the course as well as individual assignments.** This was demonstrated by many emails to me requesting clarification, students posting confused messages in the student forum, and turning in assignments that missed the mark in terms of my expectations. **Second, students struggled to make their own connections between what we were doing in class and their future professional lives.** Their assignments were done in a perfunctory way with all the trappings of an "A" or "B" but without signs of deep engagement with content or evidence of some of the higher levels of engagement with content—such as applying and connecting knowledge beyond the explicit requirements of assignments. In short, many students were not truly grasping what I expected of them, both in terms of specific requirements and the "so what?" or why this content matters.

Previous Design Approach	UDL Design Approach Students were provided:	Outcomes Students:
• For each topic, content is delivered in a single way that is determined by the instructor (e.g. readings, lectures, podcasts). • Supportive learning tools and technologies are pre-selected by the instructor and the same for every student (unless they are getting ADA accommodations).	*Multiple means of Represented Content • Options for Perception (visual, audio, "hands-on") • Options for Comprehension of Content ("novice" to "expert") • Options for Comprehension of Course Expectations (e.g. checklists, video email instructions, student examples, etc.)	• Access multiple means of represented content throughout the course. • Heavily used most of the tools with almost 100% using them at the beginning and 50% at the end.

• All students complete the same assignments in the same way to meet the course objectives.	**Multiple Means of Action and Expression** • Options for Expressive Skills and Fluency (given choices for major assignments) • Options for Executive Functions (tools for organizing and prioritizing work such as checklists, overviews, calendars, and planning options)	• Express satisfaction with choices, but selected the more familiar kinds of assignments. • Rely heavily on planning tools, especially at the beginning of the course.
• Students primarily responsible for their own motivation to invest in the course. • Students had some options for self-regulation, such as feedback on assignments.	**Multiple Means of Engagement** • Options for Recruiting Interest (pre-survey and multiple surveys throughout course to engage student investment in the course) • Options for Sustaining Effort and Persistence (interactive checklists show % completed) • Options for Self-Regulation (modules semi-flexible with hard end-deadlines but opportunities to structure work within those deadlines, timely instructor feedback, options to re-do some assignments, multiple quiz attempts, examples of student work)	• Perceive the course as unique to their needs and express enthusiasm for the design • Use interactive checklist with almost 100% participation in first half of the course and 50% in second half, but are consistent to end in their efforts (except for 2 who dropped out immediately) • Show variation in how they regulate their timing, utilizing flexibility of the design • Heavily utilize second attempts, feedback, and re-do options

*Middle column adapted from CAST (2011). *Universal Design for Learning Guidelines version 2.0.* Wakefield, MA: Author.

Universal Design for Learning paradigm shift. I remember a day when I was frustrated by receiving assignments that did not meet requirements, complaints from students, and the constant stream of student emails to justify their poor work and try to renegotiate grades. I thought about going to the faculty lounge to complain to colleagues about how unprepared students are, how they don't bother reading the syllabus thoroughly, and everything they lacked from motivation to perseverance to email etiquette. But before doing that, I decided to make some changes in the module for the following week, based on the exhausting (and agitating!) student feedback. Interestingly, my students became much more responsible, intelligent, and hard working the next week, and I wondered, "Is it possible that it was ME and not THEM who was working ineffectively?"

I am not saying that students are never responsible for failure to learn or do well in a course, but I am saying that sometimes, much of the time, I was unwittingly putting up barriers to student learning by obliviously designing courses guided by my own ego and projecting my unique learning preferences onto my students—students who had unique needs of their own that I was not bothering to discover and incorporate. This reflexivity on my teaching led me to wonder if I could "get into" the learning experiences of my students so I could see my courses from their point of view, and make them better. This is what I refer to as the UDL paradigm shift. Instead of thinking about poor performance in terms of student deficits, we think about how course design either facilitates or frustrates opportunities for success and learning afforded to our students.

This is why, when the opportunity for training on Universal Design for Learning came up at my institution, I applied right away. My first project in applying UDL principles was a Participatory Action Project of a student-designed course: Introduction to Human Development and Family Studies (HDFS 101).

Design: By Students for Students

My goal was to engage students in the design of the course before the course began so that the course would be constructed from the students' perspectives and perceived learning needs. I also intended to elicit regular feedback so that I could effectively respond to student learning needs as they emerged instead of making changes based on student evaluations at the end of the course—when the current students could no longer benefit from the changes.

Although the design was guided by teaching and learning strategies that had proven effective in other contexts (e.g., by my own experience or outcome research), the specific design came directly from what the students in the class said worked for them. The goal for this first project was not to construct a "universally designed" course that would work for every kind of learner, but to construct a course that would work for every learner *in this course* as an entry point into universal design that would help me anticipate a broader range of learners for future courses. I hoped to address the learning gap in two ways. **First, I hoped that the expectations would be clearer to them if the course was designed based on strategies that they claimed were effective for their learning. Second, I hoped that if students were involved in constructing the course, they would perceive the content as meaningful to them and connected to their professional goals.**

Student profile. The course in which I chose to apply the UDL framework was HDFS 101—a one credit, fully online course for transfer students in the first semester of a degree completion program. Over half of our students in the online degree completion program are non-traditional students who are getting a second chance at a degree or making a career change. They are much more likely than the on-campus students to be caregiving for family members, working full time, and/or providing the primary financial support for their households. I chose the course because it is their first exposure to courses in our program and to me as their program director, advisor, and instructor. I am the only person who teaches it online in our department, and every new admit takes it in the first semester. This means that I get every student in our online program in their first semester and have sole responsibility for designing and executing the course.

Project description and assessment plan. I used a Participatory Action Research (PAR) approach to designing, implementing, and assessing this UDL project. PAR is embedded in a critical paradigm that highlights the inequities in power and opportunity that privilege some people at the expense of others (Levin & Greenwood, 2011). PAR fits within this paradigm by actively deconstructing the "traditional" process of research that places the expert researcher at the top of the hierarchy and the passive (and disempowered) participants at the bottom. This is done by involving the participants in the design, implementation, and (ideally) dissemination of the research findings. Controlling bias in order to produce generalizable results is not the intent of PAR. Rather, the goal of PAR is to incite change, especially empowering participants to enact the changes that are important to them. This was a very suitable approach to this project as it parallels UDL's approach of designing courses from the student rather than instructor perspective.

UDL requires that educators make continual efforts to understand learner differences so they can anticipate and design courses accessible to all potential learners (Meo, 2008). This is a daunting and potentially overwhelming task as we are all bound by our own experience and egos. We have some knowledge of what works for us, for others who we speak with directly, and others to whom we have been exposed to through indirect sources (e.g., books, media, descriptions from others). But how can we possibly design for *all potential* learners? This laudable goal threatened to discourage me until I decided to work at it one class at a time, beginning with this class and gradually building my repertoire of diverse learners that I could anticipate and for whom I could design.

In summary, for this UDL pilot project, students were empowered to reflect upon, articulate, and co-design a course that fit their learning needs and met their educational goals and objectives as well as the requirements of the department and university. I planned to give them opportunities to revise the course throughout the semester and to learn visually and audibly through different types of lecture deliveries. When the course finished, I intended to have them reflect on where the design succeeded and failed and how it could be revised to maximize opportunities for them to flourish.

This student-led approach to the course design resulted in (at students' request): diverse modes of content delivery, diverse opportunities to demonstrate skills and knowledge, and a variety of tools to support learning. These preferences became part of the course design, and were developed and implemented throughout the course.

Develop

Two weeks before the semester began I emailed students informed consent forms with a brief explanation of the student driven design. A survey link for reflecting on learning preferences was also emailed. Responses to survey (Appendix A) and reflections were requested within 5 days. Nine days before the semester began I followed up on and summarized student feedback from the pre-survey, which included preferences for content delivery, modes of assessment, pace and timing, structure/flexibility, tools, etc. Then I created and distributed a syllabus that was responsive to the student preferences and suggestions. Five days before the semester began I emailed students the syllabus, asking for any final feedback within three days. Two days before the semester began I finalized the syllabus, based on student feedback, and revised the course design and course shell in the Learning Management System (LMS) to meet the expressed needs of the students.

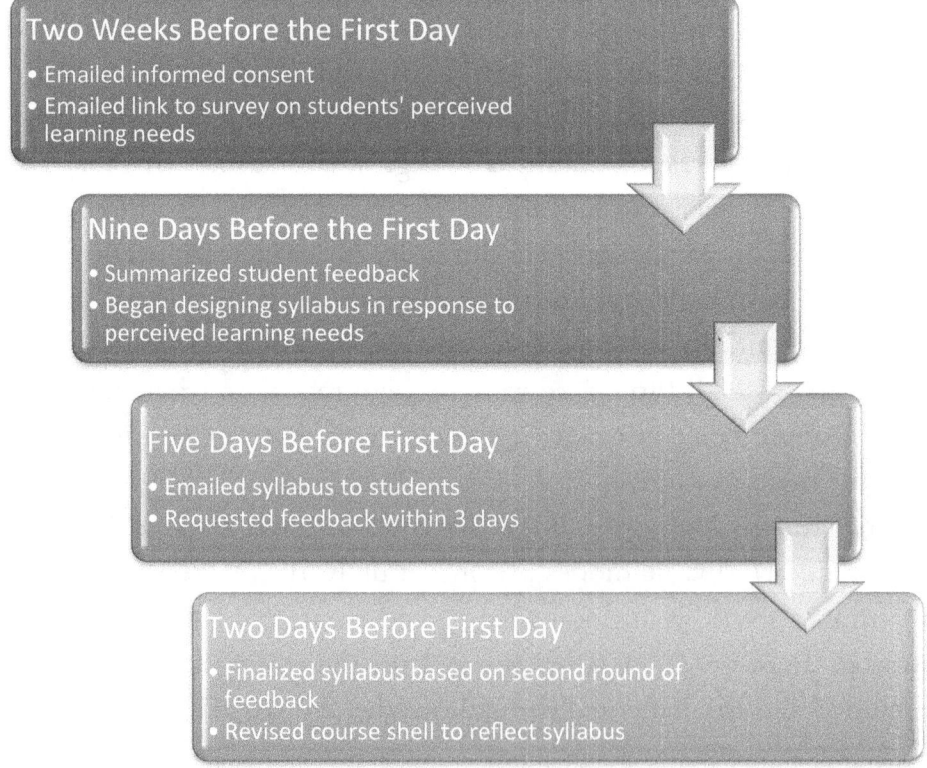

Simply put, students wanted diverse, meaningful options for receiving content, expressing learning, and engaging. They also wanted *every* available tool option to support their learning. In response, I provided a variety of diverse and meaningful options and opportunities, described below.

STUDENTS' EXPRESSED NEEDS	DESIGN RESPONSE
Multiple Means of Representation	
Diverse sensory ways of receiving information - auditory, visual and hands-on. *Note: It came out that I had a deaf and a blind student in this class, which became a good test for the universally accessible learning.	• **Provided audio and visual options for content** to the extent possible. E.g. written assignment guides and recorded "talk throughs" • **Provided content at various levels of entry.** E.g. Complex readings accompanied by audio/visual summary of
Content delivery in order of importance was: 1. Lectures from Instructor 2. Audio-visual Media 3. Textbook 4. Popular Articles 5. Audio Only Media 6. Academic Articles Wanted choice in how to receive content.	main points. Students encouraged to use summaries as scaffolds to the articles. • **Favored lectures, audio-visual media and the textbook for representing content.** Since learning to read academic articles was a learning objective, I did assign them, but with scaffolding supports.
Multiple Means of Expression	
Ways to express learning in order of importance were: 1. Discussions 2. Untimed Study Activities/Worksheets 3. Projects with flexibility and options 4. Writing a Paper 5. Traditional Exams (timed, closed book) 6. Presentations Wanted choice in how to express learning.	• **Discussions** were included in most weekly modules. • **Open book, untimed reading quizzes** with application and critical thinking questions replaced traditional timed exams. Students were given two attempts on the quizzes. • **Choices** for expressing learning were included for the three major assignments. *See Appendix B*
Engagement with Other Students	
Small majority preferred to work alone rather than in groups – expressing concern about fairness, different work styles, dependability and communication.	Discussions were used as a means for students to get and provide feedback on each other's ideas, but assignments were completed independently.
Helpful Learning Tools	
Every tool listed on the survey was checked as "helpful" to students, as indicated by the percentages below: 1. Written rubrics for assignments (100%) 2. Written and/or Verbal Feedback on Work (100%) 3. Detailed *written* explanations of assignments (100%) 4. Scheduled chat time with instructor (91%) 5. Weekly course announcements from instructor (91%) 6. Weekly checklist (82%) 7. *Verbal* explanation of assignments (64%) 8. Examples of quality work from former students (64%) 9. Student forum to discuss class work with peers (64%)	**All of the tools were provided in the course.** This resulted in significant overlap and reinforcement of material. For example, weekly expectations would appear in: 1. Written instructions in the module 2. Recorded "talk through" of instructions in the module 3. Weekly announcements 4. Example of former student work 5. Weekly checklist (briefly) Additionally, expectations were reinforced via: 6. Feedback (post submitting the assignment) 7. Scheduled chats with the instructor

Implement

During weeks 1-15 the course was implemented according to plan with scheduled feedback, discussion, and (potential) course revisions at Week 8. During Weeks 15-16, data was collected on the learning experience through audio and written reflections and a post-survey. This data, along with data collected throughout the course, was used to evaluate the design.

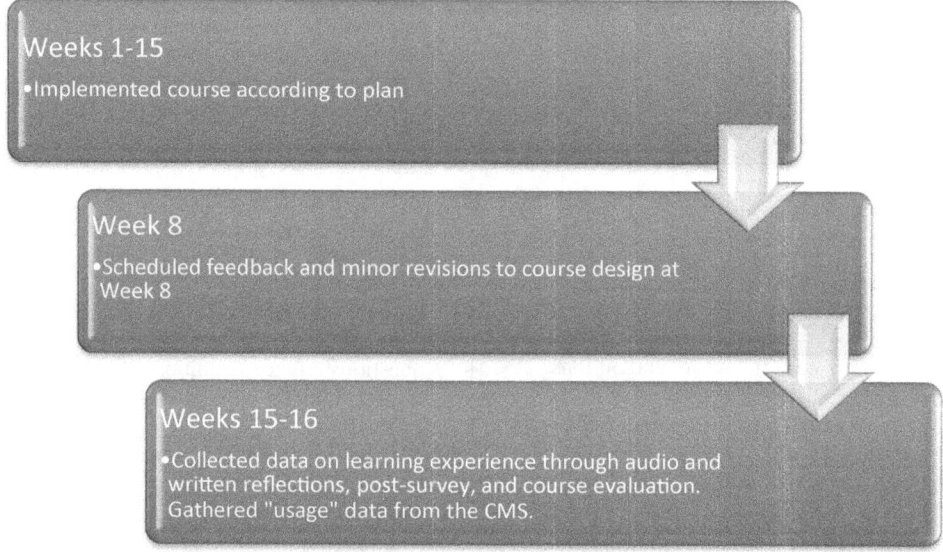

Evaluate: Method of Assessing the Effectiveness of the Design

Evaluation of the course design focused on the students' perceptions of how effective the design was in helping them learn. In the pre-survey and discussions before the class began, I invited students to tell me their learning preferences (in terms of content delivery), the most effective way for them to express their learning, and what kinds of tools they thought would support their learning. Although we cannot conclude from the data gathered if their learning happened as a result of specific UDL element/s of the course, we can infer if students found the content delivery and tools useful by examining how the students used the various methods of delivery and tools. Descriptive data on student usage of UDL course elements were gathered and examined to see if students actually used the elements that they said they would find useful.

Students were also asked via survey midway through the semester (Week 8) and at the end if the course design was effective in helping them learn.

The following data was collected to evaluate the course design:
1. Mini surveys and/or requests for open feedback after major assignments and at Week 8 of the course.
2. Analytics from LMS (D2L) that showed what and how course elements were being used by students (e.g., frequency of clicks, sequence of clicks).
3. Qualitative data from D2L discussion posts, our class Facebook page, surveys, assigned writings that were relevant to the objectives of this evaluation, and reflective discussions at the end of the course.
4. Overarching project pre- and post-survey responses (see Chapter 3).

Student use of Multiple Means of content delivery. Much of the content was available in multiple modes (audio, video, text, etc.) and at different levels of entry to accommodate students with diverse experiences, knowledge, and abilities. This section uses student usage of these means of content delivery to infer what they found useful. Besides posting the syllabus, I provided three mini-lectures (video screen capture with voice over) to give the students an overview of the course syllabus, assignments, and instructor expectations. The chart below shows student access to these lectures.

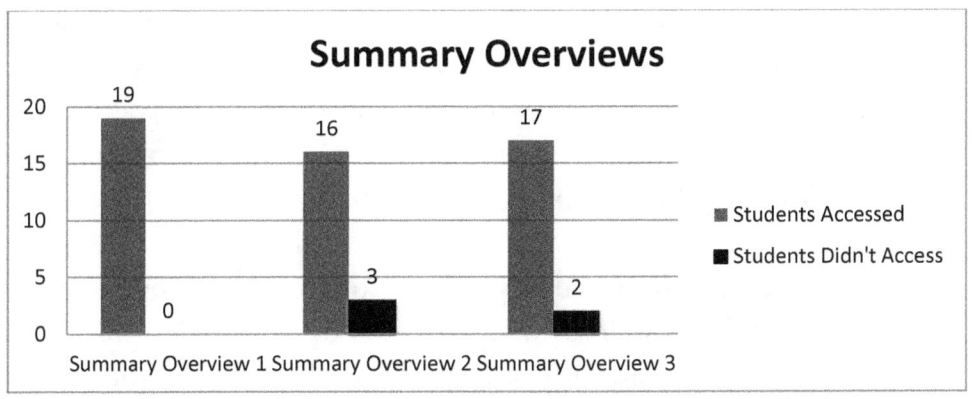

The first major content delivered in the course was a complex academic article on the history of the field. All of the students accessed the article. Below are the results for how many students accessed the six mini-lectures (5 minutes each), summarizing the article.

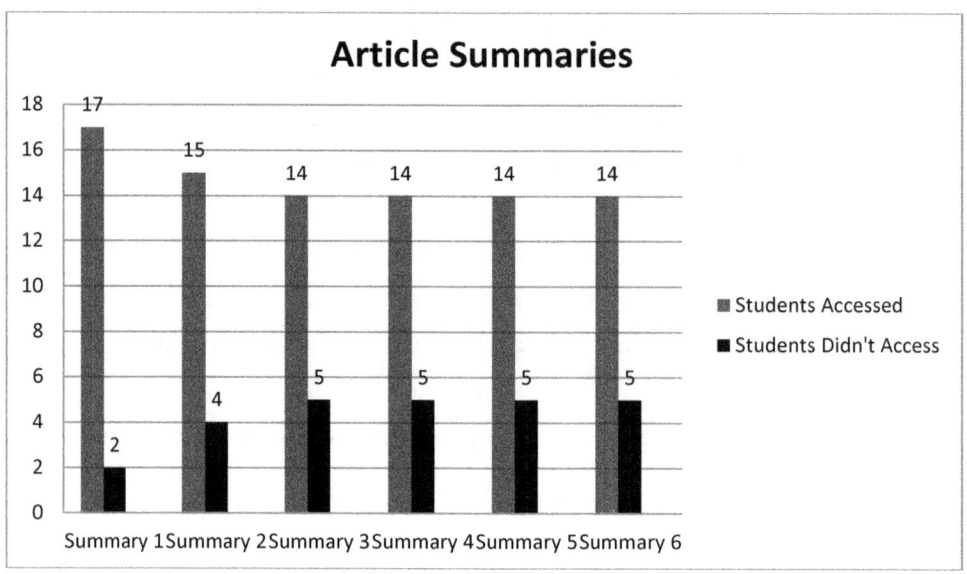

Students were almost evenly mixed regarding the order in which they accessed the article and the article summary. About half of them first looked at the article and then went to the audio/visual summaries, and the other half started with the summaries and then went to the written article. Although there was some attrition in finishing the article summaries, 14 of 19 followed the summaries through to the last one. Only two students did not access the summaries at all, and these two ended up discontinuing the course early. If we do not consider the students who discontinued the course, 100% of the students accessed the first summary and 82% (14/17) accessed all six summaries. This was in addition to 100% of them accessing the written article. (Note that we have no way of knowing how many students actually read the article after accessing it.)

Students were also provided library links to tutorials on how to search for scholarly articles as well as an audio/visual demonstration that I customized for this course. Similarly, students were given a link to the Purdue OWL website on how to write a reference entry in APA style as well as an audio/visual explanation by me that "talked through" APA citation examples. All of the active students (17/19) clicked on the general tutorial links as well as both of the tutorials that I had customized for them.

This data suggests that students really do value multiple means of content delivery. In all cases, students accessed all of the content delivery modes provided, even though the information overlapped. There was also very little attrition in content delivery that was broken into a series of small chunks.

Multiple Means of Expression: Assignment choice. Students had choices for how to complete the three major assignments in the course (Appendix B). In all cases, the majority of students opted for the more conventional choice, and for the first assignment (article summary), I surveyed the students on why they made the choice they did. Of the 13 students who wrote the paper, here are the reasons they gave for making this choice and the number of times each reason was given:

- I am most comfortable with this choice (5)
- This was the best way for me to convey my thoughts (4)
- I am more skilled at writing papers (2)
- This choice helped me gain professional skills that I value (2)
- I learned better by making this choice (2)
- I was not ready to use the technologies necessary for the other choices (2)

Students who made the less conventional choices said that they wanted to challenge themselves, learn different technologies, thought it would be less "dry," and/or thought they would learn better using visual manipulations and creativity to express ideas.

This data suggest that more exploration of these assignment choices is needed. Perhaps the choices need to be more relevant or I need to better explain the different benefits of each choice. If I implement these types of choices again, I will have a good example of each, provide my thoughts on what kinds of skills each choice requires, encourage students to consider both the value of doing something they are good at and the value of trying something new, and try to remove technology barriers before introducing the assignment.

Student use of tools to support learning. Students ranged from 64% to 100% on requesting each of nine learning tools, and so every tool was provided in the course. Below is a comparison of what percentage of students said that they wanted a learning tool and an approximation of what percent actually used them.

Learning Tool	% Requested Tool	App. % Used Tool
Rubrics	100	100
Feedback on Assignments	100	100
Written Assignment Explanations	100	100
Scheduled Chat Time with Instructor (via Facebook and Skype)	91	50%*
Weekly Course Updates/Reminders	91	62%**
Weekly Checklists	82	68%
Verbal Explanations of Assignments (Recorded)	64	100%
Examples of Quality Work	64	89
Student Forum	64	100***

*About 50% used Facebook and Skype chat regularly while the other half relied on email as the primary way of communicating with me.

**These updates were the "talk through" versions. See charts below for how many students accessed the written weekly overviews, which covered much of the same information.

***Our student forum was on a class Facebook page. All students used it at some point in the semester to discuss class assignments, but many used it mostly at the beginning and not very much by the end. A few used it extensively all the way through the course.

Some tools—like the module overview and checklist—were used in every module over the course of the semester. I thought that students might use them more at the beginning and then abandon them as they acclimated to the course and expectations. To examine use over time, I charted which students clicked on module overviews and checklists over the semester. The overview and checklist give the same information but from different perspectives. The overview at the beginning of each module provides module readings, activities and assignments as they align with module objectives. The checklist at the end of the module repeats the readings, activities and assignments with their due dates that also appear on the class calendar. The following charts show the number of students who accessed the Module Overviews and Checklists over the semester. Note: By week three, there were 17 active students in the course.

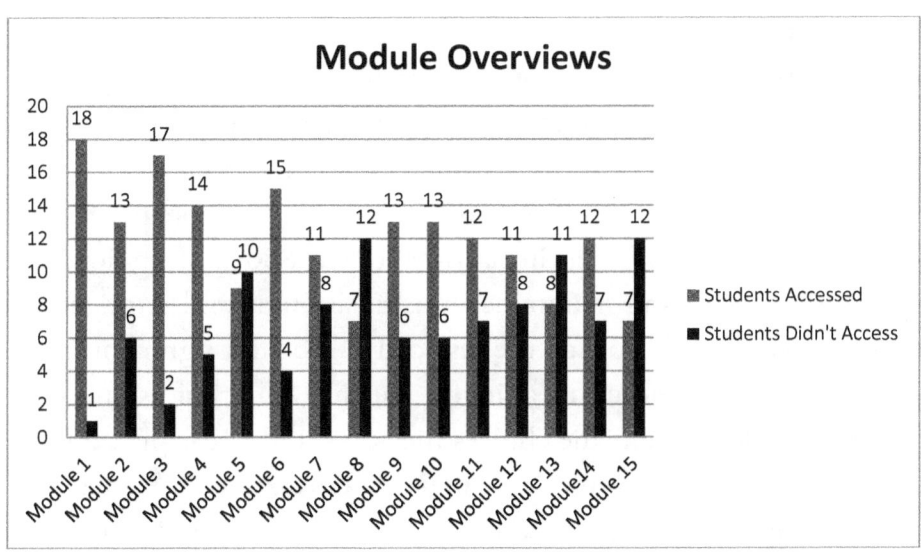

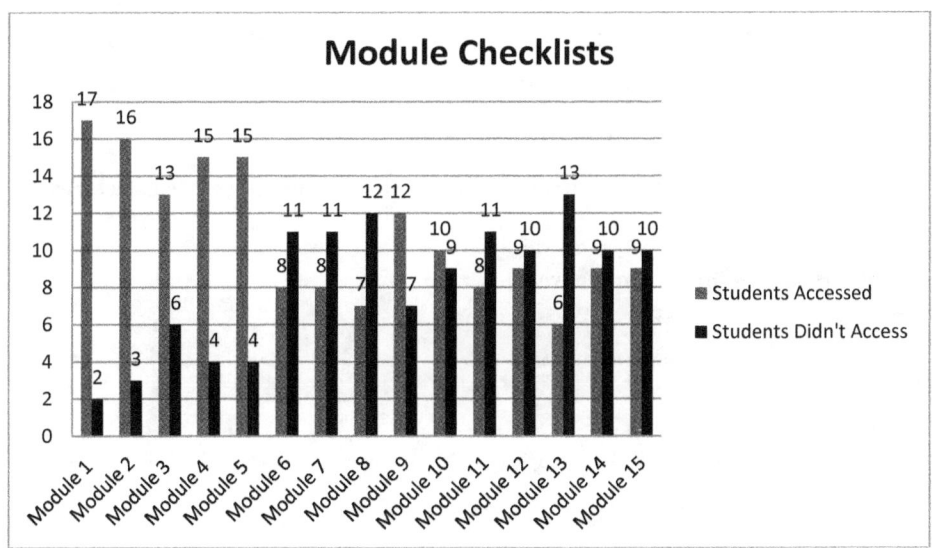

In both cases, student access of the tools declined from nearly all of them accessing the tools at the beginning to about half of them from mid semester to the end. This is likely due to the students gaining familiarity with how the course is run and becoming more confident in their ability to manage course requirements without the supportive tools.

Summary of access data. Student access to the course delivery options and tools was generally high. It appears that students really did want multiple modes of content delivery and tools to support their learning if we can gauge "usefulness" of these options by whether or not students accessed them. Although access to the overviews and checklists declined over the semester, they may have served their purpose in helping students understand the structure of the course and expectations as almost all of the students continued to meet instructor expectations to the end of the semester. The question of providing choice needs more examination. Most students were very enthusiastic about the idea of choice before the semester began and maintained this position at mid semester, even though most did not opt for the less conventional assignment choices. The question of providing meaningful and relevant choices and discovering why students make the choices they do should be explored further.

Student perceptions of course delivery effectiveness. Students were asked for their perceptions of course effectiveness on a mid-semester survey and on the course evaluation at the end. They also participated in a discussion at the end of the semester where they reflected on the course and their learning. All of the active students in the course participated in the mid-semester survey with results charted below.

How satisfied are you with how content is DELIVERED in the course? (e.g. lectures, readings, etc.)

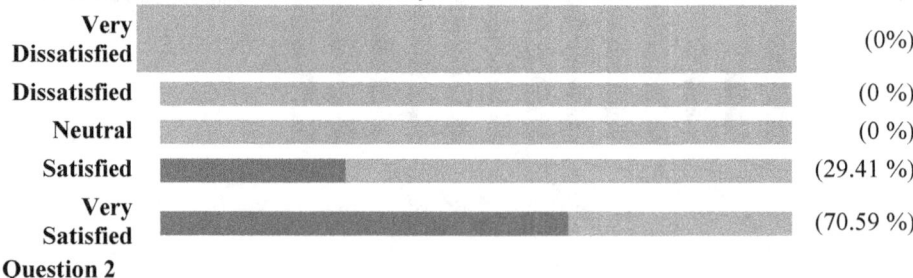

Level of satisfaction for content delivery

Very Dissatisfied	(0%)
Dissatisfied	(0 %)
Neutral	(0 %)
Satisfied	(29.41 %)
Very Satisfied	(70.59 %)

Question 2

Please indicate your level of satisfaction for how you can demonstrate your competence of course material. (e.g. choices for assignments)

Level of satisfaction for expressing competence.

Very Dissatisfied	(0%)
Dissatisfied	(0 %)
Neutral	(0 %)
Satisfied	(47.06 %)
Very Satisfied	(52.96 %)

Students were also invited to comment on what was working or not working well in the course. I have coded and summarized their comments and included the number of times each type of comment was mentioned in the short answers.

Comments about what was working well:
1. Choice for completing assignments (6)
2. Audio/visual explanations of each week (5)
3. Multiple ways of viewing/accessing class materials (4)
4. Checklists (3)
5. Quizzes (untimed, open book, two attempts) (3)
6. Using new technologies (2)
7. Written weekly overviews (1)
8. Responsiveness of instructor to questions (1)

Comments about what was not working well:
1. Would like more technology support (2)
2. Assignment details should be up a few weeks ahead, when the modules open (1)
3. Does not use enough technology (1)
4. More choice would be better (1)

In response to the mid-semester survey, I sent out a reminder about where to get technology support and was sure to put assignment details up three weeks ahead, when the modules opened.

The course evaluation at the end of the semester also included some questions about student perceptions of the course delivery. The following chart shows those results. Eleven of 17 students did the course evaluation.

#	Question	Poor	Below Average	Average	Above Average	Excellent	Responses	Mean
1	Organization of subject matter	0	0	0	2	10	12	4.83
2	Ability to communicate concepts	0	0	0	2	9	11	4.82
3	Style of delivery	0	0	1	2	9	12	4.67

| 4 | Availability to students | 0 | 0 | 0 | 2 | 10 | 12 | 4.83 |
| 5 | Online presence | 0 | 0 | 0 | 2 | 10 | 12 | 4.83 |

There were three written comments from students about what could be changed—one saying that the technology was overwhelming and another saying that technology was not used enough. Additionally, there was the following comment: "I did not feel that assignment details, outlines, and expectations were described well enough and suggest more detailed rubrics and assignment examples in the future."

Student reflections on the course design. Throughout the course, students made comments (many unsolicited) on Facebook, email, class discussions, and survey questions left open throughout the course. Here are some comments that were especially relevant to Universal Design for Learning:

- *I am totally blind and was struggling immensely at my previous university to obtain proper accommodations in order to learn effectively. I honestly could not bear to attend classes at my previous university another semester and ended up withdrawing and taking a semester off to try and find a better program. I wish that I could have found out about Stout's online degree completion sooner, as I would have chosen to attend Stout from the beginning if I had been aware that this was an option. The teachers have been amazing, and I have needed little accommodating as the program is set up in a way that allows for total accessibility from day one.*

- *I have a learning disability but I don't think it will affect me too much in your classes. I don't comprehend what I read very well so the classes that I have with you that have no time limits on quizzes and open book [help]. I thank you.*

- *For me, having two attempts of the quiz really works. It forces me to go over the material a second time, and the information stays with me much longer than if I was only allowed one attempt.*

- *I think that the way it is delivered and the options that are available are great. It gives everyone a chance to use something different and work with what is best for them.*

Overarching Survey Outcomes Specific to this Course. The broad survey that went out to students in every course participating in this project yielded some very promising results specific to the design of HDFS 101. As described in Chapter 3, this survey was intended to measure student's perception of course accessibility in a way that would compare their experience of the current course to courses taken in the past. The pre-survey went out at the beginning of the semester and asked students questions about "previous courses" they had taken. The post-survey went out at the end of the semester and reframed the questions to ask about the specific course they were finishing—in this case, HDFS 101. I have summarized the results of the matched-pairs data analysis below. There were a total of seventeen active students in this class, and twelve of them took the pre and post-survey so that the difference in their responses could be measured and tested for statistical significance. Because the sample size was so small, statistically significant results indicated a large effect size that is of practical as well as statistical significance.

Table: Course Accessibility Compared to Previous Courses

Questions:	Cohort	Mean	Standard Deviation	N	Mean Difference	Effect Size (d)
Course Materials and Assignments In previous courses that you have taken, the instructors created course materials and assignments that were accessible and easily used by people with diverse individual abilities (sensory, intellectual, physical and communication). *Note that in the post-test, all of these questions were revised to say, "in the current course."*	Pre	3.17	1.19	12	1.33**	1.13
	Post	4.50	1.17			

Instructor Used Variety of Teaching Methods Your previous instructors used a variety of teaching methods (lectures, group activities, projects, etc.) to help students learn and experience course knowledge in different ways that were designed to accommodate a wide range of individual abilities (sensory, intellectual, physical and communication).	Pre	3.33	.99	1 2	1.33*	1.24
	Post	4.67	1.16			
Instructors' Expectations Were Clear Past instructors have laid out their course expectations for exam performance, papers, or projects in a straightforward, clearly understandable and predictable manner.	Pre	4.00	1.28	1 2	.42	.34
	Post	4.42	1.17			
Sensory Abilities In previous courses, the instruction was designed in a way so that essential information was communicated effectively to all students regardless of their sensory abilities (vision, hearing, learning attention, etc.).	Pre	3.25	1.29	1 2	1.33**	1.08
	Post	4.58	1.17			
Practice Assignments and Feedback Past instructors routinely divide long-term course assignments into smaller parts or offer "practice" exercises and provide constructive feedback that will help students learn more effectively.	Pre	2.83	1.34	1 2	1.41**	1.08
	Post	4.25	1.29			
Use of Technology Your past teachers intentionally designed the course assignments/projects to allow for the use of technology and other tools that focused students' attention more on learning and less on requiring physical effort to complete them (ex., use of Internet for text editing versus hand-written editing, etc.).	Pre	3.33	1.23	1 2	1.08**	.88
	Post	4.42	1.24			
Environment Accommodates Difference In your previous classrooms, your teachers designed either the physical classroom space or the on-line learning environment to accommodate differences in students' physical, intellectual and communication needs.	Pre	2.75	1.36	1 2	1.58**	1.22
	Post	4.33	1.23			
Environment Promotes Interaction Your past teachers created a learning environment that promoted interaction and communication among students and between students and instructors.	Pre	3.33	1.50	1 2	1.33**	1.00
	Post	4.67	1.16			
Welcoming Environment In previous courses, your instructors created a welcoming class environment by encouraging students to discuss any special learning needs with them.	Pre	3.67	1.44	1 2	.75	.53
	Post	4.42	1.38			

Individual Learning Needs Met In the past, previous teachers created a classroom environment and course materials that effectively satisfied my individual learning needs.	Pre	3.00	1.41	12	1.33*	.96
	Post	4.33	1.37			

Note: ** *statistical significance at the .01 level;* * *statistical significance at the .05 level.*

There was a statistically significant difference and large effect size on all measures except for two: welcoming environment and clear expectations of the instructor. For these two, the students did rate the current class higher than previous courses, but the generally high rating on previous courses made the difference smaller. There was an improvement in all mean scores for this course compared to previous courses, and the means on all measures were between "agree" and "strongly agree" that the course fit the statement.

Summary of Outcomes. Data from the course level surveys; open-ended comments on discussions, emails, and the class Facebook page; overarching project survey; and course evaluations indicated students' strong satisfaction with the accessibility of the course and their ability to learn with the course design. They also made a strong, favorable comparison of this course to courses they had taken in the past. Student use of multiple means of represented content (audio, video, scaffolding at various levels, etc.) was high, suggesting that they did find it helpful to access content in different ways. Students frequently used the majority of the learning tools they requested throughout the course and especially during the first half, suggesting that the tools were, indeed, helpful to them. Although students liked the idea of choice for assignments and commented favorably on it throughout the course, few did the less typical options, indicating that the choices for assignments should be re-examined to make them equally appealing to students.

Limitations of Outcomes. All of the outcomes were based on student reports of their perceived accessibility to the course, satisfaction with the course, and frequency/duration of accessing course content and tools. We do not know if students learned more because of how this course was designed or which features of the design contributed most to their learning. Since the design was holistic and involved students from the beginning, we cannot know how many of their favorable attitudes toward the course were from their initial engagement and continued investment in the course design or the actual course design features. The course design was a success from the participatory action approach because positive change occurred with the help of the participants and in a way that they perceived as beneficial and meaningful to them. Whether positive change comes from participant investment in good outcomes (considered a strength in PAR and a "bias" in traditional research) or the intervention itself is not relevant in PAR. The fact that positive change occurred is relevant, regardless of how it occurred.

Impact of Pilot on Next Semester of HDFS 101

At the time of writing this chapter, I have designed for and taught subsequent semesters of HDFS 101 and learned some important things relative to this study. Because students in the pilot requested such broad and diverse learning opportunities (representation of content, expression of content, and supportive tools) it was very effective in providing a more universal design for future classes. The semester after this pilot, I used the information from this class to design the most universally accessible class that I could with active anticipation of diverse learners. I sent out the survey to the next class, asking them to identify needs, but did NOT change the class as I had designed it in order to investigate two things: 1) How well had I anticipated student needs prior to them enrolling in the class and 2) would surveying students ahead of time serve to ENGAGE students and elicit investment, even though I did not intend to redesign for their specific needs (assuming I did a good job of anticipating those needs, according to Goal 1)?

The second class also rated the instruction and accessibility highly. They perceived that the class was attentive to their *unique* needs, even though it had not been designed for them uniquely as in the pilot study. This suggests that we can begin designing more universally by starting with the students we have and, over time, increasing our awareness of diverse student needs and repertoire for meeting those needs. While I have continued to design "universally" prior to meeting my students, I have also continued surveying each class and getting feedback primarily as an engagement tool as well as to aid my anticipation of diverse learners when designing future courses.

Reflections for Practice

The following reflections encapsulate the thought and practice that my students and I experienced together throughout this project.

Focus First on a Solid and Simple Design. It is critical to begin with a clean, clear and integrated course. If a course is disorganized or illogical, the UDL application should begin there. How can the content be designed in a way that flows logically and is intuitively laid out for the greatest number of students? UDL, as I applied it, included adding many options for content, assignments, and learning tools, but this would not have been successful without a solid, simple foundation. In fact, all of the additions that proved helpful might have undermined learning if the course was already difficult to access due to being conceptually and/or structurally "messy."

Elicit Student Feedback Early and Often. It has always seemed ineffective to me that students' primary way of providing feedback on their courses is when the course is finished! It may be a way to pay it forward, but that assumes that the students who come after them will have the same kinds of preferences and experiences as the students who evaluate the course before.

For HDFS 101, I elicited student feedback two weeks before the course began because I wanted a student-designed course. But, in other classes I ask for feedback within the first couple of weeks and again in the middle of the semester. Of course, I only do this because I am fully committed to responding to the feedback within the current course. It would seem pointless to me and even dismissive to students to ask for feedback during a course with no intention of responding to it.

It is possible that students may not know what they need or want sometimes—especially if I am asking them for their general preferences in the absence of something specific. But once students are in a course, I find that they really do know what is not working for them and that they have great suggestions for making it more accessible. The role of instructors, then, is to use their teaching expertise as a way to guide students into reflection on their own learning and consider possibilities that they may not be able to conceive on their own. The course cannot be completely student designed because students do not have the knowledge and skill in designing an effective course. But, they are experts on their own learning if we as instructors can help them access the wealth of knowledge they have about what works and does not work for them. It is an iterative, reflexive process that also has inherent value for students who can translate their reflexive skills to other educational, personal, and professional contexts (see Chandler's example of reflexivity in learning, Chapter 7).

Balance Responsiveness with Consistency. One thing I learned long before doing this course design project is that students do not like change—especially mid-stream! I was perplexed the first few times that I made accommodating changes for students and then read my course evaluations with comments like, "It was really unfair how the teacher changed the course from what the syllabus said." I felt like students were punishing me for trying so hard to respond to their needs. There were also times that I asked for feedback and decided against incorporating it into the class—resulting in another stream of disgruntled comments on course evaluations such as, "The instructor asked what could be changed in the course and then didn't bother to listen. I felt like giving my opinion was a waste of time with this instructor." In this way, asking for student feedback during a course seems like a Catch-22.

Interestingly, in HDFS 101, I was very flexible with the course design and changed it in response to student feedback throughout the semester. Yet, I got only positive comments on making changes and not a single complaint. I think it is because I was responsive to their needs while maintaining enough consistency to help them feel like they were on solid ground. They wanted the predictable, clean design that I advocated for earlier, but they also wanted to know that the work they put into the reflective feedback was being heard and honored.

I am careful not to ask for feedback on something that I am unwilling to change. I don't ever ask for feedback that I do not respond to *in some meaningful way*. In the case of students' preference to not read scholarly articles, I responded with my appreciation of their feedback, my rational for assigning scholarly articles anyway, and my plan for making the assignment more accessible and meaningful to them, based on their feedback. Every time I asked for feedback in this course, I prepared a brief summary of the feedback to present back to students along with my appreciation of their thoughts and how I planned to respond. I would reinforce this in the actual course (weekly announcements, explanations of assignments, overviews of weekly work, etc.) with phrases like, "In response to your feedback, I added..." or "As I promised, I am now providing you with the kinds of examples that you find helpful. You can locate them...". I suspect that this helped students still feel in control of a course that was being modified.

There were some things in the class that were very consistent and not open to change—like the course objectives, general timeline, grade structure and criteria, instructor responsiveness to student needs (response to email, grading turnaround, etc.). The things that were subject to change were stated from the outset and generally involved adding more supportive tools, means of representing content, and means of expressing learning. This meant that students could continue through the course in the same way they planned to from the beginning, ignoring the changes if they chose. They did not HAVE to use the checklists, listen to the assignment "talk- throughs," read additional feedback on discussions, or take advantage of additional choices of assignments. For those students who become anxious with ambiguity, this was very helpful. I assured the class that the "clear, integrated, and clean course" that we started with is the foundation and would remain consistent. The things I built onto that foundation in response to their feedback were to enhance their learning and expand their access to the course. With this solid footing, the students did tend to explore and use the many tools and means of representing content and expressing learning. I attribute the curious lack of student resistance to the solid footing that they sensed beneath the changing features of the course.

Be Kind to Yourself. Designing a course like HDFS 101 is a lot of work, and I could not have done it without a graduate assistant. Now that I have all of the learning tools and supportive features created, I can run the course quite easily, making adaptations as needed to respond to a new cohort of students. But I teach other courses, and I am always educating myself on new ways to make learning more accessible to students. The problem is that when I learn something new that really seems to work, my standards for course design and delivery are raised. Other courses that I felt proud of seem far less impressive until I have raised them to my new standards. The more I learn and the more successful my design strategies, the less successful I feel in some ways because I do not have the time resources to thoroughly incorporate the changes into all of my courses. Maybe you feel like this when reading this chapter or the other great design ideas in this book. Here is how I am trying to balance my commitment to my students and my commitment to a balanced life.

Each semester I choose either A) one course or B) one course design option to focus on and then count myself a success if I follow it through. If a course is changing texts, that makes the decision easy. I will focus on creating a clear, integrated, clean design for that course. If I learn a very impressive and effective learning technology, I might apply the new technology to relevant elements from every course I teach. When I am tempted to criticize other parts of my course design or be hard on myself, I am an aggressive defender (to my critical self) of my competence and desire for a balanced life. I choose to think of "excellence" as an approach or "way of being" rather than a destination. I want to have an excellent approach to teaching and trust that my courses and instruction will usually *be* excellent as a result of that approach. This shift in my conceptualization of excellence has led to an approach in designing and executing courses that allows me to be "excellent" and "developing" at the same time (two words that never show up together in rubric categories!). It allows me to work well but also to stop working before everything is "just right" so that I can do the other important things I want to do in life. My ego says I can do it all. But I know better.

Conclusion: From "Evaluate" back to "Analyze"

The evaluation of my course design brought me back into the "Analyze" phase for the next semester when HDFS 101 would be offered again. The rich feedback from students and evaluation of what worked and did not work helped me to revisit "where things are" and "where things should be." This brings me right back to the beginning point about my ego and the need for humility and insight. Putting more trust in my students to help me understand their learning needs has come back around to putting more trust in myself. It takes confidence to let go of my preferred ways of teaching in order to privilege my students' preferences. It can be a professional risk to accommodate students in a way that some colleagues view as "enabling" or "pandering." I need to possess 1) strong insights into my own motivations for designing courses the way I do, 2) humility to respond openly and without defensiveness to challenges from students and colleagues on my course designs, and 3) willingness to set aside my ego in order to adopt an "excellent approach" to course design characterized by responsiveness to diverse student needs. I am committed to taking this approach to teaching and continually re-analyzing my goals and process based on the evaluation of the previous semester. Aristotle conveyed as summarized by Durant, "We are what we repeatedly do. Excellence, then, is not an act, but a habit. (Will Durant, n.d.)"

About the Author

When this chapter was first drafted, Dr. Julie A. Zaloudek was an assistant professor in the Human Development and Family Studies (HDFS) program at the University of Wisconsin-Stout. She served as program director for the HDFS Online Degree Completion program.

Zaloudek's training specific to this project included: graduate of the Preparing Future Faculty Program (focused on teaching in higher education) at the University of Minnesota; Master Reviewer for Quality Matters (applying best practices in online course design using evidence-based standards); participating in the advanced cohort in the Universal Design for Learning program (University of Wisconsin-Stout's Nakatani Teaching and Learning Center); coursework in instructional design, distance education, and technology enhanced learning; and currently served as the Family Social Science Graduate Curriculum Development Coordinator (doctoral curriculum innovation project at the University of Minnesota). At that point, Zaloudek had been teaching in higher education for six years, administrating an online program for four years, and actively conducting research on teaching and learning. She has since taken a position as Dean of Online and Extended Learning at Minnesota State University-Moorhead.

References

Butler, C. (2009, April). *You don't find anything out until you start showing it to people.* Retrieved from https://www.newfangled.com/newfangleds-iterative-website-prototyping- process/

Butler, C. (2012, March). *Your ego is a bad designer.* Retrieved from http://www.newfangled.com/your_ego_is_a_bad_designer

Center for Applied Science Technology [CAST]. (2011). *Universal Design for Learning guidelines version 2.0.* Wakefield, MA: Author.

Levin, M., & Greenwood, D. (2011). Revitalizing universities by reinventing the social sciences. In N. K. Densin & Y. S. Lincoln (Eds.), *Qualitative research* (pp. 27-42). Thousand Oaks, CA: SAGE.

Meo, G. (2008). Curriculum planning for all learners: Applying universal design for learning (UDL) to a high school reading comprehension program. *Preventing School Failure, 52*(2), 21-30. doi:10.3200/PSFL.52.2.21-30

Will Durant quotes. (n.d.). Retrieved from https://www.brainyquote.com/quotes/quotes/w/willdurant145967.html

Appendix A: Pre-Test Survey Results

Question 1

Which description of learning most fits you? Please rank order the following three learning styles so that one = <u>most</u> preferred and three = <u>least</u> preferred.

I sometimes think in pictures and learn best from visual displays. I often prefer to take detailed notes to absorb the information.

1   (36.36%)
2   (18.18%)
3   (45.45%)

I learn best through verbal lectures, discussions, talking things through and listening to what others have to say. I often benefit from reading text aloud.

1   (45.45%)
2   (27.27%)
3   (27.27%)

I learn best through a hands-on approach, actively exploring the physical world around me.

1   (18.18%)
2   (63.64%)
3   (18.18%)

Question 3

Mark the degree to which you agree or disagree with the following two statements so that 1=strongly disagree and 5=strongly agree.

I prefer to work in groups or with other people.

1   (18.18%)

2	(27.27%)
3	(27.27%)
4	(27.27%)
5	0 (0%)

I prefer to work alone and use self-study.

1	(9.09%)
2	(9.09%)
3	(18.18%)
4	(9.09%)
5	(54.55%)

Question 5

Think about how you like information to be presented to you. Rank order your preferences so that 1 = favorite way to receive information and 6 = least favorite way to receive information.

Academic Articles (e.g. from scholarly journals)

1	(0%)
2	(0%)
3	(20%)
4	(30%)
5	(30%)
6	(20%)

Textbook

1	(20%)
2	(20%)
3	(10%)
4	(40%)
5	(0%)
6	(10%)

Popular types of articles (e.g. similar to a Wikipedia or web-based magazine article)

1	(0%)
2	(20%)
3	(10%)
4	(20%)
5	(30%)
6	(20%)

Lectures from the Instructor

1	(50%)
2	(30%)
3	(10%)
4	(0%)
5	(10%)
6	(0%)

Audio Media (e.g. podcasts from radio program)

1	(0 %)
2	(10 %)
3	(20 %)
4	(20 %)
5	(20 %)
6	(30 %)

Audio/Visual Media (e.g. YouTube or other video clips)

1	(30 %)
2	(20 %)
3	(20 %)
4	(0 %)
5	(10 %)
6	(20 %)

Question 7

Think about how you like to express what you have learned. Rank order your preferences so that 1 = favorite way to express learning and 6 = least favorite way to express learning.

Traditional, closed book, timed exams.

1	(18.18 %)
2	(0 %)
3	(18.18 %)
4	(18.18

No Accommodations Needed: 105

		%)
5	▬	(9.09 %)
6	▬▬▬▬	(36.36 %)

Study guides I can fill out on over a period of time.

1	▬▬▬▬▬	(45.45 %)
2	▬	(9.09 %)
3	▬▬	(18.18 %)
4	▬	(9.09 %)
5	▬	(9.09 %)
6	▬	(9.09 %)

Writing a paper.

1	▬	(9.09 %)
2	▬▬	(18.18 %)
3	▬▬	(18.18 %)
4	▬▬▬	(27.27 %)
5	▬▬▬	(27.27 %)
6		(0 %)

Participating in an online discussion with other students (written or voice recorded)

1	▬	(18.18 %)
2	▬▬▬	(45.45 %)
3	▬	(18.18 %)
4	▬	(9.09 %)
5		(0 %)
6	▬	(9.09 %)

Doing a presentation.

1		(0 %)

2	(0 %)
3	(18.18 %)
4	(27.27 %)
5	(27.27 %)
6	(27.27 %)

Creating a project with a lot of flexibility about what to include (e.g. visuals, sounds).

1	(9.09 %)
2	(27.27 %)
3	(9.09 %)
4	(9.09 %)
5	(27.27 %)
6	(18.18 %)

Question 9

Some tools can be helpful to support learning. Please check any tools that you think would support your ability to learn effectively.

Written Rubrics for Assignments	(100 %)
Examples of Quality Work from Former Students	(63.64 %)
Weekly Checklists	(81.82 %)
Detailed Written Explanations of Assignments	(100 %)
Verbal Explanation of Assignments	(63.64 %)

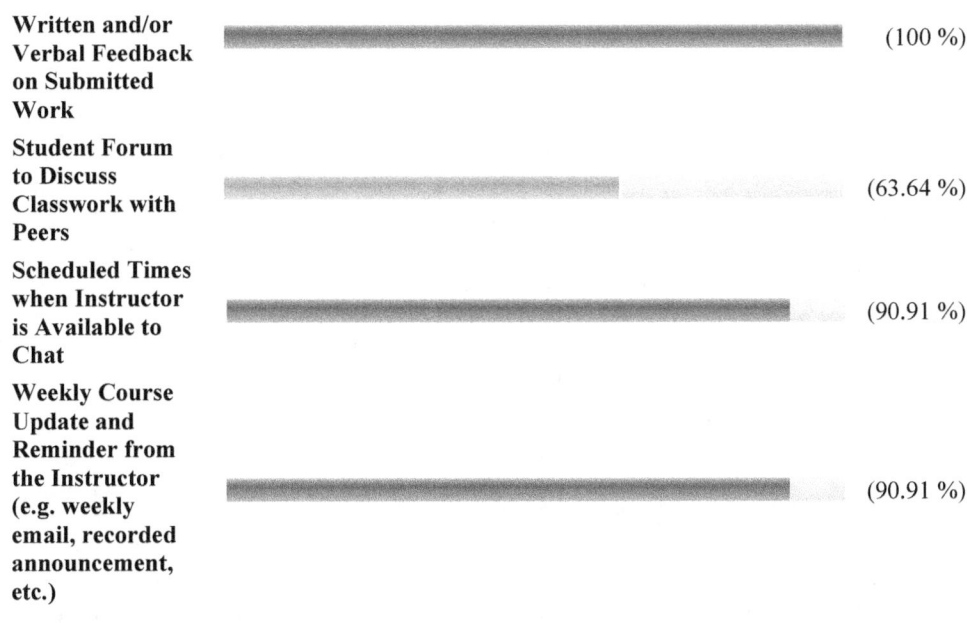

Written and/or Verbal Feedback on Submitted Work	(100 %)
Student Forum to Discuss Classwork with Peers	(63.64 %)
Scheduled Times when Instructor is Available to Chat	(90.91 %)
Weekly Course Update and Reminder from the Instructor (e.g. weekly email, recorded announcement, etc.)	(90.91 %)

Question 11

Mark the degree to which you agree or disagree with the following statement so that 1=strongly disagree and 5=strongly agree.

If my instructor offered choices for how I receive information (e.g. choice among readings and/or lectures) and how I express learning (e.g. choice between writing a paper or doing a presentation), I would learn better.

1	(9.09 %)
2	(0 %)
3	(0 %)
4	(9.09 %)
5	(81.82 %)

Appendix B: Assignment Choices

Assignment Choices for Article Summary, Career Exploration, and NCFR Exploration

Article Sum: Paper	Career Explore: Profile	NCFR: Attend
Based on your article, write a three page paper (double spaced) that includes: 1) Purpose, 2) Summary 3) Your Reaction *Must include APA reference for article	Explore two careers and then make a professional profile of yourself in each career (as if you are already a professional in the career) – like what you might find on a professional networking site like Linked In.	Attend Wisconsin Council of Family Relations or other major HDFS professional event this semester.
Article Sum: Presentation	**Career Explore: Compare Grid**	**NCFR: Scavenger Hunt**
Based on your article, prepare a five-minute presentation in Jing (visual AND audio) that includes: 1) Purpose, 2) Summary 3) Your Reaction *Must include APA reference for article	Explore two careers and construct a matrix to compare and contrast various elements of the careers.	Explore NCFR website and hunt for items listed in the scavenger hunt (posted in quizzes).
Article Sum: Visual	**Career Explore: Cover Letter/Resume**	**NCFR: Commercial**
Based on your article, prepare a visual representation of the information that includes: 1) Purpose, 2) Summary 3) Reaction *Must include APA reference for article	Explore two careers and design a cover letter and resume for each career. Be sure to tailor your qualifications to the duties and work environment of that career. Also, be sure to include all required info (e.g. expected salary)	After exploring the NCFR website, make a commercial (using narrated Power Point, Jing, Voice Thread, or a technology of your choice) that "sells" people on becoming a member of NCFR.

5. Rethinking Environmental Education

Kitrina Carlson, Ph.D.

UDL for Today's Biology Student

Is education possibly a process of trading awareness for things of lesser worth? The goose who trades his skin is soon a pile of feathers.
—Aldo Leopold (1949), Sand County Almanac

As a botanist teaching the next generation of scientists at a polytechnic university with a heightened mission to "pursue innovation and technology that serves society," I find myself focused on training and assessing students on their tangible and marketable skills and perhaps not often enough asking them to evaluate their own understanding of the environment and to reflect on their role within the natural world. This is most problematic in our introductory, general education science courses where over the past decade I have anecdotally perceived students to be increasingly disinterested in exploring their relationship to the environment. For example, I've become a well-known instructor to avoid for students who don't want to identify, by common name and scientific name, 100 of Wisconsin's common plants and important plant families. "Does spelling count?" and "Can't you make this multiple choice?" are common refrains on exam day. My thought has been, if students don't value them enough to learn their names, they won't care enough to protect and value their habitat.

Student performance on the common plants exam has been underwhelming, and scores tend to plot-out in an inverted bell curve, the majority falling into the lower half of the curve, more than a handful failing entirely. Having grown up in northern Wisconsin, learning these plants on hikes with my dad and later inheriting his well-used field guide for my own when I went off to college, I had difficulty realizing many of my own students were challenged to appreciate the inherent value and importance of the plants they were asked to learn.

In all prior semesters, I blamed their poor performance on the common plants exam and their growing disinterest in environmental topics that required anything beyond superficial effort, on their overall lack of preparation and dearth of opportunities to actually engage with the environment before they got to my class. The opportunity to reevaluate my course through the lens of Universal Design for Learning (UDL) helped me better understand my own responsibility for the students' apathetic response to the common plants exam and environmental issues of importance in general. Understanding UDL principles helped me to identify the "ego-design" that's inherent in my class and possibly inherent in many environmental science courses.

Meaning, I started to question whether the way I was taught and the way I learn was really the best way to educate others in the environmental sciences. More importantly, I started to ask myself why someone else would care to conserve the trails *I* had hiked, the vistas *I* had beheld and the plants, animals and other wild things *I* had encountered on my adventures. Of course, I could appreciate the importance of studying, conserving and enjoying the plants and places that were fundamental parts of experiences that helped to shape and define the person I am today. But who am I to assume that asking students to learn plants I valued and structuring learning experiences that support my environmental ideology would be the right way to provide environmental science learning opportunities for *all* students. Perhaps a more effective way to educate a new population of scientists and citizens of the world who can make informed decisions about important environmental issues is to create classroom experiences that allow them to establish their *own* environmental ethic and have a foundation in their own existing relationship with the natural world, not one I dictate to them based on my own values and experiences.

Background

The contrast between the rapidly declining state of the global environment and the annual celebration of Earth Day's 40-something anniversaries has caused some to question the effectiveness of environmental science education in our country (Sobel, 2012; Saylan & Blumstein 2011; Sanera, 2008). Despite billions of dollars directed towards environmental science education in the United States, largely as a result of the United Nations Conference on the Human Environment *(*1972), UNESCO-UNEP (1975), UNESCO-UNEP (1977), and implementation of the Environmental Education act of 1990, only 20% of U.S. citizens are considered to be literate in the environmental sciences (Miller, 2004).

Reevaluating my environmental science-based courses through the lens of UDL helped me to recognize that I had unintentionally been presenting students with my own environmental ideology and had embedded opportunities for environmental action through service-learning experiences that *I* believed were meaningful rather than providing possibly more effective opportunities for students to gain knowledge and establish their own values through a more active role in the critical evaluation of environmental issues. Engaging students in the complex, non-linear and often poorly understood consequences of human interactions with the environment and empowering them with the knowledge, skills and abilities to take action *they* determine to be meaningful is vocally espoused as a best practice by a small but emerging number of environmental scientists (Saylan & Blumstein, 2011).

Previous Design Approach	UDL Approach	Outcomes
Students are given a service-learning project meant to inspire and engage them in conversation practice and offer opportunities for hands-on experience.	Students determine for themselves their motivation for learning and practicing in conversation practices.	Students have improved attitude and behaviors towards environmental conversation.

The goal of this project was to increase student access to environmental science knowledge and experiences by implementing principles of UDL across the course and ultimately better equip students to formulate their own standards for an ethical relationship with the environment. It has been well documented that students learn more from natural science laboratory experiences when they can relate it to something with which they are familiar and are building their understanding based on a scaffolding of prior information (Paas, Renkl, & Sweller, 2003, 2004; & Sweller, 1999, 2004). I use "citizen science"-based research opportunities in many of my introductory courses to provide this scaffolding. There are many variations on citizen science projects and definitions, ranging from projects that focus on the overarching philosophy of public discourse to projects that are designed specifically to enhance the research efforts of scientists by empowering and training a corps of engaged citizens to assist in data collection. In biology and the environmental sciences, citizen science projects tend to focus on environmental data collection. Notable examples include the Water Action Volunteer (W.A.V.) program initiated by the University of Wisconsin-Extension to empower citizens to gather water quality data across the state, and Project Budburst (Project Budburst, 2017), a National Science Foundation-supported activity that trains citizens to record and report flowering times in order to evaluate global climate change across the country. For this project, I hypothesized that students who were offered opportunities to gather citizen science data in natural areas that were meaningful and accessible to them would be better equipped to establish their own environmental ethic.

The project was developed from three primary objectives, to 1) assist students in understanding and acknowledging their own existing connections to their environment; 2) identify barriers to student access to natural areas they had self-identified as meaningful; and 3) provide a series of opportunities for students to proactively engage with the environment in ways that would support knowledge and skill development related to environmental conservation.

Project Overview

This project was implemented in *Plants and People* (BIO 141), an introductory, general education biology course with three 55-minute lectures and a two-hour lab period each week.

The course examines the role of plants in the daily lives of humans and the impact of humans on the environment of plants. In addition to general plant science and ethnobotany, it has recurring themes of environmental conservation and social justice. The typical student in this course is a freshman or sophomore, non-science major who is taking the course for their general education, natural sciences and contemporary issues requirement.

Project Design: Infusing UDL Principles Across the Course

Because BIO 141 was an existing course I had originally developed and taught numerous times prior to the UDL project, revamping the entire course to meet UDL standards did not seem like a reasonable or manageable approach for a one-semester activity. Instead, to imbed the principles of UDL across the course, I chose to incorporate a UDL-based activity that wove through the majority of the semester (Fig. 1). Following pre-assessment, students in the treatment group were first introduced to concepts of UDL through a "tic-tac-toe" activity designed to help introduce them to a new teaching style early in the semester and provide a series of options for students to learn background knowledge essential for the course. The primary "UDL" project in the treatment section took place over a five-week period and was followed by a second project component where students could demonstrate their enhanced knowledge and skills set at a different location.

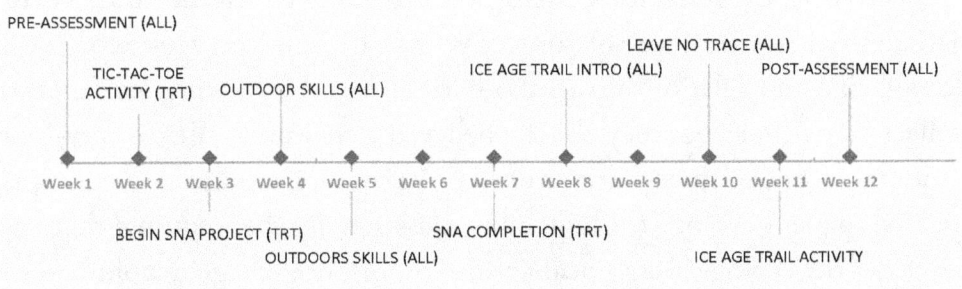

Figure 1. Timeline of UDL project implementation in treatment and control group.

Prior to beginning any aspects of the embedded UDL activity, students completed a "pre-assessment" of their knowledge, current behaviors and attitudes about and towards environmental conservation (Appendix). Two sections of the course did not participate in the activity and were included as the control group (Table 1).

Table 1
Attributes of the UDL Project That Were Included in the Control and Treatment Sections of BIO 141.

"Treatment" BIO 141 24 students in sect 2*	"Control" BIO 141 48 students in sect 1, 3
UDL Implemented across project	X
Students ID an SNA** to visit individually	X
Develop site visit plan	X
Learn skills for data collection	✓
Collect data at individual SNA	X
Collect data at Ice Age Trail SNA	✓
Assess attitude and behaviors pre/post	✓
Assess skills and knowledge pre/post	✓

*different instructors taught each section of BIO 141
**SNA Scientific and Natural Areas

The course contained three objectives:
1. Understand existing connections to the natural world,
2. Identify and overcome obstacles to accessing scientific and natural areas, and
3. Provide opportunities for students to meaningfully engage with the environment.

Objective 1) Understand existing connections to the natural world. The desired outcome of this objective was to build on students' prior knowledge and relationship to the natural world by asking students to reflect on natural areas they already believed were important. Twenty-four students in one of three sections of BIO 141 were introduced to concepts related to plant ecology through an in-class activity that required them to consider the ecological significance and importance of a geographical area students self-identified as important to them. More specifically, they were asked to identify a natural area that they felt a positive prior connection towards, perhaps a location they had previously hiked, hunted or camped or simply visited as a child. Examples of natural areas that were important to the course instructor and why were shared with the class to clarify, but not define, the concept. After a brief lecture introducing students to the biological and ecological concepts related to regionally important plant communities, students were directed to several resources to identify the different plant communities found in the geographical area they had self-selected. Students were required to complete a brief assignment on their selected region including assembling a short PowerPoint describing the plant communities unique to the area and an explanation of what is "important" to them about the area. Class time was provided to complete the presentations, and these were shared with their classmates in small groups, with each student having approximately five minutes to share their selected areas with a group of 3-5 peers.

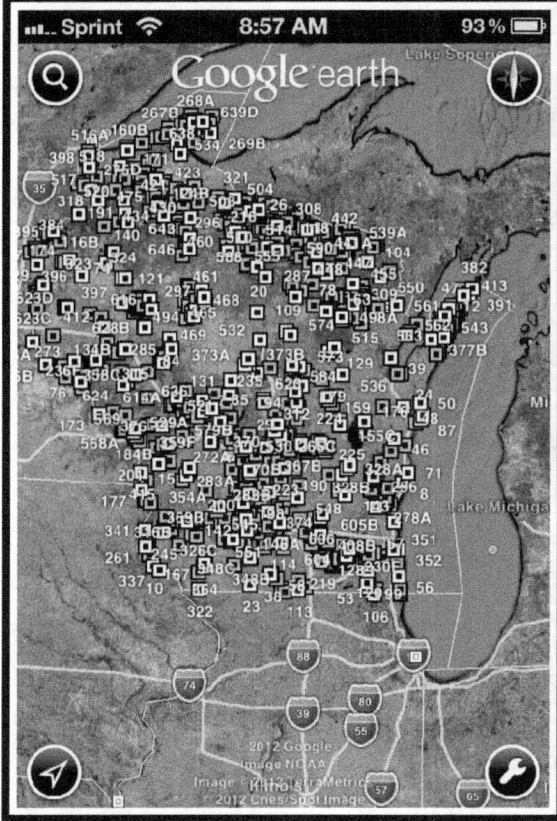

Figure 2. Following the UDL Principle of Multiple Means of Representation, students were provided numerous ways to access information. Innovative smart phone technology, such as the use of Google Earth with embedded SNA locations, along with training to use the new resources, provided novel access opportunities for students.

Objective 2) Identify and overcome obstacles to accessing scientific and natural areas. The desired outcome of this objective was to ensure student interaction with their self-identified "natural area of importance" by making a site visit plan to overcome access barriers. After initially identifying a specific geographical region that held personal significance, students were instructed on the history and relevance of State-designated "Scientific and Natural Areas" (SNAs). The geographical area that all students were most familiar with (Wisconsin and eastern Minnesota) maintains over 1,000 publicly accessible SNAs, each with unique, well-described attributes. With the assistance of two additional staff with extensive knowledge and background in the topic, students were asked to identify an exact SNA they would like to visit and to make a plan to visit their selected SNA to collect citizen science data. All students completed site visit plan worksheets including how students would get to the site, when they would arrive and specific materials and supplies they would need to take with them. Students could choose any site designated as an SNA in Wisconsin or Minnesota, and advised to select an area that was interesting to them but also reasonably accessible within the provided time allotment. Students were aware of the assignment five weeks prior to the project deadline and could visit their site at any time prior to the due date. Following the UDL principle of "multiple means of representation," students were provided numerous "entry-points" to the information about their selected site, including additional expert staff, step-by-step PowerPoint instructions they could work through on their own, links to DNR-hosted websites and interactive/smart phone maps that displayed the geographical locations of all SNAs relative to any other location, a description of the SNA that could be used to generate driving directions, as well as tutorials on how to use the materials (Fig. 2). Students were also instructed on the legal and social responsibilities associated with visiting SNAs and given self-guided instructions and data sheets for collecting data at the site.

Objective 3) Provide opportunities for students to meaningfully engage with the environment. The desired outcome of this objective was to provide students with the knowledge, training and resources required to interact with the environment in a manner that was important and meaningful to them. Students had the opportunity to visit two different SNAs, one individually, and one as a class to collect citizen science data. Prior to their site visits students were trained in a series of skills including:

basic orienteering, compass orientation and declination determination, GPS for navigational use, setting up transect lines, and basic plant identification. Before visiting the site all students completed the "Leave No Trace" online training certification process to learn strategies to reduce their impact on a natural area. Once on site, students used their skills to collect basic biological survey data and additional information on any facet of the natural area that was of interest to them. They were provided with data sheets to conduct a simple survey of native and invasive plants, and following the UDL principle of "Multiple Means of Engagement," were able to conduct any biological species survey or site investigation they found interesting or meaningful. Finally, following the UDL principle of "Multiple Means of Expression" students were able to disseminate their findings in a variety of different formats including an in-class PowerPoint presentation, poster presentation at STEM research day, a microblog, or even as an interpretive dance or skit.

Assessment Methods & Outcomes

Assessment tools to measure attitude and behavioral changes pre/post experience were used to evaluate students' progression towards understanding their own relationship or connection to the natural world. Basic knowledge questions and skills assessments were incorporated to determine if having an opportunity to participate in conservation practices and citizen science data collection in an area the student was emotionally invested in would translate into engagement in citizen science activities in a natural area students were not invested in.

Attitudes and behaviors. The pre/post assessment of attitudes and behaviors in the treatment group showed significant positive changes for a majority of the assessed behaviors and attitudes. Importantly, there were no declines/negative outcomes from the pre to post-assessment in the treatment group.

Table 2
The BIO 141 "Treatment" Class Indicated Significant Positive Changes for the Following Behaviors and Attitudes (a = .05, n = 16*, paired T-test)

Attitude/Behavior	Pre / Post	(SD)
Purchased products in reusable or recyclable containers	Pre: 3.3125 Post: 3.875	0.24
Picked up litter that was not your own	Pre: 3.065 Post: 3.6875	0.287
Composted food scraps	Pre: 2.0625 Post: 2.8125	0.326
Voted for a candidate who supported environmental causes	Pre: 1.467 Post: 3.2	0.370
Engaging in environmental behaviors is important to me	Pre: 3.375 Post: 3.75	0.2016
In general, being part of the natural world is an important part of my self-image.	Pre: 3.5 Post: 3.938	0.2016
I take pride in the fact that I could survive outdoors on my own for a few days.	Pre: 3.1875 Post: 3.8125	0.204
I keep mementos from the outdoors in my room, like shells, rocks or feathers.	Pre: 3.3375 Post: 3.0625	0.176

Knowledge and skills. Based on comparative outcomes between treatment and non-treatment classes as well as pre-and post-assessments of knowledge, students in the treatment section appeared to have better mastered core learning outcomes. Some examples of this include:

1. Over 50% of students in the treatment section correctly answered the question "list three invasive plant species" versus only 10% of the students in the other sections, though all classes were trained with the same skills stations that specifically required identification

of these invasive plants. Furthermore, students in the control sections were not only unable to list three invasive plants, some of the plants listed were obviously guesses: "cactus", "weeds like tumbleweeds", and "mosses" were among some of the incorrect responses from the control groups. These types of guesses were not observed in the treatment responses. The most typical incorrect response in the treatment group was listing only two of the three invasive plants required.

2. A very surprising observation from the pre-assessment was that only ≈60% of all students were able to correctly name the county, city/town, and state they considered their "hometown" because many students did not know which county their city/town was located within. In the post-assessment there was no improvement in the control group, but almost all (98%) students in the treatment group knew their home county, city/town and state and were able locate it on a map.

Although a skills station competency assessment activity was embedded into the all-group field trip, on-site it became unexpectedly difficult to implement the quantitative assessment of skill competency of each participating student. However, it can be reported that all 76 students who participated in the Ice Age Trail Site Visit, in both the treatment and control groups, demonstrated at least the minimal level of skills competency required to participate in the field trip activities. Anecdotally speaking, students in the treatment group completed the activities with significantly less confusion, more quickly, and with less assistance from fellow group members.

Student reflections. There was no observed difference in the theme of student reflections between treatment and control groups of the Ice Age Trail field visit experience. Within the 76 student reflections collected, only two students reported strong negative experiences indicating they were not interested in participating in a similar activity in the future. Interestingly, the negative reflections were from students in a control section working in a group that was the least prepared for the visit in terms of dress/attire (one student wore sandals, for example). Students who did not dress appropriately were either not allowed to participate and would receive no grade for the activity, or had the option to change their attire/footwear to something appropriate and safe. Students had been informed of this requirement multiple times before the activity. While some of the students indicated only a moderate interest in the actual on-site activities of the Ice Age Trail field day, in both the treatment and control groups, students almost universally reported that they enjoyed the outdoor site visit and appreciated learning and using the skills station activities. Examples of their comments include:

- *YES!!!*
- *I really liked learning how to use the GPS and compass.*
- *My favorite part was taking out my aggression on the invasive buckthorn.*
- *I enjoyed everything about the trip.*
- *I didn't have a least favorite part.*

When students in the treatment group were asked to reflect specifically on their SNA site visit, similar themes emerged with no explicitly negative feedback and a consistent indication that students appreciated the skills they learned with only a few students reporting anything specific about appreciating the opportunity to visit their selected SNA. There was also a theme of reflecting on the attributes of the SNA they visited, both positive and negative, though most were presented as relatively neutral observations. Most comments related to SNA attributes were related to the limited accessibility of the site they selected, disappointment at the lack of maintenance occurring at their selected SNA or surprise at the lack of "user-friendly" site attributes like signage, benches, trails, etc.

For both activities, an interesting sub-theme observed within even "positive" reflections was that some students reported that they didn't perceive or define themselves to be "outdoors" types. This reflection often correlated with students who reported that they enjoyed the outdoors experience, but not the actual data collection activities that took place on-site.

Overarching UDL impact. The overall goal of this activity was to implement UDL across the course to broaden my students' ability to cognitively access the knowledge, skills and abilities they needed to begin to establish their own standards and values for an ethical relationship with the environment. Success of UDL implementation within this course was assessed through an overarching survey of the UDL experience the students perceived in this course relative to prior courses. Quantitative data was collected via online surveys emailed to students at the beginning and end of the spring 2012 semester. Results were analyzed by the UW-Stout Applied Research Center using SPSS (Statistics Package for the Social Sciences). For the pre-post comparisons, data analysis was conducted only with respondents who completed both the pre-survey and the post-survey (N=24/100% return rate)

Table 3
Assessment of Student Perceptions of UDL in BIO 141 Relative to Previous Courses

	Cohort	Mean	Standard Deviation	N	Mean Diff	Effect Size
Questions:						
Course Materials and Assignments Instructors created course materials and assignments that were accessible and easily used by people with diverse individual abilities (sensory, intellectual, physical and communication).	PRE	3.38	.97	24	1.08**	1.30
	POST	4.46	.66			
Instructor Used Variety of Teaching Methods Your teacher used a variety of teaching methods (lectures, group activities, projects, etc.) to help students learn and experience course knowledge in different ways that were designed to accommodate a wide range of individual abilities (sensory, physical, intellectual and communication).	PRE	3.54	.88	24	.79**	.93
	POST	4.33	.82			
Instructor's Expectations Were Clear Your instructor laid out his or her course expectations for exam performance, papers, or projects in a straightforward, clearly understandable and predictable manner.	PRE	3.46	1.10	24	.58	.56
	POST	4.04	.96			

Sensory Abilities For this particular course, the instruction was designed in a way that effectively communicated essential information to all students regardless of their sensory abilities (vision, hearing, learning attention, etc.)	PRE	3.50	.93	24	.54**	.57
	POST	4.04	.96			
Practice Assignments and Feedback Your teacher divided long-term course assignments into smaller parts or offered "practice" exercises and provided constructive feedback	PRE	3.38	1.25	24	.75	.69
	POST	4.13	.90			

Note: ** *statistical significance at the .01 level;* **statistical significance at the .05 level.*

Student perception of UDL implementation was significantly improved for 9 of the 10 UDL characteristics measured within the treatment BIO 141 course, relative to prior courses (Table 3). It's evident from these data that students in the treatment section perceived the course and course materials to have been designed and implemented in a manner that was conducive to learning and met their individual learning needs. While the intentional UDL nature of the course correlates with improved attitudes and behaviors and knowledge skills and abilities associated with the environmental sciences, further assessment is required to elucidate the precise relationship between UDL and student ability to establish their own environmental ethic.

Changes in Practice

I'm leaving this experience with many more questions than answers. Reevaluating my course through the lens of UDL allowed me to see some of my inherent teaching biases, areas that I may have been too blinded by my own personally held values and ideology to create a classroom experience that allowed students to access information by building from their own experiences rather than forced to "appreciate" the information I shared in the way I shared it. Had someone suggested to me prior to this UDL project that my own love and passion for a topic could actually negatively impact my course outcomes, I would have laughed. Prior to this experience I believed my personal investment in the field was my strongest attribute as an instructor. While I think I've always been a reflective instructor, and open to new teaching and learning pedagogies, it was really hearing the term "ego-design" that triggered my ability to see how my personally held values regarding the environment and conservation were skewing every aspect of my classroom environment, from the ways I shared information, the types of activities I expected students to participate in and the ways I wanted students to express information back to me. Interestingly, this experience has caused me to retool my own environmental ethic, and understand and appreciate that everyone can and should be encouraged to learn about the environment in order to interact with the environment in a manner they find most rewarding. It's not my job to shape their environmental ethic, but give them the tools to establish their own standards for an ethical relationship with the environment. Prior to this experience I wasn't aware of how the way I shaped my course was overly driven by my own prior interaction with the environment and the ways I valued and appreciated interacting with the natural world.

I believe a big reason for the need to unknowingly attempt to shape the foundation for my students' environmental ethic was my own lack of trust in my students to make good choices in their future roles and my confidence that my values were "right" and therefore should also be held by them. With my own increasing awareness of how my class had been largely shaped by my values, I am more able to see this same flaw inherent in much of the field of environmental science. As scientists, it's our job to objectively present the tools to access knowledge, and the skills and abilities to critically evaluate that information to come to our own conclusions. While I believed my courses were always fact driven and accurate and as a scientist I've always been extremely careful to present no intentional bias on a topic in my courses, the UDL experience allowed me to see the hidden bias inherent in my course design. The material I was teaching, the way I was teaching the course was clearly biased in favor of my own ideology. Requiring students to participate in a service-learning activity of my own design and report back to me on the outcomes and importance of the activity does not allow for unbiased learning outcomes and certainly does not allow for adequate opportunities to critically examine an environmental issue.

In the field of environmental sciences, I often see prescriptive, overly detailed and maybe even condescending lessons on the "appropriate" ways to interact with the natural world. But when I asked my students to identify and report on an SNA that held personal value, I could "hear" the sense of ownership and pride many of the students already felt towards these sites when they presented on them. While this sense of personal ownership wasn't expressed in their written reflection activities, it was obvious to me when they spoke about the sites, especially when they expressed to me all the times they may have visited the site or some similar site as a child, or how they hunted in that location every deer season, etc. They didn't need to be told of the importance of protecting and conserving these sites because it was just as obvious to them as it had been to me about the sites that I held dear. Intentionally meeting students where they were at and acknowledging their own existing appreciation for the natural world rather than making assumptions was a much more effective way to help them expand these attitudes and behaviors to natural areas that were more foreign to them. I believe this activity allowed them to more consciously reflect on the ways they interact with the environment and even perhaps consider themselves as a part of the natural world rather than an observer.

It is clear that attitudes and behaviors towards the environment changed significantly for students in the treatment section. The behavior most significantly, positively improved was related to political protections for the environment. Students indicated being significantly more likely to vote for a political candidate who supported environmental issues following their SNA/Ice Age Trail experience. This result is of particular interest to me because I am always extremely careful not to discuss political biases in my courses and this semester there was literally no mention of political/civic engagement as a mechanism for environmental protection/change. This result may suggest that students do recognize the issues associated with our environment, but may believe political/civic engagement through voting is the only meaningful way for them to take action. This outcome, combined with the almost universal student feedback indicating their appreciation for the outdoor skills development, suggests to me that one way I can be a more effective environmental science teacher is to focus on 1) data driven analysis of environmental issues, 2) development of skills and abilities associated with remediation of environmental problems, and 3) increase student access to a wide-array of opportunities to interact with the environment in a manner they determine to be most useful based on their own analysis of an issue.

The past year of UDL research and the resulting awareness of my own bias, initially affected my confidence as an instructor. It's both exciting and scary to realize all the ways you can grow as a professional in your field. With a growing sense that I need to teach environmental science in a manner that was somewhat not the accepted "status quo" and a better sense of my own biases and shortfalls as an instructor, I began to question a lot of my once normally accepted teaching strategies. I realized that I was formerly very confident as a professor because I was very confident in my own knowledge, values and beliefs. I received teaching awards and excellent evaluations and, while I always knew I had shortcomings and areas for improvement and personal growth, I thought I was pretty good at this teaching thing! However, this experience has caused me to rethink *"what is good teaching?"* and frankly, to better appreciate the importance of my work. It really does matter to me if my students think they've learned something that's simply parroting my own paradigm versus teaching the next generation of students who can actually *THINK* for themselves.

About the Author

Dr. Kitrina Carlson was a Professor of Biology at the University of Wisconsin-Stout and the Director of the UW-Stout Sustainability Sciences Institute. She was actively engaged in course design, teaching and learning, and scholarship with an emphasis on service learning as a way to transform the way students think and learn. As a Wisconsin Teaching Fellow, she investigated attitudes of faculty and community perceptions regarding service learning. Her teaching and research were student-focused as evidenced by numerous awards for her student researchers. Dr. Carlson also participated in the advanced cohort in the Universal Design for Learning program through the University of Wisconsin-Stout's Nakatani Teaching and Learning Center. Dr. Carlson left UW-Stout to accept an administrative and teaching position at the University of Wisconsin-Madison, Madison College.

References

Environmental Education Act of 1990, § 20 USC 5501-5510-104 Stat. 3325 (1990). Leave No Trace Center for Outdoor Ethics. (2007). *101 ways to teach leave no trace.* Boulder, CO: Center for Outdoor Ethics. Retrieved from https://lnt.org/shop/product/101-ways- teach-leave-no-trace

Leopold, A. (1949). *Sand County Almanac.* United States: Oxford University Press, Inc.

Mayer, R. (2004). Should there be a three-strikes rule against pure discovery learning? The case for guided methods of instruction. *American Psychologist, 59,* 14-19.

Miller J. D. (2004). Public understanding of, and attitudes toward, scientific research: What we know and what we need to know. *Understand Sci, 13,* 273-294. doi: 10.1177/0963662504044908

Overdevest, C., Orr, C., & Stepenuck, K. (2004). Volunteer stream monitoring and local participation in natural resource issues. *Journal of Human Ecology, 11*(2), 177-185. Retrieved from http://www.humanecologyreview.org/pastissues/her112/overdevestorrstepenuck.pdf

Paas, F., Renkl, A., & Sweller, J. (2003). Cognitive load theory and instructional design: Recent developments. *Educational Psychologist, 38,* 1-4.

Paas, F., Renkl, A., & Sweller, J. (2004). Cognitive load theory: Instructional implications of the interaction between information structures and cognitive architecture. *Instructional Science, 32,* 1-8.

Project BudBurst. (2017). *Project BudBurst: An online database of plant phenological observations*. Boulder, CO: Project BudBurst. Retrieved from http://www.budburst.org/results_attribution

Sanera, M. (2008, September). *The problem with environmental education today: Is the tail wagging the dog?* Paper presented at the Free Market Forum of the Center for the Study of Monetary Systems and Free Enterprise, Dearborn, Michigan.

Saylan, C., & Blumstein, D. (2011). *The failure of environmental education (And how we can fix it)*. Berkeley, CA: California Press. Retrieved from http://www.jstor.org/stable/10.1525/j.ctt1pnv79

Sobel, D. (2012, July). Look, don't touch: The problem with environmental education. *Orion Magazine*, Retrieved from http://www.orionmagazine.org/index.php/articles/article/6929

Sweller, J. (1999). Instructional design in technical areas. *Australian Education Review*. Camberwell, Australia: Australian Council for Educational.

Sweller, J. (2004). Instructional design consequences of an analogy between evolution by natural selection and human cognitive architecture. *Instructional Science, 32*, 9-31.

UNESCO-UNEP. (1975, October 13-22). *The Belgrade Charter*. Retrieved from http://unesdoc.unesco.org/images/0001/000177/017772eb.pdf

UNESCO-UNEP. (1977, October 14-16). *The Tbilisi Declaration of 1977*. Retrieved from https://www.gdrc.org/uem/ee/tbilisi.html

UN General Assembly. (1972, December 15). *United Nations Conference on the human environment*, (A/RES/2994). Retrieved from http://www.refworld.org/docid/3b00f1c840.html

Appendix: Attitudes Towards Environmental Conservation

This survey is designed to measure your interest in conserving, protecting and interacting with the environment. It will be used to improve curricular experiences for BIO 141 and BIO 242 students. There are no wrong answers.

DO NOT PUT YOUR NAME ON THE SURVEY. By filling out this questionnaire, you are giving your consent as a participating volunteer in this study. The information in this study is being sought in a specific manner so that no identifiers are needed and so that confidentiality is guaranteed. You have the right to refuse to participate in this study or to withdraw from participation at any time during the study. Your decision not to participate will be respected with no coercion or prejudice. If you have questions or concerns regarding this study, please contact the Investigator, Dr. Kitrina Carlson. If you have any questions, concerns, or reports regarding your rights as a research subject, please contact the IRB Administrator.

INVESTIGATOR:
Dr. Kitrina Carlson
261 Tech Wing
UW-Stout
Menomonie, WI 54751
232-2540
carlsonki@uwstout.edu

IRB ADMINISTRATOR:
Michael Tzaruzka
152 Vocational Rehabilitation Bldg.
UW-Stout
Menomonie, WI 54751
232-2477
tzaruzkam@uwstout.edu

1. What county and state do you consider "home"?

2. List 5 plant species and 5 animal species you *should* find in an undisturbed natural area near where you live:

3. List 3 plant species that are found in natural areas near where you live that are non-native invasive plants that *should NOT* be found there:

4. What "plant communities" are found in your county?

6 Improving Access through Choice

Debbie Stanislawski, Ph.D.

Providing "Choice" in GE Courses

Does looking out at the sea of faces the first day in a college classroom continue to bring you excitement and a nervous sense of anticipation about how to meet the diverse audience's needs? If so, you are much like me! As a teacher educator who constantly deals with primarily upper level major classes, teaching general education courses for the first time came with both huge rewards and new challenges and opportunities. One challenge/opportunity revolved around designing instruction to meet the needs of diverse college-aged learners, more specifically, first semester freshmen to seniors one semester away from graduating.

Designing this course to be accessible to an academically diverse audience was at the forefront of the project described in this chapter. After reading a book and research articles, and attending a workshop on universal design, access for learning took on an entirely new meaning for me. The idea of making learning accessible, allowing for multiple means of representation and multiple means of engagement, pushed my thinking beyond my somewhat historic paradigm of accommodations only being available for those with a documented need (Center for Applied Special Technology [CAST], 2011) to consideration of the proactive design of curriculum that teaches to the broadest range of student learners. The idea that learning can be designed to benefit all was liberating! While learning about universal design challenged my former ways of thinking, it provided new opportunities to revise my curriculum.

Analysis: The Way Things "Were" and the Challenges

The pilot project was conducted in two sections of EDUC-210 Impacts of Technology on Learning. This is a general education technology elective course with a diverse target market.

Although a majority of the students in the course are education majors, the balance of students spans across all majors on campus and the age group ranges from freshmen to seniors. In addition, some students' senior status means they are not able to fit the course into prior schedules, for others it means they may have a minor aversion to the course content. It is not uncommon to hear on the first day of class that several students held off taking the course as long as possible. Their reasoning usually revolves around a self-professed lack of technology skills or simply not liking to use technology. Not only does this mean students come with varying skill sets, they also bring a broad range of attitudes and motivations for learning course content.

The course has both a heavy theoretical component and a strong focus on examining contemporary literature. Specifically, the course aims to examine the impacts of technology on the education of the individual and society; the role technology plays in both the informal and formal education of individuals; and contemporary developments and issues related to the use of technology in the learning process. The methods used in the course include reading, lecture, q/a, discussion, papers, and a heavy reliance on oral directions given during class time.

In the way that the course was implemented, the History and Impacts on Learning Project served as a summative assessment and required students to demonstrate learning across all course objectives. At the completion of this course, students had to know how to, and be able to:

1. Define technology and its impact on education, individuals and society.

2. Synthesize current research and literature involving the use of technology in learning.
3. Describe the tools and devices used to enhance learning and manage educational enterprises.
4. Compare and contrast diverse viewpoints on issues concerning the use of technology in learning.
5. Forecast potential impacts new technological developments may have on future learning environments.
6. Apply problem-solving strategies to access and analyze information.

Prior to the planning and implementation of universal design, the summative assessment was a research paper. This research paper consisted of several small scaffolded assignments that were then brought together as a compiled research paper. The development of this research paper was sometimes painful for the students and me. Some days I would tell myself, learning is challenging and these challenges (pain) are necessary to get to the end-product of a culminating research paper. It wasn't uncommon to have multiple appointments with students during the semester to discuss/show how they could work their ideas into my concept of what the research paper needed to be. Typically, complaints included a lack of clarity on how to focus or pick a research topic, difficulty finding a range of resources to meet expectations, and synthesizing the research to make key points about the research findings.

What was the problem with the research assignment as it existed and the instruction that occurred along the way? First, the academic diversity in the course meant that students not only brought a wide variety of skills to the classroom, they also brought a wide range of misconceptions. For example, relative to teaching technology such as interactive whiteboards, some students were aware of them but thought about them only as tools used in formal PK-12 educational settings, while others had either actively used them in teaching and learning settings or had no experience with them at all. This is only one example, but it could be easily replicated for other tools such as video, speech recognition software, iPads, etc. In summary, the academic diversity and curricular design caused challenges in providing student access to the course content, motivation for learning, and demonstration of learning. Another challenge with the original project design was the project directions and the learning opportunities that were scaffolded leading up to the final project. Although there was a rubric for the original project, there was a heavy reliance on providing context for the project through oral explanation in class. Providing only auditory information relative to project directions did not allow all learners to equally access the learning (Center for Applied Special Technology [CAST], 2011).

Previous Design Approach	Multiple Means of Action and Expression*	Outcomes
• All students read the same course materials or watched the same videos as determined by the instructor. • For the summative research project, all students completed the same assignments regardless of program major or area of interest.	• Options for Expressive Skills and Fluency (given choices for major assignments) • Options for Executive Functions (tools for scaffolding learning)	• Pre and post survey results documenting students perceptions of access to learning. • Student reflections on assignment "choice". • Ease or perception of choice and amount of choice was evaluated. • Impact of choice on student's perception of learning was obtained. • Limited impact on development of Critical Thinking skills. • Instructor reflections on the experience.

*Middle column adapted from The Center for Applied Science Technology (CAST) (2011). *Universal Design for Learning Guidelines version 2.0.* Wakefield, MA, Author.

Design and Develop

As previously stated, the academic diversity and curricular design of the course caused challenges both in the access to the course content, motivation for learning, and demonstration of learning. Choice was used to overcome these challenges through multiple means of representation and multiple means of engagement (CAST, 2011). After deciding to participate in the UDL project, the History and Impacts on Learning Project was revised to include "choice" through a modified bingo format.

In addition, efforts were made to provide written direction, recorded narrations throughout the course to support written directions (Jing) on major assignments, and the syllabus was formatted to be user friendly to screen readers. Elements of choice included choice in access and expression, although some required elements remained consistent for all students throughout the project (Appendix A). Essentially, a semester-long project with six discreet steps incorporated elements of choice for three of the six components. Along the way students chose different readings to access, different technologies to utilize, and different options for conducting research. Upon conclusion of the assignment, students produced an oral, digitally narrated presentation. The presentation was chosen as a way to provide multiple tools for construction and composition (CAST, 2011). It did this by using current media (screen capture) to allow students to articulate what they learned in a contemporary way (CAST, 2011). In summary, the summative assessment of a presentation was chosen as part of the strategic universal design for all students even though choice was not involved; the steps to get to the final project had multiple choices along the way.

Not only was the project revised, but the opportunity to think about and gather perceptions of students relative to "choice" was also an important element of the project's design. It was important for me to think about the choices students made in accessing and demonstrating their learning and why they made those choices. To do so I tracked their choices for each choice-related assignment and included a reflective activity with each one. The questions focused on asking students about what choice they made, why they selected that option and their beliefs about if their choice was the best option for their learning (Appendix B). I believed that this would help improve choices for future classes and help students reflect on their choices relative to how they affected their learning. In addition, I have always been passionate about developing critical thinking skills in my students and these revised assignments allowed me to scaffold opportunities for further development of those skills. This supports the idea that engaging students in actively thinking about their thinking can support the development of critical thinking (Jones, 2012).

Implement and Evaluate

Some of the issues that arose during the implementation stage provided me with a great deal of excitement, but also tested my fortitude. The ongoing formative feedback through the analysis of choices and the reflection on choices provided data and motivated me to continue with the project. This process helped me think about metacognition and the development of students' ability to self-monitor their own learning. Even the opportunity to discuss metacognition with an academically diverse group of college students can be rewarding. At the same time, clearly, for some students this might have been their first foray into UDL-related "choice" and having the ability to choose. The anxiousness exhibited by some students came across as trying to please the teacher. It gave me the opportunity to continually reflect on the ultimate purpose of providing access without creating an accommodation for an individual student.

The course design and the students' perceptions of the impact of intentional use of universal design were evaluated through multiple measures. They included the following methods of data collection:

1. An overarching survey pre- and post-survey (Chapter 3) to assess student perceptions of effective teaching and learning.
2. Tracking of choices selected by each student for each assignment where a choice was given.
3. Reflective activity after each choice assignment where students were asked to reflect on their choice, which included a rationale for the choice and a perception of the impact of that choice on learning.
4. End of course survey regarding course design.
5. Instructor evaluations using a departmental evaluation tool.

Outcomes

The broad goal of creating more accessible, effective curriculum at UW-Stout was measured using an overarching survey as previously mentioned in Chapter 3. Of the ten characteristics measured in this pre- and post-survey, four had statistically significant mean ratings for the course (See Table 1). Those statements indicated that the instructor: 1) used a variety of teaching methods, 2) routinely divided long-term course assignments into smaller parts or offered "practice" exercises and provided constructive feedback, 3) intentionally designed the course assignments/projects to allow for the use of technology and other tools that focused classmates' attention more on learning and less on requiring physical effort to complete them, and 4) designed either the physical classroom space or the on-line learning environment to accommodate differences in students' physical, intellectual and communication needs. The UDL idea of "choice" was supported by these statements. Specifically, the fact that statistical significance was found for the statement on accommodating differences was personally exciting. The goal of designing a course that is useful to an academically diverse audience was at the forefront of this project.

The lack of statistical significance on course expectations that were clear and well laid out was both disappointing and thought provoking (See Table 1). In an effort to make the learning accessible to all students, efforts were made throughout the course to provide written, oral, and narrated directions. This was part of the intentional design of the course. After reading and thinking about why students perceived the course to be lacking clarity, I turned to my course instructor evaluations to help make sense of this. What I learned is that not all students were comfortable with choice. This may have affected their perception of clarity relative to the ability to pick the "right choice". For example, a student stated, "Personally I like being told what to do, so having a choice affected me negatively because I struggled to choose one or the other".

Table 1

Overarching Survey Results from Assessment of Student Perceptions of UDL Implementation in EDUC-210 Relative to Previous Courses

Questions:	Cohort	Mean	Standard Deviation	N	Mean Difference	Effect Size (d)
Instructor Used Variety of Teaching Methods Instructors used a variety of teaching methods (lectures, group activities, projects, ect.).	Pre	3.84	1	31	.65*	69
	Post	4.48	.85			
Practice Assignments and Feedback Instructors routinely divided long-term course assignments into smaller parts or offer "practice" exercises and provide constructive feedback.	Pre	3.30	.95	30	.93**	.93
	Post	4.23	1.04			
Use of Technology Teachers intentionally designed the course assignments/projects to allow for the use of technology and other tools that focused classmates' attention more on learning and less on requiring physical effort to complete them.	Pre	3.23	.82	30	1.13**	1.30
	Post	4.37	.93			
Environment Accommodates Difference Your past teachers designed either the physical classroom space or the on-line learning environment to accommodate differences in students' physical, intellectual and communication needs.	Pre	3.30	1.15	30	.73**	.73
	Post	4.03	.81			
Instructors Expectations Were Clear Your instructor laid out his or her course expectations for exam performance, papers, or projects in a straight forward, clearly understandable and predictable manner.	Pre	3.84	.93	31	.39	.42
	Post	4.23	.92			

Note: **statistical significance at the .01 level; *statistical significance at the .05 level.*

The tracking of choices was especially powerful from a course improvement perspective. After careful reflection, I realized that my descriptions of the assignments may have influenced or swayed choices. In addition, the actual assignment choices made by the students helped me better understand their perception of choice. What I mean is that when I described the choices verbally in class, the tone of voice that I used or my enthusiasm for the choices was likely not indifferent.

The choices of students at first surprised me. Rather than finding their own resource when given the choice, most chose a reading provided by the teacher. The data from the reflective assignment after each choice assignment was insightful in understanding choices that students make when given options. For example, the first-choice assignment in The Technology and Learning Project was to interpret the definitions of formal and informal learning by writing several paragraphs on the topic. Students had choices for accessing learning that ranged from reading an article preselected by the instructor, reading information in a web format, or finding their own article on the topic. Table 2 demonstrates the choices made by students. The majority of them chose the website followed by choosing their own article and reading the one provided by the teacher. As mentioned, students were asked to reflect on their choice by giving a rationale for it and the perception of the impact that it had on their learning (Appendix B). Student comments about their choice included:

- *I selected this option because I knew that already it was a good source for the assignment because it was given by the teacher.* (Option chose: teacher selected article)
- *The lay out seemed less intimidating and overwhelming than a long scholarly article.*
- (Option chose: teacher selected website)
- *I searched for my own article but I did not find any articles I liked.* (Option chose: teacher selected article)
- *Because it looked like it would be the easiest of the options to do.* (Option chose: teacher selected website)

In section EDUC-210-01, 11 students' choices were affected by the "ease" or perception of time it would take to read from the website vs. the research article approach. This demonstrated that further care needs to be taken in making sure that choices are similar in effort required and complexity (Fulton & Schweitzer, 2011). In contrast, students who did choose their own article commented on being able "to read about something that I wanted to learn more about and not what was chosen for me". Students also reflected on their perceptions about whether their choice was the best for supporting their learning. Again, in this same section of EDUC-210- 01, 14 of the 17 students selected the website option and indicated that they did so because it best supported their learning.

Table 2
Choice tracking for Assignment one of Technology and Learning Project

	EDUC-210-01 (Percentage)	EDUC-210-02 (Percentage)
Article of choice	8 (25.8)	3 (13)
Knowledge Jump Website	17 (54.8)	16 (36.6)
Article provided	6 (9.7)	4 (17.4)
Total Students Completing Assignment	31	23

The end of the semester survey was administered to collect additional student perceptions of their assignment choices (Appendix C). Students were asked to select "the statement that best describes your feelings about the amount of choice used in EDUC-210 during the semester." Students' answers to this question reflected that they felt that overall the amount of choice was about right (Table 3). This is supported by research by Patall, Cooper, and Robinson (2008) that states "The largest positive effect on choice on intrinsic motivation was found when participants made two to four choices in a single experimental manipulation compared to when only a single choice or five or more choices were made" (p. 95). Choice was not provided on all assignments throughout the course, only on the Teaching and Learning Project Assignment.

Table 3
Results of End of Course Survey on Perceptions of Choice

	EDUC-210-01 (Percentage)	EDUC-210-02 (Percentage)
Way too much	0	1
Too much	3 (10.3)	1 (5.6)
About right	22 (75.9)	15 (83.3)
Not sure	4 (13.8)	1 (5.6)
Too little	0	1 (5.6)
Way too little	0	0
Total Students completing End of Course survey	29	18

Overall, student comments on the final course survey also supported the impact of choice on their learning. For example, student comments included:

- *I was more motivated and interested to learn about the material.*
- *It gave me more of a chance to become engaged in the class. There were also different ways to learn this way.*
- *I was able to communicate my learning more clearly by having a choice of how to communicate my learning.*
- *It didn't seem to really affect me while I was doing it but I can reflect on how not having options in other courses has negatively affected me. I really like to get involved with things physically and be interested in the subject so being able to choose was a HUGE advantage. GREAT CLASS.*
- *Having a "choice" affected my learning because I got to do things in a way that I understood them, and explain how I learned from the assignment without only having one option.*

There were several student comments on the final course survey that deserve additional analysis and reflection, for example:

- *Having options on assignments gave me the choice of which I felt I would be more efficient at doing.*
- *Personally, I like being told what to do, so having a choice affected me negatively because I struggled to choose one or the other.*
- *It affected my learning because I was able to choose what I wanted to do, however it did not force me to choose to do an option that was new to me. I knew how to make a Prezi and completed that part so that did not force me to learn anything new.*

The previous three comments demonstrated that students did choose assignments based on their perceptions of time and ease, as previously mentioned. In addition, the notion of having a choice was sometimes difficult for a portion of students. The intent of Universal Design for Learning is to provide a plan for "simple and intuitive use" (Burgstahler & Corey, 2010). The notion of ease could be considered positive in relationship to the overall intent of UDL.

Using a departmental survey tool, my instructor evaluations were also a source of interesting and beneficial information relative to the course design and implementation. For example, across both sections, themes emerged about the amount of work being too much for a one-credit class (7 comments in EDUC-210-01 and 5 comments in EDUC-210-02). In fact, on a 5- point scale with 5 being high and 1 being low students rated the course as 3.92 (01) and 3.33 (section 02) relative to the level of the appropriate course difficulty. So, although students thought the level of choice was appropriate, the overall level of difficulty they expected was too much relative to the course objectives and 200 level nature of the course. The majority of the other ratings were strongly agree or agree (about 4.0), but the perception of "too difficult" does stand out relative to the ratings of other course factors. This feedback was part of an impetus to revise the course to three credits; yet, there was also celebration when interpreting this as course rigor.

Critical thinking is an underpinning to all courses I design and implement. It was my hope that the approach taken to improve access would also support the development of critical thinking. On the course evaluations the statement, "The course requirements and content challenged me to think critically," was rated by students overall as 4.14 and 4.17 on a 5-point scale. Course evaluations of critical thinking did not improve from previous semesters in the two sections of EDUC-210 where this intentional design was implemented. I may have been overly optimistic about the ability of this project and its design to make improvements in this area.

Reflections for Practice

Choice as a method of implementing Universal Design for Learning and access for an academically diverse student audience will continue to be part of my teaching practices in all courses. The majority of students in the research project felt that the "choice" given throughout the semester was about right in both sections (78% and 83%). No students felt that there was an inadequate amount of choice in the class. This means that

I will continue to offer choice for some assignments, but not all assignments throughout the semester. Having students reflect on their choices encourages metacognition and can help develop a knowledge base about 1) the choices given and 2) how to modify choices for the future. As I work to improve the implementation of choice, it will be paramount to reflect on aspects of choice that provide challenges and confusion for students. Options include evaluating rubric options, as sometimes the amount of information and grading detail on the rubric may be overwhelming for students.

The lack of improvement in critical thinking relative to students' perceptions on course evaluations was troubling. As a researcher interested in critical thinking I am always trying to underpin my course design to develop and improve critical thinking skills. I now must ponder if there can be a connection between Universal Design for Learning and improving critical thinking. Or, must critical thinking and pedagogy relative to improving it be a separate assault. I do realize that critical thinking may have taken place, but it develops slowly and is not always apparent. Perhaps future survey responses will document observable improvements in my students' critical thinking skills.

This foray into universal design has opened my mind to planning for access. It has changed the way I think about access for all relative to multiple means of representation, multiple means of expression, and multiple means of engagement (CAST, 2011). It has made me aware of how much further I have to go relative to planning for access in all of my courses.

Researching other methods of providing access beyond choice is also an important next step. Simply, I keep reminding myself that one revision at a time will help improve each of my courses!

About the Author

Dr. Debbie Stanislawski is a professor in the Teaching, Learning, and Leadership Department at the University of Wisconsin-Stout. Her background includes teaching business education in public high schools and teaching in higher education for more than 15 years. Dr. Stanislawski's research interests include preparing future business teachers for the comprehensive role of being an educator, student teacher supervision and digital supervision, critical thinking, and Universal Design for Learning (UDL). She strives to inform her teaching through research.

References

Burgstahler, S., & R. Corey. (2010). *Universal design in higher education: From principles to practice.* Cambridge, MA: Harvard Education Press.

Center for Applied Science Technology (CAST). (2011). U*niversal Design for Learning Guidelines version 2.0.* Wakefield, MA: Author.

Fulton, S., & Schweitzer, D. (2011). Impact of giving students a choice of homework assignments in an introductory computer science class. *International Journal for the Scholarship of Teaching & Learning, 5*(1), 1-12.

Jones, R. (2012). What were they thinking? *Science Teacher, 79*(3), 66-70.

Patall, E. A., Cooper, H., & Robinson, J. (2008). The effects of choice on intrinsic motivation and related outcomes: A meta-analysis of research findings. *Psychological Bulletin, 134*(2), 270-300. doi:10.1037/0033-2909.134.2.270

Appendix A: Tools and Devices to Impact Learning Unit

Explore, Learn, Apply and Demonstrate Assignment

Each student is responsible for completing three activities. One activity must be chosen from each row.

1. Develop knowledge of informal vs. formal learning. Pick one from this row	Find and read an "quality" article defining/describing informal vs. formal learning.	Read a website that defines formal vs. informal learning http://www.knowledgejump.com/learning/informal.html	Go under content at learn@. Read the pages 1-14 article on formal vs. informal learning. Title "Informal Learning Review "
2. Application of Knowledge Pick one from this row	Create a 10 question true false or multiple choice "hot potatoes" quiz about informal vs. formal learning. (10 examples of informal vs. formal learning that demonstrates you understand the difference of each). http://hotpot.uvic.ca/ (Requires you to download and install the software).	Create a hard copy "collage" of 5 examples of informal learning and 5 examples of informal learning. You may cut "pictures" out of magazines, newspapers, etc to create your collage. Label each informal or formal. Explain why each is informal vs. formal learning based on the definitions of each.	Create a digital poster using http://www.glogster.com/ of 5 examples of informal learning and 5 examples of informal learning. Label each informal or formal. Explain why each is informal vs. formal learning based on the definitions of each.
3. Explore and Learn	Locate at least six quality references that will discuss the technical means from a less personal standpoint. I expect you are going through the source analysis process we learned about in class and that you developed a flow chart for as you select each reference (content and internet analysis). These references should be used to provide some introductory background information on the topic for your final report. It should also help when planning the interview. Pick references that speak both to a **historical perspective** and a **research/learning perspective**. Develop an annotated reference list. See Handout for Directions on preparing an annotated reference list.		

4. **Demonstration of Knowledge**	Write Your Research Paper. This will provide the formal background on the technology using the references listed in step 1. This section of your paper should include an 1) Background Information on Use, 2) Historical Perspective, and 3) overview of the multiple perspectives related to the impacts of the tool or device on learning based on research. The background is to be 3 pages in length. Please limit to 3 pages double spaced. (See Separate Rubric).	
5. Pick one from this row **Explore, Learn, and/or Apply**	Interview, compare and contrast of interview to research, and the development of a presentation using multiple tools, such as Prezi, Jing, Etc. Please note: You will need to identify an individual who has experienced learning in new and different ways by using the tool or device that you have been chosen. That person should have interacted with the tool or device in either formal or informal learning environments.	Expand research paper length to 7 pages, not including references. Go deeper into research on historical perspective and multiple perspectives. This must be using "research based articles".

6. **Demonstration of knowledge**	A. Prepare a final digital report.
	
	1) Visual
	  a) Prepare a visual that captures the following:
	    i) Biographical Sketch of the Interviewee
	      (1) Why is this person worthy of interviewing? Background? Credentials?
	    ii) Overview of Key Finding from the Interview (Based on questions)
	    iii) Analysis
	      (1) Did the interview validate what you found in your research paper? Was the interview counter to what you found in your research paper? Essentially, compare and contrast the background research for your paper that you completed to the information you gained about technology and learning from your interview.
	  b) Use one of the following tools for the visual
		A. Prepare a final digital report.
		
		1) Visual
		  i) Prepare a visual that captures the following:
		    (1) Biographical Sketch of the Interviewee
		      (a) Why is this person worthy of interviewing? Background? Credentials?
		    (2) Overview of Key Finding from the Interview (Based on questions)
		    (3) Analysis
		      (a) Did the interview validate what you found in your research paper? Was the interview counter to what you found in your research paper? Essentially, compare and contrast the background research for your paper that you completed to the information you gained about technology and learning from your interview.
		  ii) Use one of the following tools for the visual
		    (1) Prezi

	i) Prezi
	ii) Glogster
	c) The visual should be used only as an "outline" for your oral presentation
	   i) Consider text load 6x6 rule
	   ii) Layout and Design
	2) Narration and Explanation – Time limit – 5 minutes.
	   a) Use "Jing" to create an oral narration of your presentation
	     i) In essence, provide the detail that your visual lacks
	     ii) Include an introduction, body, and conclusion
	     iii) As you narrate, move through the visual
		(2) Glogster
		iii) The visual should be used only as an "outline" for your oral presentation
		   (1) Consider text load 6x6 rule
		   (2) Layout and Design
		2) Narration and Explanation – Time limit – 5 minutes.
		   i) Use "Jing" to create an oral narration of your presentation
		     (1) In essence, provide the detail that your visual lacks
		     (2) Include an introduction, body, and conclusion
		     (3) As you narrate, move through the visual

Appendix B: Choice Reflection Survey Format

Which of the following choices did you select?

	List Choices				
YToxOntzOjc6IIF:	1	QID3	1|2|3	TE	ML

Why did you select that option?

What part of the option you chose most helped you learn?

After completing that option, was that the best choice to support your learning? Why or Why not?

What specific, practical change would you suggest to improve this assignment and options?

Appendix C: End of Course Choice Survey

My learning was influenced because there were different options for assignments.

Agree	Somewhat Agree	Don't know	Somewhat Disagree	Disagree
☐	☐	☐	☐	☐

I understood expectations for most assignments.

Agree	Somewhat Agree	Don't know	Somewhat Disagree	Disagree
☐	☐	☐	☐	☐

There was enough support (teacher explanation, website links, etc.) for me to learn my best throughout the project.

Agree	Somewhat Agree	Don't know	Somewhat Disagree	Disagree
☐	☐	☐	☐	☐

Assignments encouraged me to use various forms of nontechnical tools (e.g., graphs, diagrams) and technology (concept mapping tools, visual slides).

Agree	Somewhat Agree	Don't know	Somewhat Disagree	Disagree
☐	☐	☐	☐	☐

I could accurately show my learning because I had options of how to demonstrate my learning.

Agree	Somewhat Agree	Don't know	Somewhat Disagree	Disagree
○	○	○	○	○

The particular assignment options had enough challenge for me.

Agree	Somewhat Agree	Don't know	Somewhat Disagree	Disagree
☐	☐	☐	☐	☐

I was able to learn in a way that was best for me because I had options of how to complete assignments.

Agree	Somewhat Agree	Don't know	Somewhat Disagree	Disagree
○	○	○	○	○

My ability to demonstrate what I learned in the course was enhanced by the various formats available for assignments (oral, written, and graphic products, video demonstration, etc).

Agree	Somewhat Agree	Don't know	Somewhat Disagree	Disagree
○	○	○	○	○

I felt more motivated to complete assignments because I got to choose how to complete them.

Agree	Somewhat Agree	Don't know	Somewhat disagree	Disagree
○	○	○	○	○

Having assignment options improved my learning.

Agree	Somewhat Agree	Don't know	Somewhat Disagree	Disagree
○	○	○	○	○

There were choices available for assignments and demonstrating learning in this course.

Agree	Somewhat Agree	Don't know	Somewhat Disagree	Disagree
○	○	○	○	○

Please describe how having "choice" affected your learning in this course? (If it did not, respond: It didn't)

[   ]

Which statement best describes your feelings about the amount of "choice" (assignment options, etc.) as used in EDUC-210 this semester?

Way too much	Too much	About right	Not sure	Too Little	Way too little
○	○	○	○	○	○

Please explain your rating for the previous question in the space below. [The previous question was: Which statement best describes your feelings about the amount of "choice" (assignment options, etc.) as used in EDUC-210 this semester?]

[   ]

7 One Size Does Not Fit All

Renee Chandler, Ed.D.

From Special Education to UDL for All

"I loved this class" and "I learned so much in this class" are both comments that instructors like to read on their course evaluations. When I was a beginning instructor in higher education I accepted both statements as equal validation of my teaching skills. As a veteran teacher who focuses on learning outcomes, my primary concern is that students are mastering the course material, so I would much rather hear "I learned so much in this class." It is a wonderful bonus when students also enjoy the course as this certainly has a positive impact on motivation and persistence.

Decades of teaching both children and adults have confirmed my belief that not all students learn in the same way or at the same pace. Unfortunately, the traditional model of instruction in higher education is a one-size-fits-all approach that ensures that some students will succeed and others will fail. Included in both groups are students who are not engaged in learning because the instruction is not relevant or challenging. Although experience and logic tell us that this approach to learning is not reasonable, we continue to assign instructors large classes of students who have wide ranges of interests, abilities, and background knowledge without a framework that allows all students to be successful learners. How do you ensure that every student in a class is engaged and learning?

Prior to teaching in higher education, I taught both general education and special education in PK-12 public schools. In these roles, I became adept at making appropriate accommodations and modifications to my instruction for students with disabilities. I was proficient at taking the general education curriculum and making it accessible to students on a case-by-case basis. When I was a general education teacher, the special education teachers loved me because they knew I would provide good instruction to the students on their caseloads.

When I was a special education teacher, the general education teachers loved me because they knew I would work hard to create the accommodations needed so that my students could be successful in their classrooms. Then I moved into higher education and taught undergraduate teacher education students how to develop these same skills for their future teaching contexts. I was the expert when it came to designing appropriate accommodations.

I gained significant insights during my work as a teacher. Making accommodations and/or modifications on a student-by-student basis is very time-consuming. I had to put in a lot of time to help students with disabilities achieve success academically. I learned that students do not always appreciate this hard work, especially when it makes them feel singled out or "different." I discovered that what worked well for students with disabilities often worked equally well for students without disabilities. In fact, when I presented a task with accommodations to my general education colleagues they started asking, "Can I use this with all of my students?" I did not know about Universal Design for Learning (UDL) in a formal sense, but I was beginning to discover one of its primary constructs: Good design for people with disabilities benefits everyone (Edyburn, 2010).

Analysis: Who are my students and what do they need?

I teach graduate level education courses in an online program. The course that is the focus of this chapter is a required class in the Master's in Education program titled "Assessment for Learning." An instructor might mistakenly assume that this is a homogeneous group of students comprised mainly of PK-12 teachers. In reality, the course included individuals such as teachers in public school systems, instructors in postsecondary institutions, instructional designers who work in business/industry settings, program coordinators for various public and private organizations, a pastry chef, a dental hygienist, and other individuals who are seeking skills that will help them provide meaningful learning experiences for the learners with whom they work. In addition, the undergraduate degrees of these students ranged from education to psychology to business and student ages varied from mid-twenties to mid-fifties.

Initially, UDL was appealing to me because it reduced the workload involved in providing individual accommodations for students with identified disabilities and did not single students out as "different." My motivation for infusing UDL into my current coursework, however, did not stem from a desire to reduce the number of individual accommodations that needed to be made. Very few of my graduate students request accommodations for disabilities. My goal was to make the course as accessible and relevant as possible to a group of students who wanted to apply the content to a wide range of contexts. I wanted my course evaluations to say, "I learned a lot in this class and it was relevant to my specific situation."

Prior to UDL implementation, student evaluations of courses in my program often cited the need for content and activities that were more relevant for students who work in adult education rather than PK-12 settings. This is an instructional challenge because I also have a large audience of students who teach children. In the past, I created coursework that was primarily focused on the needs of the PK-12 teachers and attempted to add on additional readings and references that made the content more relevant for people working with adult learners. My goal with UDL implementation was to create a course that was meaningful to all students. I examined the course objectives and determined that they were applicable to educators across the wide range of settings. What I needed to change were the activities used to meet the course objectives.

Design, Develop, and Implement

Given the diversity of the learners who comprised my class, I was determined to provide all of these students with learning and activities that were relevant and purposeful. As I designed my course, I discovered that I moved back and forth among the ADDIE stages of design, develop, and implement (Chapter 2). I needed to constantly re-evaluate my design and development as I was implementing the course. Although the ADDIE model appears to present distinct stages of course development, my experience demonstrated that I needed to be flexible in how I approached the stages.

Assessment for Learning (EDUC-745) is comprised of six distinct modules that provide the students with the knowledge and skills that they need to produce their final project, a learner assessment plan. The modules and learner assessment plan are designed to meet eight course objectives:

At the completion of this course, students will know how to, and be able to:
1. Articulate the purposes of assessment, including the historical, philosophical, legal, ethical, and social principles underpinning current assessment practices.
2. Evaluate a wide range of assessment techniques (e.g., formative, summative, and standardized tests) to determine which assessment tools are appropriate for specific purposes.
3. Analyze the effects of assessment practices on under-represented or diverse learners.
4. Demonstrate how to locate, evaluate and select the most valid and reliable instruments to aid in instructional decision making.
5. Analyze the role assessments play in guiding classroom and district decisions regarding instructional planning, differentiation, curricular design, and curricular implementation.
6. Develop a learner assessment plan intended to demonstrate the effect of instruction on learning in a field-based setting.

7. Interpret assessment results to evaluate and articulate the effects of instruction on identified learner outcomes.
8. Interpret assessment results to inform the instructor's professional goals and development.

Because my students had such diverse backgrounds and teaching contexts, I determined that giving all students the same assignments would not be appropriate. I had some highly effective materials that would benefit PK-12 educators but would be irrelevant for other students in my class. I either needed to eliminate these tasks from the course or find additional tasks that would be appropriate for the other students.

Based on my premise that "one size does *not* fit all" and the diverse population of students who take my course, I chose to implement student choice as a primary UDL strategy. Within the framework established by the Center for Applied Special Technology (CAST), "student choice" can best be categorized under CAST's Principle 3: Provide Multiple Means of Engagement. This principle includes checkpoints such as optimizing individual choice and autonomy, heightening the salience of goals and objectives, and developing self-assessment and reflection (CAST, 2011). In addition to providing multiple means of engagement, I infused aspects of multiple means of representation and multiple means of action and expression, the two other principles of UDL.

As indicated in this table, I infused multiple UDL principles across several of the guidelines outlined by CAST. Student choice was the critical element of my design across all three principles.

Table 1
Example of Student Choice within the CAST framework

Previous Design Approach	UDL Design Approach Students were provided:	Outcomes Students:
• For each topic, content is delivered in a single way that is determined by the instructor (e.g. readings, lectures). • Supportive learning tools and technologies are pre-selected by the instructor and the same for every student (unless they are getting special ADA accommodations).	**Multiple means of Representation** • Options for Perception (visual, audio, text) • Options for Comprehension of Content (activated prior knowledge through online discussions, highlighted critical ideas through module overviews) • Options for Comprehension of Course Expectations (e.g., text-based syllabus that was accessible to screen readers, expectations stated in multiple places throughout the LMS)	• Access module overviews through multiple media (audio, video, text) • Engage in conversations and experiences that allow them to connect new material with what they already know and what they are experiencing in their daily lives. • Access consistent information about expectations from multiple places (checklists, syllabus, module content, discussion board prompts).
• Students are responsible for monitoring their own progress in the course	**Multiple Means of Action and Expression** • Options for expression and communication (discussion board posts provide scaffolding for the final project) • Options for Executive Functions (tools for organizing and prioritizing work such as checklists, overviews, calendars, and planning options)	• Engage with their final project throughout the semester, receiving feedback from peers and the instructor through online discussions • Monitor their own progress throughout the course
• Students rely on the instructor for assessment of their performance. • All students complete the same assignments in the same way to meet the course objectives.	**Multiple Means of Engagement** • Options for Recruiting Interest (optimize individual choice and autonomy) • Options for Sustaining Effort and Persistence (heighten salience of course objectives, foster collaboration and community) • Options for Self-Regulation (progress toward course objectives is self-assessed at the end of each module)	• Students select tasks that are engaging and relevant to their context and unique needs. • Engage with course objectives in every module. • Participate in peer review and collaboration. • Provide statements of how their work demonstrates competence of course objectives.

* Middle column adapted from CAST (2011). *Universal design for learning guidelines version 2.0*. Wakefield, MA: Author.

For each module, students had some required assignments (typically participation in an online discussion board) and earned the rest of their points by selecting assignments from a menu of options (Appendix A). I attempted to provide a plethora of options that allowed students to demonstrate their learning using multiple modes of expression (i.e., written, audio, visual, etc.). I also allowed them to access information using multiple modes of representation by giving them options such as reading the text, listening/viewing a PowerPoint or Prezi presentation with audio narration, reading a transcription of the PowerPoint/Prezi narration, viewing online videos, and locating websites and/or other resources that met their particular context. In some cases, this meant that students were accessing similar content but with different examples. In other cases, students were acquiring the same content through different modes (i.e., seeing, hearing, etc.). Sometimes similar themes were explored through different case scenarios that were context specific.

When I was in the design and development stages of this project, I started to ask myself, "How will I know if they all learned the same thing?" The more I pondered this question, the more I realized that instructors never really know if their students have learned the same things and perhaps it is not important or even possible for everyone to learn the same things. As I grappled with this line of thinking, I decided that all students needed to master the course objectives, but how they went about mastering the objectives and demonstrating their learning could be very different. With a more open approach to course completion, I needed a way to document that students were indeed meeting all of the required course objectives, regardless of which assignments they chose to complete. I designed a Course Alignment Summary and a student self-reflection piece to accomplish this task (Appendix B). For each module, students were required to self-report their progress on the course objectives by completing the Course Alignment Summary and justifying their choices with rationale statements explaining how their work demonstrated progress on course objectives. At the end of the semester, students also submitted a self-reflection paper in which they reported their own perceptions of their work for the semester.

Evaluation

I assessed the success of the course design with multiple measures including student feedback, student performance on module assignments and a final project, and student self-assessment.

Outcomes. The outcomes of this project can be evaluated from multiple measures that were employed during two academic semesters, Spring 2012 and Spring 2013. The midterm survey was instructor-created and anonymous. It elicited responses regarding students' preference for choice but did not directly measure learning outcomes. I asked students to respond to the following statements using a Likert scale that ranged from "strongly agree" to "strongly disagree":

1. The amount of work assigned is appropriate for a 700-level course.
2. I make assignment choices that are appropriate for my learning needs.
3. I enjoy the level of choice offered in this course.
4. I would prefer fewer choices and more direct instruction.

In Spring 2012, 22 of the 30 students responded. Of the 22 respondents, 21 indicated Agree or Strongly Agree to the statement: "I enjoy the level of choice offered in this course." When asked to respond to the statement "I make assignment choices appropriate for my learning needs," 20 of the 22 students selected Agree or Strongly Agree. In contrast, when presented with the statement "I would prefer fewer choices and more direct instruction," 17 students disagreed or strongly disagreed with four answering "neutral" and one student indicating strongly agree.

Responses for Spring 2013 were similar. Twelve of 20 students responded. Of the 12 respondents, 11 indicated Agree (1) or Strongly Agree (10) to the statement: "I enjoy the level of choice offered in this course." When asked to respond to the statement "I make assignment choices appropriate for my learning needs," 11 of the 12 students selected Agree (1) or Strongly Agree (10). In contrast, when presented with the statement "I would prefer fewer choices and more direct instruction," nine students disagreed or strongly disagreed with three answering "neutral."

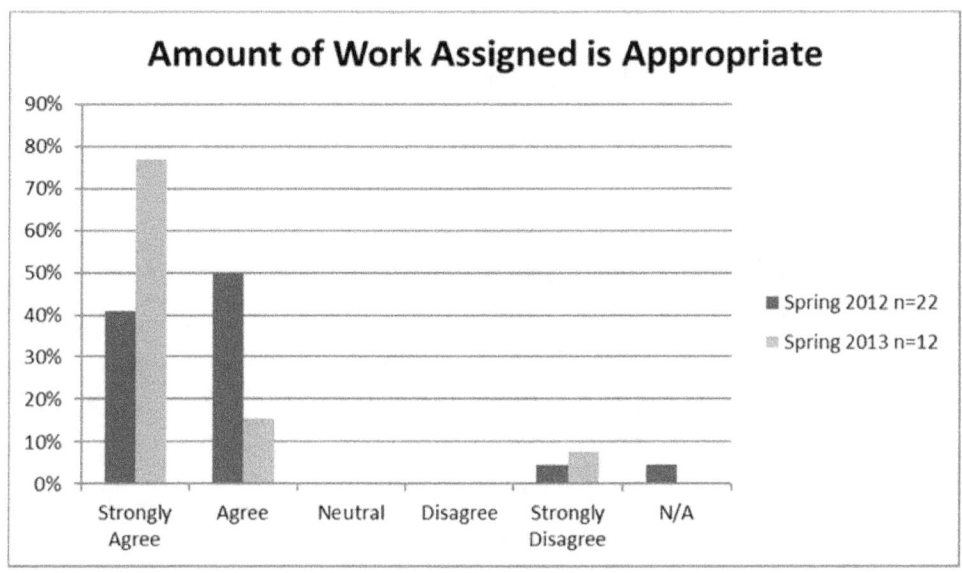

Figure 1. Midterm survey results for "The amount of work assigned is appropiate for a 700-level course."

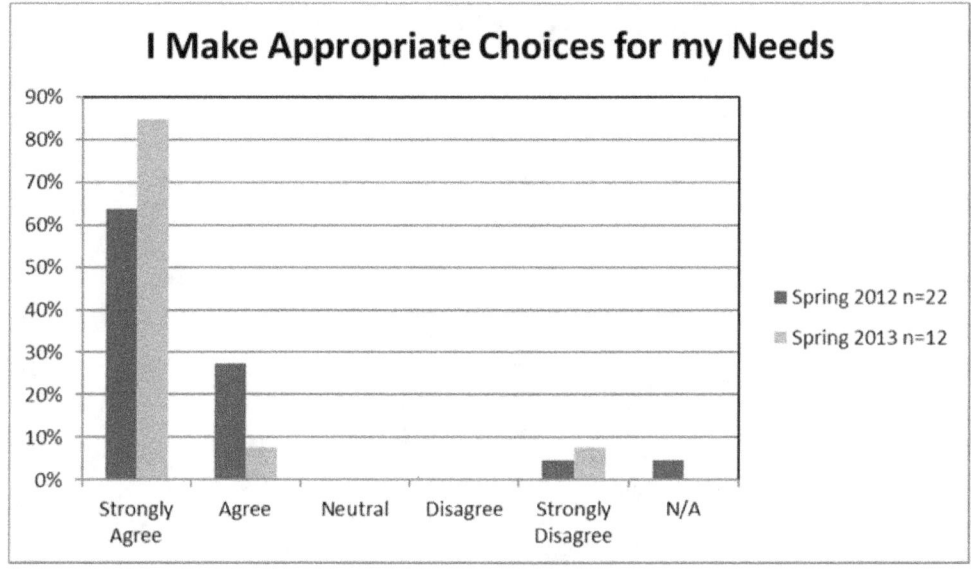

Figure 2. Midterm survey results for "I make assignment choices that are appropiate for my learning needs."

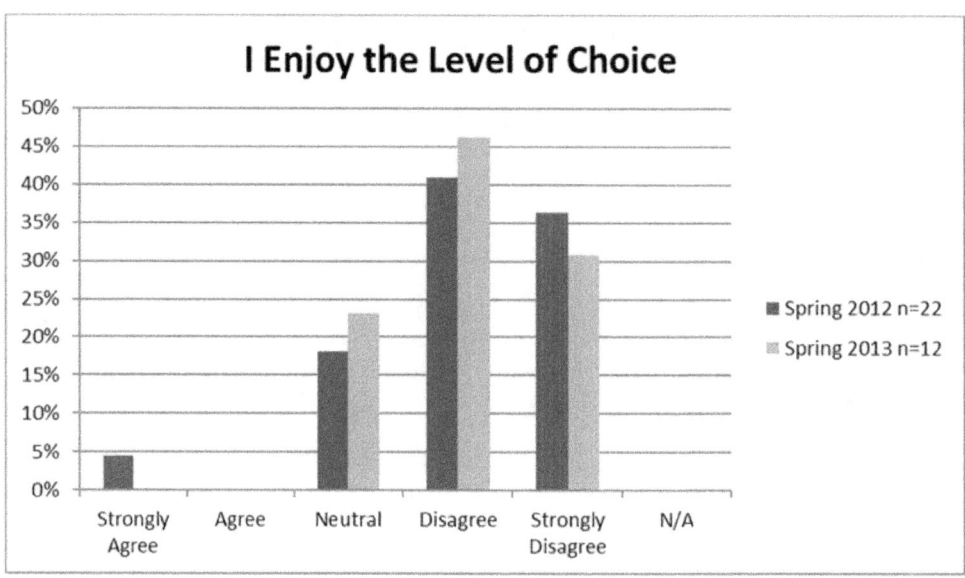

Figure 3. Midterm survey results for "I enjoy the level of choice offered in this course."

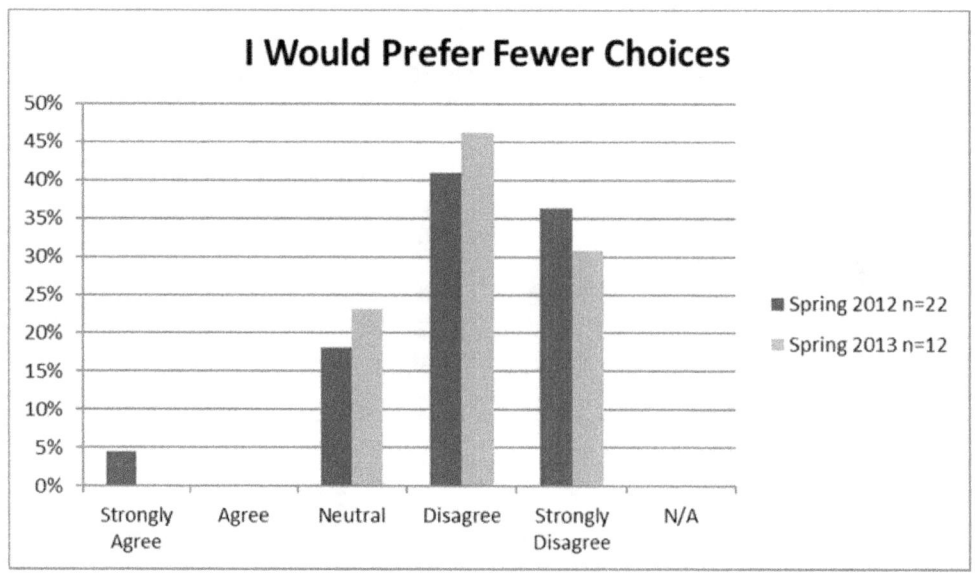

Figure 4. Midterm survey results for "I would prefer fewer choices and more direct instruction."

The results from Spring 2012 and Spring 2013 reveal that I had one student each semester who could be considered an outlier. These students provided responses that indicated a strong dissatisfaction with the level of choice offered. The survey was anonymous so I have no way of identifying these students for clarification on their responses. I was worried about having a student in each class with such negative responses, particularly because my goal was to create a course that was appropriate for ALL learners. I sent out a general e-mail to both classes and asked that students who had concerns to please contact me individually so that I could address their issues. I did not receive any replies to these e-mails. In addition, the open-ended responses all indicated positive reactions to the level of choice offered. I suspect that there was a student in each class who simply read the scale incorrectly.

As mentioned previously, open-ended responses indicated general satisfaction with the level of choice offered in the course:

- *The best part of this class is that I have the freedom to explore the information I feel I need to explore to gain a better understanding of how it applies to my own education/career/situation. It doesn't feel like "busy-work" or that I'm just completing random assignments- instead, I'm doing the research or applying the concepts to areas that affect me and my own field. Purposeful education.*

- *I have found this course to be a great learning experience. I appreciate the differentiation and the ability to align my learning to my professional career. I love the options given for each module and appreciate your feedback.*

- *The options for assignments have been very helpful in my learning more about my individual learning style. It is nice to have choices and not just be told to do the same thing as everyone else.*

- *I enjoy the choices allowed in module assignments as this forces me to reflect and evaluate the assignments. I choose those which best serve my goals.*

Qualitative data was also collected from students' written work, especially their final reflection papers and their completed alignment summaries. Themes gleaned from the analysis of qualitative data include an appreciation of choice, instructor modeling of best practices, and the implicit value of utilizing choices as part of a comprehensive assessment system. Specific statements that support these themes include:

> *I absolutely loved the element of choice that was included into the assignments for this class. I've never had an instructor allow for this type of individualized learning before. Being able to choose what assignments to work on allowed me to pursue work that was more attuned to my interests and my background.... having a choice in what assignments to complete also allowed me to specifically choose content that covered gaps in my knowledge in order to give me a fuller picture of educational assessment.*
>
> *Angie, Assessment Developer*
> *Western Governors University*

> *First off, let me say that I really enjoyed having the choices in assignments this semester. Sometimes, in these classes, I feel like the assignments are mundane and that I am simply checking a box by doing the assignment. Having the choice allowed me to tailor the class to my needs and holes in my education.*
>
> *Dena, Special Education Teacher*
> *Washington State*

> *One of the things I liked best about this course was the flexibility of choosing the course assignments to demonstrate competence of the modules from the list of options. This allowed me to choose what helped me best demonstrate my comprehension of the materials.*
>
> *Dianne, Technical College Instructor*
> *Wisconsin*

As we began the course and the element of choice was introduced, I was admittedly a bit nervous. I am typically a student who likes to have the specific requirements outlined clearly for me and am then careful to meet or exceed those requirements. This element of choice, and the variety of choices presented, presented me with an initial pause. I wasn't entirely sure how to proceed. As I have worked through the modules, however, I have grown to genuinely enjoy the opportunity to select my own projects and ways to deepen and demonstrate my learning of the material. I liked the width of opportunity within each 'menu' of assignment options and the flexibility of selecting point values.

Jessica, 4th grade teacher
Mason City, Iowa

The comments students made regarding the importance of choice were affirming, but even more exciting were the comments that indicated that students grasped what I was modeling for them and intended to use some of the same strategies with their own students. Some of the students even began to make connections between the content of the course (assessment) and the UDL framework that I had adopted. Their comments reflect an appreciation for the use of student choice as a means of promoting student engagement:

This was the first time in my academic career where I was given the opportunity to choose the type of assignment that I would be completing. In regard to assessment I think that is one of the most important aspects. You need to provide your students with multiple ways to display their understanding of the material. Everyone learns in different ways. While some prefer to read others like to visualize or hear the material.

Chase, Physical Education Instructor
University setting

I have decided to try and implement this idea of course work completion flexibility in one of the courses I teach. I have shared this with other instructors at the college where I work and we all had similar responses of, "That is genius! Why didn't we ever think of this!" I feel l learned teaching techniques from the instructor as well as the content of the course.

Dianne, Technical College Instructor
Wisconsin

I also think students should be given multiple opportunities to meet the class requirements. The focus should be on achieving success for all of the students rather than achieving student success that follows a learning curve where some students succeed, and some students fail. The former results in wins for everyone (and I believe this extends beyond the classroom) and the latter results in win for some-lose for others.

Ann, Online Education Developer Mayo Clinic, Minnesota

The impact of choice on student learning was demonstrated through the final reflection papers and the final project of the class, the learner assessment plan (LAP). The LAP is essentially a research proposal that students take forward with them as they move into an action research course. As such, it is a formal written report with standard expectations. The LAP does not contain the elements of choice evident in the earlier modules of the course. It is the high-stakes summative assessment for the course that demonstrates student mastery of the course content as well as their ability to apply it. All learner assessment plans were graded using the form presented in Figure 5.

EDUC-745 Learner Assessment Plan
Project Grading Criteria

	Points Possible	Points Earned
Section 1: Context		
Description of setting: Rich description that includes enough details to provide the reader with a clear picture of the larger setting (i.e., the school and school district, the university, the clinic, etc.) and the more specific setting (i.e., the classroom, the program, etc.)	5	
Description of learners: Rich description that includes enough details to inform the reader (e.g., age, achievement level, background knowledge, disability status, etc.)	5	
Description of curriculum: What are the goals for the entire year/semester/program of study? What are the "big rocks"?	5	
Description of assessor/instructor: Who is conducting the assessment? What relationship does the assessor have with the subjects? How much experience does the assessor have?	5	
Section 2: Student Learning Outcomes		
Tied to larger curriculum/program: Clear and plausible explanation of how the identified learning outcomes tie to the larger curriculum or program	5	
Appropriateness for learners: Author provides a convincing explanation of how the Learning Outcomes are appropriate for the learner(s)	5	
Observable and measurable: Learning outcomes can easily be observed and measured	5	
Rationale: Strong rationale clearly ties the objectives to the larger context and provides exceptional reasoning for the selection of the Learning Objectives.	5	
Section 3: Data Collection		
Description of methods: Describe the what, how, who, when, where of your data collection with enough detail that someone else could easily replicate your study	5	
Reliability/Validity: Explain how you know that your assessment methods are sound/credible	5	
Rationale: Provide a sound argument for choosing the assessment and data collection methods	5	
Limitations: Outline the limitations of your study	5	
Section 4: Use of data for decision making		
Explain how you will respond to the data. How will you change instruction/programming if the data shows that students are achieving the learning outcomes as you expected? What if they achieve the learning objectives more quickly or slowly than you anticipated? If working with a group, how will you respond if the data reveals different levels of success on the learning outcomes?	5	
Section 5: Related Literature		
10 professional and current resources listed	5	
Alphabetical order and correct APA format	5	
Explanation of each reference and how it relates to your study	10	
Additional requirements		
Draft of IRB paperwork	5	
Mechanics: grammar and spelling	5	
Organization of ideas: ease of comprehension, flow of ideas	5	
TOTAL SCORE	100	

Figure 5. Grading criteria for final project.

Evaluation of the LAP documents submitted provides evidence that all the students mastered course content at a basic level while many exceeded expectations and performed at proficient or advanced levels.

Table 2
Learner Assessment Plan results

	Spring 2012	Spring 2013
Range of scores (percentage)	85%-100%	82%-100%
Average LAP score	95.21%	95.42%
Standard Deviation	4.65	4.72

Reflections for Practice

In conclusion, I found that designing my course with the widest possible audience in mind was a great learning opportunity for both me and my students. I enjoyed working with colleagues and learning from their projects as well as my own. Here are some initial "pearls of wisdom" for other educators as they contemplate the use of UDL in their own classes:

- Give yourself permission to start small. Implementing one aspect of UDL into one unit of your course is an effective way to "get your feet wet." Start with a manageable project that will not overwhelm you. For me, it worked to design my entire course using UDL principles, but I also had to realize that I could not make every aspect of my course perfectly accessible to all possible users and still have any kind of a life. My colleagues and I joke about having "UDL guilt" because the more you learn; the more you realize how much more you could be doing. Resist UDL guilt and keep your project within reason of what you can manage.

- Always keep your focus student-centered. For each decision you make, ask yourself how it will affect students' ability to access the course and student learning. When I found myself tempted to incorporate a different technology or assignment, I had to remind myself that I should only do so if it provided students with an improved learning experience.

- Remember the "D" in UDL. UDL is about how you Design your course. It is not just another teaching method. For me, it was ideal to start with a new course that had never been taught before because I was not tempted to simply modify a course. I actually designed it from the start with a UDL framework.

- Celebrate your successes! UDL can provide a very motivating structure for students, but it can also be a lot of work for the instructor. When you see your hard work paying off, be sure to share your accomplishments with colleagues and others. For me, working with a cross-disciplinary group of colleagues gave me the opportunity to share my accomplishments.

Concluding Thoughts

I began this project with the firm belief that one size does not fit all when it comes to learning. My work with UDL has reinforced this belief and provided me with some specific strategies and tools for meeting a wide range of student needs and backgrounds. I have evidence of student learning and students have expressed appreciation for being allowed to choose tasks that were relevant and meaningful for their context. This study was not designed to establish a scientific research base for UDL or student choice, but it does provide a case study of how the implementation of specific strategies and tools impacted a particular group of learners.

Students completed my course saying, "I loved this class" and "I learned so much in this class." In addition, many of my students commented on my teaching methods and how they provided a strong model for how they want to teach in their own classrooms. To me, this is the greatest compliment a teacher can receive.

About the Author

During the design and implementation of this project, Dr. Renee Chandler was an associate professor in the School of Education at the University of Wisconsin-Stout. She was also the program director for the

Masters of Science in Education program at UW-Stout. She has since become the director of the Graduate School and UW-Stout Online. Her background includes teaching students in general and special education in the public schools for over 10 years and teaching in higher education for more than 10 years. Dr. Chandler's research interests include assessment, Universal Design for Learning (UDL), high-poverty schools, and rural education. She has presented research relative to these topics at state, regional, and national conferences and is currently participating in an Advanced Universal Design for Learning project through UW-Stout's Nakatani Teaching and Learning Center. In addition, she has advised thesis papers and an undergraduate research project on the topic of UDL. Dr. Chandler's scholarship and teaching goals are focused on improving learning for all students.

References

Center for Applied Special Technology (CAST). (2011). *Universal design for learning guidelines version 2.0*. Wakefield, MA: Author.

Edyburn, D. L. (2010). Would you recognize universal design for learning if you saw it? Ten propositions for new directions for the second decade of UDL. *Learning Disability Quarterly, 33*(1), 33-41.

Appendix A: Sample Menu of Options

√ Read Chapters 4-7 in the textbook.

√ Re-read the Word document that describes the Learner Assessment Plan, paying special attention to Sections 3 and 5

√ Review the PowerPoint slides for Module 3 (narrated or transcribed)

√ Participate in the required discussion post (in groups) where you will be working on your learner assessment plan (10 points)

√ Take the anonymous midsemester survey located under "Surveys" on our D2L site.

√ Select and submit a total of 40 points of work from the table below. _With each assignment, include a statement describing how your work demonstrates your competency in one or more of the course objectives._

10 Points
• Answer 10 of the questions from the Chapter 4-7 sections on pages 221-224 in the text (can be repeated for more than 10 points)
• Submit your notes from this module's reading assignments
• Create a graphic organizer that displays the content from this module's reading assignments
• Create a list of ten websites that address Module 3 content. For each website provide a brief description (1-2 sentences).
• Find an article or other reading relative to Module 3 content or a topic related to your Learner Assessment Plan and write a 1-page reaction paper. (NOTE: This activity will help you prepare for section 5 of the Learner Assessment Plan)
• Participate in an optional discussion post.
• Create a presentation using PowerPoint or similar software that summarizes Module 3 content for colleagues.
• Create some type of visual display (e.g., poster, brochure) highlighting the most important content from Module 3.
20 points
• Create an audio or video file that could be used to share and/or clarify Module 3 content for colleagues.
• Read articles or other readings relative to Module 3 content or a topic related to your Learner Assessment Plan and write a 2-page reaction paper. (NOTE: This activity will help you prepare for section 5 of the Learner Assessment Plan)
• Create and moderate a D2L discussion board relative to this week's content (send your prompt to the instructor so that it can be posted)
30 points
• Interview a professional in your field about their assessment practices and how they use assessment results to guide their work. Share your findings in a 3-page paper or an audio or video file.
• Survey a group of learners about their assessment experiences and report your findings.
• Complete one of the Assessment modules or case studies at http://iris.peabody.vanderbilt.edu/resources.html. Submit your answers to the questions.
• Locate and read at least 2 resources related to assessment for learning and write a 3-page reaction paper in which you compare and contrast the views expressed or facts presented in the two resources. (NOTE: This activity will help you prepare for section 5 of the Learner Assessment Plan)

Assignments may be completed individually or in groups. A dropbox is provided for submitting completed assignments.

Appendix B: Objectives & Assignment Scoring

EDUC-745 objectives & Assignment Scoring

The following form is provided for you to align your assignments to the course objectives, evaluate your own performance, and receive feedback on your performance to evaluate and inform your learning throughout the course. Please rate yourself by completing the highlighted sections below:

Unsatisfactory (U) The performance does not meet expectations (e.g. <7/10 points).	Emerging (E) The performance meets some expectations, with many errors or areas for improvement (e.g. 7/10 points).	Basic (B) The performance meets some expectations, with some errors or areas for improvement (e.g. 8/10 points).	Proficient (P The performance meets all expectations, with a few errors or areas for improvement (e.g. 9/10 points).	Distinguished (D) The performance meets or exceeds all expectations, without any errors or areas for improvement (e.g. 10/10 points).

Assignment	Course Obj.	Self-Rating	Rating	Score	Comments
e.g. Discussion Board (10 points)	1	p			
Total score in module (50 Points Possible)					

Course Objectives: At the completion of this course, students will know and be able to:

1. Articulate the purposes of assessment, including the historical, philosophical, legal, ethical, and social principles underpinning current assessment practices.
2. Evaluate a wide range of assessment techniques (e.g., formative, summative, and standardized tests) to determine which assessment tools are appropriate for specific purposes.
3. Analyze the effects of assessment practices on under-represented or diverse learners.
4. Demonstrate how to locate, evaluate and select the most valid and reliable instruments to aid in instructional decision making.
5. Analyze the role assessments play in guiding classroom and district decisions

regarding instructional planning, differentiation, curricular design, and curricular implementation.
6. Develop a learner assessment plan intended to demonstrate the effect of instruction on learning in a field based setting.
7. Interpret assessment results to evaluate and articulate the effects of instruction on identified learner outcomes.
8. Interpret assessment results to inform the instructor's professional goals and development.

8 Universal Design for Learning in Group Projects

Diane Olson, Ph.D.

UDL's Impact on Group Dynamics and Student Learning

The dynamics of a group project are determined by its strategies, work plans, team processes, team behaviors, and individual human factors. These components are integrated, but operate on three different planes or spaces. Space refers to a conceptual boundary of human interaction as illustrated in Figure 1, on page 5.

Organizational space is the broad interaction of people and systems which the organization controls. Organizational space is unemotional, logical, and objective. Team space includes people's interactions with each other, as well as team processes and behaviors which the team owns and controls. Personal space involves the individual team member's inner self where internal interactive thinking occurs and human factors are formed. Human factors make individuals unique and include genetics, values, personalities, experiences, culture, beliefs, and the way individuals respond to people and things. Individuals choose how to respond to the world each day.

In project management, it is critical that individual team members as well as team leaders understand the dynamics of human factors and develop effective interpersonal skills in the individual, team and organizational spaces. Industry advisors for degree programs have stressed the importance of group projects to provide practice in interpersonal skills, as well as working in and leading project teams. However, effective delivery of group projects within a classroom or online can be a challenge due to the wide variety of personalities, experience, backgrounds, and ages in today's student population. An Advanced Project Management course delivered online was used in this study. Advanced Project Management is required for the Project Management Minor degree and several major degrees such as Information Technology Management. The course involved advanced planning, control, and leadership of technical projects. Topics covered include a systems approach to definition, analysis, and management of cost, schedule, quality, customers, and risk management. The course resides under the Operations and Management Department in the College of Science, Technology, Engineering, Mathematics and Management.

In conjunction with the prerequisite, Project Management, the Advanced Project Management course also prepares students to take Project Management Institute (PMI) certification exams as appropriate based on actual project experience. The course has five objectives which coincide with the PMI Body of Knowledge (PMBoK). Since the course is all about projects, it is important for students to gain direct experience working together with a team on a project to fulfill course requirements. Upon completion of this course, students will be able to:

- Manage projects based on the systems development cycle.
- Analyze and manage cost, schedule, quality, and customers using a systems approach to planning and control throughout the project life cycle.
- Evaluate project risk using quantitative methods and a systems approach.
- Evaluate and manage challenging situations involving tracking, scope change, and replanning of projects.
- Utilize advanced methods of a project management application.

Course Analysis

Student achievement is measured by successful completion of assignments, course participation, assessment testing, and at least one group project. Graduate-level students are additionally evaluated on the analysis and management of a project in a real organizational setting. In the past, limited Universal Design for Learning (UDL) methods had been incorporated on an informal basis. This UDL research project made every attempt to be very purposeful to identify appropriate UDL methods, incorporating best practices.

Performance gap. Students in the Advanced Project Management course are typically at the senior and graduate level. Major areas of undergraduate study for students enrolling in this course include Business, Supply Chain Management, Information and Communications Technologies, Information Technology Management, Packaging, and Graphic Communications Management. Major areas of study for graduate students enrolled in this course include Operations and Supply Management, Information and Communication Technologies, and Manufacturing Engineering. Anticipated student needs include:

- Differing interpersonal skills and comfort levels of team members and leaders working in groups. In addition, group collaboration tools were limited by the current Learning Management System (LMS).
- Acceptance of a variety of types of diversity. For example, a student wished to be moved to another project team as everyone on his team was older. Specifically, "I am completely not getting along with my team already, we are polar opposites. My fellow teammates are all old people with the typical old people problems you see in every class. They don't understand the basics, have a million questions, can't seem to grasp easy concepts, and most importantly are stuck in their ways and have to have things their way."
- Mismatched schedules. It is difficult for students to work together on projects due to mismatched schedules. The challenge was to

create teams with varying skills and diversity, while meeting the schedule demands.
- Real world experience. Appreciation for project management varies dependent on experience (good or bad). The challenge was to blend varieties of experience for appreciation of the discipline by all.
- Projects can be overwhelming. Real life projects are too long in duration to complete during one semester while also learning project management skills. In addition, projects may not be understandable for all students due to a variety of backgrounds and experience.

Based on student needs the problem gap involves providing student choices in group projects to enable buy-in and a successful learning experience. Student choices include self- selection of team members based on background and availability, collaboration methods and tools, and the assigned group project. In addition, there is a gap in the capability to receive feedback and improve based on individual and group performance. These gaps may be addressed with UDL methods.

Design

While several UDL features were implemented for the Advanced Project Management course, the main objective was to focus on improving the group project experience utilizing CAST UDL guidelines "http://www.udlcenter.org/sites/udlcenter.org/files/updateguidelines2_0.pdf" and methods to provide multiple methods of group engagement. Specifically, the research project included UDL inspired "Choice": choices for team member makeup, choices for group study project selection within specific guidelines, choices for team communication, and scaffolding for the group study project content (Table 1, CAST Universal Design for Learning Guidelines version 2.0).

Table 1
Universal Design for Learning Guidelines version 2.0

UDL Guideline	Previous Strategy	New UDL Strategy
Guideline 7: Provide options for recruiting interest		
7.2 Optimize relevance, value, and authenticity	Instructor defines groups and group projects for students.	Grad student select group members. Student groups select a group project within defined parameters.
7.3 Minimize threats and distractions	Utilize standard technical support for the standard LMS.	Utilize additional dedicated technical support for trial LMS with various collaboration tools.
Guideline 8: Provide options for sustaining effort and persistence		
8.1 Heighten salience of goals and objectives	Students complete 1-2 pieces of a project with no opportunity for rework.	Students complete part of a project each 1-2 weeks, receive feedback, improve and compile overall project at end of term.
8.3 Foster collaboration and community	Utilize standard LMS with asynchronous Discussion Board and Chat.	Utilize pilot LMS with additional group social networking collaboration tools such as Facebook, online meetings, and teleconferencing with instructor.
Guideline 9: Provide options for self-regulation		
9.2 Facilitate personal coping skills and strategies	Instructor provides feedback on group project.	Students provide peer feedback separate from instructor feedback.
9.3 Develop self-assessment and reflection	Instructor provides feedback on group project.	Students develop and share peer feedback format and process after each assignment to improve personal and group performance.

Development: UDL Methods and Technology Utilized

Universal Design for Learning concepts incorporated into this course focused on transforming project groups into high performing teams. CAST UDL guideline strategies and intended outcomes are detailed in Table 2, (CAST Universal Design for Learning Guidelines version 2.0, 2011).

Table 2
Universal Design for Learning Guidelines version 2.0

UDL Guideline	Previous Strategy	New UDL Strategy
Guideline 7: Provide options for recruiting interest		
7.2 Optimize relevance, value, and authenticity	Grad student select groups. Student groups select a group project within defined parameters.	Students have greater value and ownership of a project that ties more closely with their education and experience.
7.3 Minimize threats and distractions	Utilize additional dedicated technical support for trial LMS.	Receive immediate technical assistance to reduce and eliminate technology issues that may impede learning.
Guideline 8: Provide options for sustaining effort and persistence		
8.1 Heighten salience of goals and objectives	Students complete sub-section of a project each 1-2 weeks, receive feedback, improve the section, and compile the overall project at the end of the term.	Scaffolding with immediate feedback on pieces of projects with opportunity to rework to build on previous work and improve final deliverable and grade.
8.3 Foster collaboration and community	Utilize pilot LMS with additional group social networking collaboration tools such as Facebook, online meetings, and teleconferencing with instructor.	Provide options for communication so groups can utilize tools they prefer to enable easier collaboration. Scheduled direct communications with instructor enables students to ask questions frequently and easily.
Guideline 9: Provide options for self-regulation		
9.2 Facilitate personal coping skills and strategies	Students provide peer feedback separate from instructor feedback.	Students learn from each other and improve teaming skills working in a group project setting.
9.3 Develop self-assessment and reflection	Students develop and share peer feedback format and process after each assignment to improve personal and group performance.	Enables individual and group ownership and buy-in for improvement of teaming skills and project results.

Specific methods to accommodate the class included:

- Seven graduate-level students were enrolled in the course. Graduate students assumed the team leader role for a Group Study Project

Assignment (Appendix A). All students introduced themselves on the discussion board and provided their available times to meet as a group. The leaders chose team members based on availability to meet as well as skills and backgrounds from the personal introductions. The graduate students were responsible for facilitating the transformation of their groups into well performing teams through an appropriate group project. The additional responsibility also met the graduate requirement for the course.

- Groups created and administered their own peer reviews. Sample peer reviews were provided and students researched further examples to create the group peer review format. A midterm peer review was submitted, but not graded, providing students an opportunity to improve. A final peer review was incorporated into a graded team summary report. Similarly, graduate leaders received leader evaluations at midterm and the end of the course. The leaders did not receive points based on their evaluations, but a very negative evaluation could result in the loss of points of their personal grade for the Group Study Project final report.

- Group study projects were chosen by student groups and approved by the instructor based on provided guidelines. Scaffolding was incorporated with weekly questions from the course regarding the group projects. They were intended to encourage continuous work on the projects and help ensure that projects were on track. There were intermediate submissions for the project plan, interim report, final report, and final team summary report. Guidelines and categories for group study project selection included:
    - Studies of particular in-progress or completed projects, including the management procedures used, planning and control procedures, stages of systems development, and so on (e.g., a railroad upgrade project, an aircraft maintenance project, an electrical contractor project, and a project to install a large payroll system). Students investigated and analyzed a current

or completed project by going on-site, interviewing the project manager and participants, reviewing documentation, and so on. They prepared a summary report of the project and discussed the strengths and weaknesses of its management.

- Studies of project management procedures practiced by companies (e.g., a construction company, an electronics corporation, and a pharmaceutical manufacturer). Students were to go into an organization, learn about their procedures for managing projects and prepare a report summarizing findings with recommendations for improving the procedures.

- Library and interview research projects (sample topics: "Computer Applications in Project Management," "Applications and Examples of Project Management," "Advanced Office Management Systems," or "Project Management in Government"). Students were to perform a research study that required them to go to many libraries and interview experts in academia and industry.

- Groups had choices of which technology to use to best interact for the Group Study Project, including chats, discussion board, web conferencing, teleconferencing, online collaboration tools, or face-to-face when possible. A pilot LMS, Canvas, replaced Learn@UWStout (aka Desire-to-Learn, D2L). Canvas provided a variety of the virtual collaboration tools described as well as private work areas for groups. The author was asked to pilot the Canvas LMS by the University of Wisconsin System and more specifically the Learning and Information Technology (LIT) department at UW-Stout. The Advanced Project Management class, Canvas LMS, and the UD research were determined to be a good combination for a total integrated solution.

Preparation. Preparation for incorporating UDL into the course required work up front to learn about UDL itself as well as course preparation to incorporate UDL concepts. In addition, training and installation of the pilot LMS software, Canvas, was required. The technology installation was significant and required training for the technical support staff at the university and university system level.

All course documentation was revised to comply with UDL standards for readability. The group project assignment was designed to incorporate choices for students in selecting group members and the specific project for the assignment. In addition, documentation was developed and acquired for the pilot LMS technology to assist with training and support. Dedicated online support was also instituted with resources assigned specifically to readily assist students and the instructor.

Implementation

The course syllabus and agenda followed the standard semester schedule for online delivery (Appendix A). The installation of the new course management system (Canvas) was scheduled to begin several months prior to the start of the semester to enable time for training and loading of course information. Unfortunately, installation of the new course management system was delayed until a couple of weeks before the start of the new semester. As a result, training and loading of course information was compressed to meet the semester start date.

Technical assistance resources from the university Learning and Technology Services (LTS) were assigned to provide technical assistance with the reduced timeframe.

Groups submitted end-of-chapter questions about their Group Study Project each week (Appendix B). Questions were graded based on 10 points per chapter and groups received feedback from the instructor on their end-of-chapter questions each week. Group meetings with the instructor were also held at the beginning, midterm, and end of semester. Students received 10 points for participating in the group meetings with the instructor.

The end-of-chapter questions, revised per the feedback, were incorporated into a Final Report, which was graded (100 points). An example of the midterm peer review and graduate project leader evaluation (Appendix B) are included at the end of this chapter. In addition, there were a number of surveys for this course. Surveys were administered at midterm and end of semester for UDL and the Canvas pilot. Students were awarded five points for each completed survey.

A team summary report incorporated the peer reviews and reflection of the group study project experience, which was also graded (25 points). In addition, there was a standard department course evaluation. However, the evaluation was geared for the D2L LMS but a different LMS, Canvas, was piloted for this project. As a result, a number of the questions were confusing and unclear for the students, so those particular results were not entirely valid.

Evaluation

To help with documenting the results of learning for this course and specifically the group study project, the Canvas LMS provides an analytics report at a summary and individual student level. It is broken down further by activity, communication, assignments, and grades (Appendix C). Reviewing the reports by individual students was most helpful. It was observed that students who participated more fully in terms of activity and communication, submitting all assignments, received better grades. In addition to students completing surveys for the Canvas LMS, there was also a related survey for instructors. Unfortunately, the Canvas LMS did not have this capability at the beginning of the course because it would have been helpful to incorporate a pre- and post-analytics report.

Analysis

Reflection on the project involved a discussion with Dave Edyburn, a subject matter expert (SME) in UDL. Edyburn indicated that the work involved in the UDL implementation of the course was ambitious. There were multiple technologies to learn as an instructor, as well as the students and the university technical support team. While providing technology choices to students to help with project implementation and communication was initially a good idea, the learning curve and technological issues were at times difficult for students, the instructor, and the LTS support team.

Dedicated instructors may be willing to try new techniques, methods, and technology to improve course delivery. However, given the wide variety of students and technical skills in each course, it is important to scope the effort required by the instructor and students. Several student feedback comments indicated the pilot Canvas LMS detracted from learning course content. If this project were done again, it would be advantageous to continue the scaffolding of project pieces and respective feedback for improvement in the final project deliverable, self-selection of group members, peer reviews, choice of project, additional collaboration tools and scheduled group meetings with the instructor.

The variety of students enrolled in the course, coupled with the online delivery, was an issue that should continue to be addressed moving forward. The course is fairly new and enrollment was increased by including on-campus undergraduates and graduates, as well as distance undergrads and graduates. The mix of on-campus and off-campus in addition to graduate and undergraduate in a totally online course was too much for many of the students. One of the feedback comments was,

I don't think that in projects this big that undergrads and grads should be working together. It was a huge struggle. Also, some of my group members were on campus and had way too many other commitments due to the content of in-class projects. On campus students shouldn't be able to take online classes.

However, for some students, the student population mix worked. Another feedback comment was,

The Advanced Project Management class was one of the best run, hands-on classes I have been a part of at UW-Stout. The Canvas system was new this semester and the instructor did an excellent job at using the resources in the new trial. I am glad I got to experience the new trial system.

In addition, there were a number of feedback comments suggesting that additional student training is needed for new technology such as the pilot LMS, Canvas. It was difficult to find a middle ground of course content and delivery methods that would work for every student. Actual outcomes related to intended outcomes are detailed in Table 3 (CAST, 2011).

Table 3
Universal Design for Learning Guidelines version 2.0

UDL Guideline	Previous Strategy	New UDL Strategy
Guideline 7: Provide options for recruiting interest		
7.2 Optimize relevance, value, and authenticity	Students have greater ownership of a project that ties more closely with their education and experience.	Students appeared to have greater ownership of a project that tied more closely with their education and experience.
7.3 Minimize threats and distractions	Immediate technical assistance to reduce and eliminate technology issues that may impede learning.	Immediate dedicated technical assistance was utilized by the instructor, but not by the students.
Guideline 8: Provide options for sustaining effort and persistence		
8.1 Heighten salience of goals and objectives	Scaffolding with immediate feedback on pieces of projects with opportunity to rework to build on previous work and improve final deliverable and grade.	Mixed results. While some groups valued and fully utilized ongoing feedback, a number of students appeared to race through initial pieces of their projects with substandard work and did not fully incorporate feedback into the final deliverable.
8.3 Foster collaboration and community	Provide options for communication so groups can utilize tools they prefer to enable collaboration. Scheduled direct communications with instructor enables students to ask questions frequently and easily.	Choices for communication and collaboration were appreciated by students. However, training to make educated choices was needed. Scheduled direct communications with instructor worked well at the beginning and end of course, with minimal student attendance mid-term.
Guideline 9: Provide options for self-regulation		
9.2 Facilitate personal coping skills and strategies	Students learn from each other and improve teaming skills working in a group project setting.	Peer reviews were valuable. Student interpersonal skills and communication improved.
9.3 Develop self-assessment and reflection	Enables individual and group ownership and buy-in for improvement of teaming skills and project results.	Individual and teaming behaviors were modified and improved.

In summary, what worked included graduate students in the role of group leaders and choosing group members, group choice of project, and team collaboration techniques.

Additionally, scheduled group teleconferences with the instructor, peer feedback, and instructor feedback on each project sub-section to build a final group project deliverable also was useful. The main area that did not work well was the Canvas LMS system and collaboration tools provided by the system. More training was needed to use the LMS and make intelligent choices of specific technology to use for group collaboration.

General perceptions of UDL in online course delivery are that it was useful to have options and incorporate scaffolding techniques. However, it is important to understand the amount of work required and scale implementation so that it is doable. In addition, students don't always want choices. For some students, it may be simpler to go with well-known technology unless steps are taken to ensure students are knowledgeable and comfortable to make choices.

Overall this project was a valuable effort and identified important factors that will help in making decisions regarding the Advanced Project Management course going forward. The group project aspect required for the course is still a work in progress. The UDL concepts appear to be valid if utilized within a smaller scope. For successful implementation, it is important to scope appropriately and try only one or two concepts at one time. Finally, the instructor needs sufficient dedicated time to devote to the UDL implementation for a successful outcome.

About the Author

Dr. Diane Olson is an associate professor and adviser for the Project Management minor at the University of Wisconsin-Stout, Science, Technology, Engineering, Mathematics and Management College (STEMM), in Menomonie, Wisconsin. She previously served as Chair of the Operations & Management Department. Diane holds a Bachelor of Computer Science degree from the University of Minnesota—School of Industrial Technology, an M.B.A. from the University of St. Thomas,

Minneapolis, MN, and a Ph.D. in Technology Management with a Quality emphasis from Indiana State University. She has over 22 years of industry experience and over 10 years of teaching experience, as well as 2 years with Stout's Economic Development Administration (EDA) Outreach Center. Courses taught are in the project management, quality, and materials management areas. She was a development engineer and sub-contract program manager at Honeywell, a manager for MECC (educational software company) and director of national network services at Qwest Telecommunications. She has a wide variety of quality, process, supply chain management and project/program management experience in mission-critical engineering, information technology, and commercial software industries. These experiences include ISO9000, Boeing's D1-9000 program, SEI CMM (Software Engineering Institute Capability Maturity Model), and 2 years as a Malcolm Baldrige examiner. Diane is certified as an ISM Certified Purchasing Manager (C.P.M.) and APICS Production and Inventory Management (CPIM), and a Six Sigma Green belt.

References

Center for Applied Special Technology (CAST). (2011). *Universal design for learning guidelines version 2.0.* Wakefield, MA: Author.

Wong, Z. (2007). *Human factors in project management.* San Francisco, CA: John Wiley & Sons.

Appendix A: 475/675-Advanced Project Management Group Study Project Assignment

A good way to learn about project management is to actually participate in project management or, failing that, at least to observe it. At the end of chapters in the Nicholas & Steyn textbook are two kinds of questions: the first are the usual chapter review questions, the second are called "Questions About the Study Project." The latter are intended to be applied to any project of the student group's choosing, referred to hereafter as the "Study Project." The purpose of these questions is to help students relate concepts from each chapter to practice and reality. These questions are due to the appropriate online submission area nearly each week throughout the course. The questions will be reviewed to help ensure the projects are on track for successful completion and the final report at the end of the semester.

The instructor is available to guide students through projects and suggest things to investigate by using the Study Project questions in the following ways:

> For *part-time* students who are actually involved in projects as either managers or project team members, the questions can be related to their current work. The questions should serve both to increase students' awareness of key issues surrounding the project as well as to guide practicing managers in what to look for and how to investigate a project.

> For students who are currently *full time* students, the questions can be applied to (1) projects that the instructor assigns as part of the course requirements (e.g., class research projects) or (2) outside projects that students are permitted to observe. Many business firms and government agencies are willing to let student groups interview them and collect information about projects. Though second-hand, this is nonetheless an excellent way to learn about project management practice (and malpractice).

Selecting a Project

Students are required to work on a "real" project, that is, a project that has a real purpose and is not contrived just so it can be investigated. It can be a project in which students are currently working (e.g., in school or with their employer) or one already completed. Whichever, it must be a project for which they can readily get information.

The instructor should approve the project and the student group should ensure that they have permission to study (collect data and interview people, etc.) as an "outsider." The project to investigate should be conducted by the project team with a project leader, and having at least a two- to three-month duration. The project should also have specific goals in terms of, for example, a target completion date, a budget limit, as well as a specified end-item result or product. Some examples of projects are described later. Virtually everyone is either working on a project in a day-time job, or has friends or family members who are working on projects. Projects are ubiquitous (everywhere)!

It is important that for whatever kind of project students investigate, it is done *in a team* of three-to-five students, with one serving as project leader (i.e., a student team performs the study). This, in essence, becomes *your student project team*, a team organized for the purpose of investigating the study project. Teams are assigned as groups in the course online site. Students can then readily apply many of the planning, organizing, team building, and other procedures discussed throughout the book to analyze how the group works as a project team. This "hands on" experience with your project team combined with what you learn from the study project will give you a pretty accurate picture about problems encountered and management techniques used in real-life project management.

Study Project Examples

Categories of study projects include:

1) Studies of particular in-progress or completed *projects*, including the management procedures used, planning and control procedures, stages of systems development, and so on (e.g., a railroad upgrade project, an aircraft maintenance project, an electrical contractor project, a project to install a large payroll system). Students actually investigate a current or completed project by going on-site, interviewing the project manager and participants, reviewing documentation, and so on. They prepare a summary report of the project and discuss the strengths and weaknesses of its management.

2) Studies of project management *procedures* practiced by companies (e.g., a construction company, an electronics corporation, a pharmaceutical manufacturer). Students go into an organization, learn about their procedures for managing projects, then prepare a report summarizing findings with recommendations for improving the procedures.

3) Library and interview research projects (sample topics: "Computer Applications in Project Management," "Applications and Examples of Project Management," "Advanced Office Management Systems," or "Project Management in Government.") Students perform a research study that requires them to go to many libraries and interview experts in academia and industry.

The best kinds of Study Projects are those in categories 1) and 2). The questions "About the Study Project" at the end of each chapter can be applied directly to these kinds of investigations. Many of the projects discussed in Chapter 2 are based on the author's previous study project assignments, and are good examples. If the Study Project is from category 3), the same questions can be used. However, these are questions the student team must ask of *itself* and about how it is conducting *its own* project.

Requirements for Student Projects

All projects carry requirements, usually related to cost, time, and technical or other kinds of performance. The student groups have similar requirements placed on their projects. Following are requirements for the student projects in this course.

Requirement 1. Team Project Plan (student's work)—25 pts. (5th week of class)
1. Project Objectives
2. Project WBS
3. Project Gantt Chart
4. Project Responsibility Matrix

Requirement 2. Project Interim Report, Written in Outline Form—25 pts. (Mid-term)

> Topics: Review of student team's MS Project plan, objectives, progress to-date, problems encountered, and next steps. Include executive summary of status.

Requirement 3. Project Final Report, Written—100 pts. (Final week of class)
1. Introduction: division of labor, responsibilities of the project you are studying.
2. Nominally 25-30 pages, typed, 12 pt font, 1.5 spacing
3. Must fit in a 1.5 inch 3-ring binder when printed
4. Professional quality (no numerical or spelling errors, grammatically correct)
5. Focus on project management
6. Recommendations for the project based on course content/learning
7. Other requirements (specific to project)
    a. Ensure all submitted documents are easily printed
    b. Appendices may be submitted in separate document(s) if needed

Here are additional project requirements:

a. Focus on Project Management: THE FINAL REPORT MUST EMPHASIZE PROJECT MANAGEMENT. The questions at the end of each chapter in the textbook can be used as guidelines about aspects of the Investigation Project that you may want to investigate. *Although your report will include some discussion of the technical nature of the study project, that discussion should be brief and only to provide background about the project. Similarly, avoid lengthy discussion about the histories or backgrounds of companies involved in the project. The emphasis of the report must be on the "how, what, why, when, who" of the management of the Investigation Project. Avoid lengthy technical discussions, or lengthy discussion about the company history, technical requirements, or details of the actual work done in the project. These are not project management topics.*

A purpose of the report is to show the instructor what was learned from the investigation project about project management. Thus, avoid discussions that could lead to the conclusion that little or nothing additional about project management was learned from the investigation project!

b. Appendices. Appendices can include any documentation or materials you wish to add to substantiate your report. However, any material you include in the Appendix must be directly referenced somewhere in the body of the report. *Do not include material in the Appendices that is not referenced in the report* (the Appendix is not a place to *dump* material). Appendices must be clearly labeled and easy to find.

c. Try to include figures, diagram, tables, charts, etc. in the body of the report. This will make the report more readable and interesting. For example, instead of describing a Gantt chart used in the Investigation Project, *include* the chart (or part of it) in the report. Show samples of actual schedules, memos, budget reports, etc. These can be included in the body of the report or in the Appendix.

d. Professional Quality: Spelling, grammatical, typing or other errors are unacceptable. As are all professional documents, your report will be judged as much for readability and appearance as for content. Carefully proof read the report before submitting it.

A poorly written report will receive a lower grade.

e. The entire report, including appendixes, must fit into a binder (3-ring or spiral) not to exceed 1 ½ inch thickness. All materials, notes, original documents, etc., should be handed in with the final report. Due to the online delivery of this course, the entire report must be submitted in electronic form to the appropriate Assignment submission area.

Requirement 4. Project Team Summary Report, Written 25 (Final week of class)

Nominally 5-8 pages, typed, 12 pt font, 1.5 spacing

Project team responsibilities, strengths, weaknesses, learning, and their suggestions to future teams. Incorporate peer reviews from mid-semester and at end of semester.

Students are required to develop a plan for their project early in the course. The plan should focus on what each student team intends to do. The team is required to specify in definite, concise language what their objectives are. The objectives must be clear enough for the students and instructor to know whether or not they have succeeded by the end of the course. The team should also be required to produce a work breakdown structure that specifies the tasks that *they* must do in their project, a general schedule of these tasks with milestones in Gantt-chart format, and a matrix defining the responsibility of everyone in the team. Students often have a tough time doing a good of these, especially the first time, and they may have to redo their objectives, WBS, or schedule several times until it is acceptable.

With respect to the above requirements, the following are "detailed specifications" for the Final the Final Written Report and the Project Summary:

Requirement 3: Project Final Report, Written—100 pts.

1. All source material must be referenced. Reference citations should be noted throughout the text giving the author and year of publication in parenthesis, as (Smith, 1998). Include at the end of each chapter or the report a complete list of references in alphabetical order, showing author, title, name of publication, publisher (for books), date, and page numbers. REFERENCES MUST BE COMPLETE AND UTILIZE APA GUIDELINES, e.g.:

    Smith, J.R. "Doing a Project Right—The First Time." Journal of Project Management. June 2007, pp. 86-92.

    Talbot, T.T. "Evaluating Review Meetings." In D.P. Jones (Ed.) Project Handbook (2nd edition). New York: McGraw-Hill, 1996, pp. 791-799.

2. The report must be of PUBLISHABLE QUALITY. Spelling, grammatical, typing, or other errors are unacceptable. As in all professional documents, your report will be judged as much for readability and appearance as for content. You will probably have to rewrite your material and proofread it several times to accomplish this.

3. Each person should contribute their proportionate share of pages to the final report. This is a modest requirement to document a full semester's work.

4. The report must focus on *project management*. Questions "About the Study Project" at the end of each chapter can be used as guidelines to help you accomplish this.

5. Use of examples or figures (e.g., Gantt charts, budgets, organization charts, etc.) is strongly encouraged. It will make the documents more interesting, readable, and understandable.

Requirement 4: Project Team Summary Report, Written—25 pts.

In addition to the final report, students also prepare a written Team Summary Report. This is an INTROSPECTIVE evaluation the team makes of itself—its strengths and weakness, what the team did, and in hindsight what the members would do differently.

List members of the class and the sections of the report for which they were responsible. The nature of their responsibility (interviews, research, writing, editing, etc.) must also be stated. It is expected that some people (e.g., the editor) will make contributions in multiple parts of the report.

It also contains a section of recommendations for future student project teams, the best of which may be distributed or made available to subsequent student project teams. Include the MS Project plan. A Project Log/Action Register may also be included if used during the semester. Length: 5-8 pages, 1.5 spacing.

Throughout the term, the document submissions will be reviewed to insure that the project work is meeting the requirements (end of chapter questions). Students sometimes get so involved in their projects that they forget about requirements. Establishing requirements early in the course, reviewing and reinforcing them is a reminder that projects are always done FOR SOMEONE (the user, in this case the instructor), and that it is essential that the project be done to conform to the user's requirements.

Group Study Project Chapter Questions
Chapter 1—What is Project Management?

1. In the project you are studying, what characteristics of the company, project goals, tasks, or necessary expertise make the use of project management appropriate or inappropriate? Consider the project size, complexity, risk, and other criteria in answering this question.

2. How does the project you are studying fit the definition of a project?

3. What kind of project management is used—program, product, matrix, pure, or other? Explain, Is it called "project management," or something else?

4. What kind of role does the project manager have—expeditor, coordinator, pure project, or matrix manager? Explain. What is his or her title?

Chapter 2—Systems Approach and Systems Engineering

1. Conceptualize the project organization (the project team and the parent organization of the team) you are studying as a system. What are the elements, attributes, environment, and so on? What are its internal subsystems—functional breakdown and management hierarchy subsystems? What is the relevant environment? Who are the decisionmakers?

2. Describe the role of the project manager with respect to these subsystems, both internal and external. What is the nature of his or her responsibilities in these subsystems? How aware is the project manager of the project "environment," and what does he or she do that reflects this awareness?

3. Now, conceptualize the output or enditem of the project as a system. Again, focus on the elements, relationships, attributes, subsystems, environment, and so on. All projects, whether directed at making a physical product (e.g., computer, space station, skyscraper, research report) or a service (e.g., giving consultation and advice), are devoted to producing systems. This exercise will help you better understand what the project is doing. It is also good preparation for topics in the next chapter.

4. If the study project involves engineering or integration of many components, was the systems engineering process used? Is there a section, department, or task in the project called systems engineering? If so, elaborate. Are there functions or phases of the project that seem to resemble the systems engineering process?

5. As described in this chapter, besides the main end-item or operating system (i.e., the output objective of the project), systems engineering also addresses the support system—that system which supports installation, operation, maintenance, evaluation, and enhancement of the operating system. Describe the support system in the study project and its development.

6. Were the stakeholder requirements clearly defined at the start of the project? Were system requirements clearly defined? What are the requirements? In your opinion, were stakeholders identified and involved early in the project? Were their needs identified and addressed? Did the project deliver a system that met their needs?

7. What aspects of the project or parent organization appear to use systems management? What aspects do not use systems management? Describe the appropriateness or inappropriateness of systems management in the project you are studying.

Appendix B: Example Midterm Peer Graduate Project Leader Evaluations

Group 1

Evaluator: Graduate Project Leader

Evaluation Criteria:

Communication:

5: was fully engaged in communication and responded to all discussions in a timely manner

3: was part of team communication and responded to discussion posts

1: was absent in team communication and discussion activity

Cooperation:

5: was fully co-operational in all team activity and volunteered to lend help where needed

3: cooperated in team activities

1: was not cooperative in team activities

Commitment:

5: was fully committed to overall team success in all required activities

3: was part of team activities

1: was not committed to the success of team

Work Ethic:

5: displayed strong work ethic in all team activities

3: was present in team activities

1: displayed weak work ethic or absence in team activities

Adaptability:

5: showed team spirit and easy adaptability in all aspects of team requirements

3: adapted to needs of team

1: did not adapt to needs of team

Team Member	Criteria	5	4	3	2	1	Comments
Tim	Communication			X			Tim has been willing to pitch in and take on required tasks. However, he does need to work on being more active in team discussions, providing feedback/input on the work of his peers, and completing work assignments within the agreed upon timeframe. His ability to be flexible and respond to changing requirements has been great.
	Cooperation		X				
	Commitment			X			
	Work Ethic			X			
	Adaptability	X					
Craig	Communication	X					Craig has been great at communicating with the team as required. He actively participates in team discussions and completes assignments in a timely manner that allows for peer/group review. He is open to feedback and incorporates it into his work.
	Cooperation	X					
	Commitment		X				
	Work Ethic		X				
	Adaptability	X					
Jared	Communication	X					Jared is very cooperative and flexible to changing requirements and timelines. He takes feedback from his peers well, and incorporates their ideas into the deliverable with ease. Jared could work at being more communicative in team discussions and offering ideas to his peers on their weekly assignments.
	Cooperation	X					
	Commitment		X				
	Work Ethic	X					
	Adaptability	X					

Graduate Project Leader Evaluation

1. This is a survey for the graduate project leader _____

2. Meeting Efficiency
    - Very Good
    - Good
    - Neutral
    - Poor
    - Very Poor

3. Project Leader Availability
    - Very Good
    - Good
    - Neutral
    - Poor
    - Very Poor

4. Project Leader Approachability
    - Very Good
    - Good
    - Neutral
    - Poor
    - Very Poor

5. Openness to New Ideas
    - Very Good
    - Good
    - Neutral
    - Poor
    - Very Poor

6. Teamwork Skills
    - Very Good
    - Good
    - Neutral

- Poor
- Very Poor

7. **Personal Organization**
   - Very Good
   - Good
   - Neutral
   - Poor
   - Very Poor

8. **Level of Commitment**
   - Very Good
   - Good
   - Neutral
   - Poor
   - Very Poor

9. **Amount of Effort**
   - Very Good
   - Good
   - Neutral
   - Poor
   - Very Poor

10. **Communication Skills**
    - Very Good
    - Good
    - Neutral
    - Poor
    - Very Poor

11. **Reliability**
    - Very Good
    - Good
    - Neutral
    - Poor
    - Very Poor

12. Grade you would give your graduate project leader:
    - A
    - B
    - C
    - D

13. Explain why you suggested the grade you did for your Project Leader

14. List one area in which your Project Leader excels.

15. List one area in which your Project Leader should strive to improve.

16. Other comments or suggestions.

Appendix C: Canvas LMS Analytics Reports

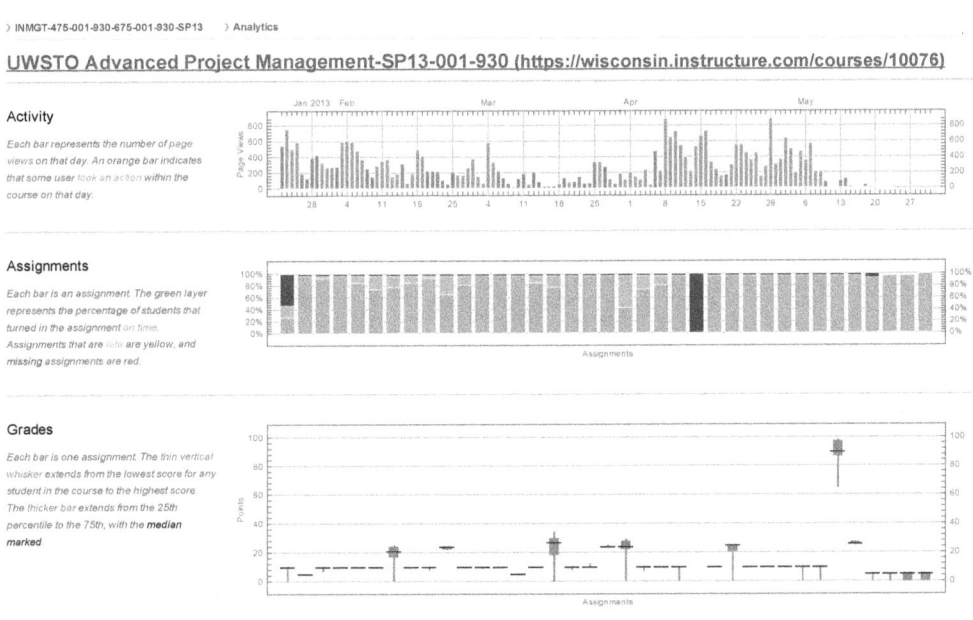

200 UNIVERSAL DESIGN FOR TEACHING **ALL** STUDENTS

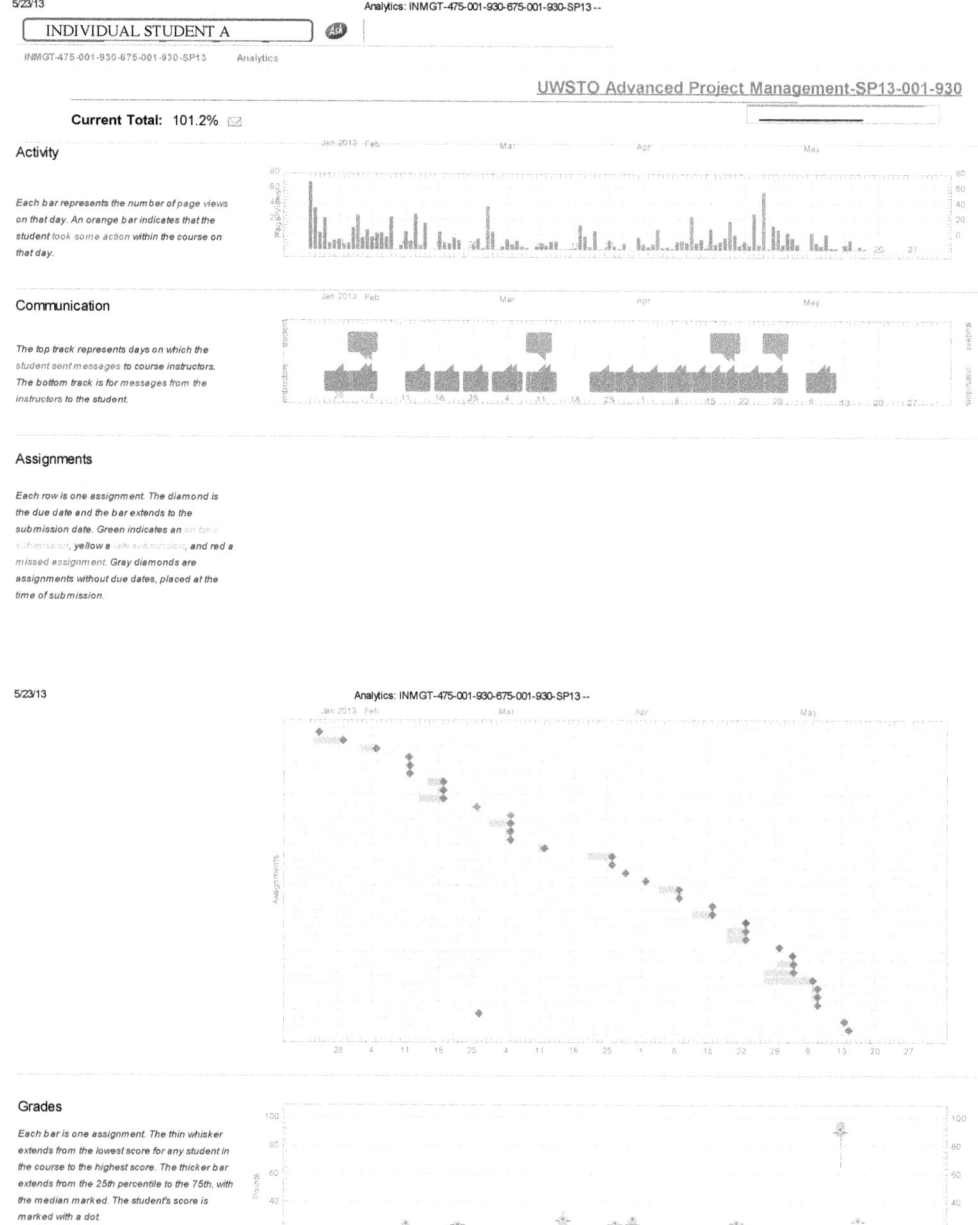

9 SELF-RELIANCE

Monika Herrmann, Architect

Applying UD: From Architecture to the Classroom

Recognizing the need is the primary condition for design.
—Charles Eames, Designer (n.d.)

"Charles and Ray Eames gave shape to America's twentieth century" (Albrecht & Billington, 1997, p.13)—with their furniture, buildings, toys and educational films; most importantly with their approach to solving problems elegantly and inclusively. I remember watching "The Power of Ten" (Office of Charles & Ray Eames, 1977) as a young person and falling in love with the playful way this film is engaging curiosity while introducing a variety of complex scientific principles. In less than ten minutes the viewer is taken on a high-speed journey through concepts of science and being left in wonder over the interrelatedness of the universe. As a young designer I found their work inspirational in its joyfulness and persistent clarity. In my career as an architect and educator, I am striving to recognize essential needs, to analyze key parameters and to creatively address challenges.

My first intimate encounter with the principles of Universal Design came through a project in my architectural practice. My client experienced rapidly progressing multiple sclerosis and all the limitations related to losing muscular strength over time. I had worked on designs for hospitals, nursing facilities and many other public buildings and I felt well versed in complying with the regulations described in the Americans with disabilities act (ADA) signed into law in 1990. Nevertheless, my client expected a more holistic approach—she expected the principles of Universal Design (UD) to be employed for the design of her home. The term "Universal Design" in architecture was coined by Ron Mace who pioneered the efforts of designing buildings and products "to be aesthetic and usable to the greatest extent possible by everyone" (Center for Universal Design, 2008, webpage). Adapting my client's home to meet her somewhat unpredictable needs was a challenge that has altered my personal and professional perspective. A residence has a purpose, primarily to shelter us and allow us to store our tools and provisions. Yes, it basically is that simple. According to the EPA, "Americans spend about 90 percent or more of their time indoors" (U.S. Environmental Protection Agency, 2009, p. 4). Should we age and become frail, or outgrow the access to our homes through unexpected events, we most often must fall back on public facilities for shelter and play.

It was crucial for my client to understand her needs and to be able to communicate those needs. The emphasis during the planning and construction process was not placed on providing the client with options to select from—rather to include her in the process of creating options that can address the changing nature of her disability and the needs of other family members.

Long story short, the challenge to design a curriculum for a freshman course that does include students with a variety of learning styles reminded me of the universal design process for an accessible home. The significant difference lays in the fact that a curriculum must be accessible to many "clients" who the instructor has never met before the course is launched.

Analysis: Is College Education a Continuity of K12?

Within the last decades, we have gotten used to accommodations in public buildings like elevators, zero-level entries, voice and motion recognition and many other perks; these make our lives easier, movement quicker and more comfortable. In addition, they are often the only way for people with impairments to have access. As occupants, able-bodied or not, we take such features for granted; they are included in construction budgets, in building codes and in architects' training. These same rights of equal access established in the ADA apply likewise to the learning environment. Certainly, a lesson plan or lecture is not as much of a long-term investment as a concrete entry-ramp; after all instructors are accountable to be flexible and to adapt curricula to current technology, industry standards and to research outcomes. Nevertheless, in compliance with the ADA, access must be provided—sometimes designed, sometimes spontaneous and always creatively. In my experience, knowing the need turns out to be the key. The class roster tells the number of students enrolled in any course but it does not disclose if students learn with barriers. Usually students present a need for accommodation within the first month of the semester. At this point there is no time to restructure a course—the student and the instructor are left with the provisions defined by the university's Disability Service and their own ability to work together. Embracing Universal Design within academic education is the attempt to design educational strategies to proactively accommodate the broadest access to the material offered to students.

I admit the participation in our group endeavor encouraged me to contemplate and ask critical questions that had irked me for a while, such as: *How would I reasonably accommodate a blind student in a graphic communication class? How would I fairly accommodate a student who can't keep up with the course's rigor because of a learning disability? How would I safely accommodate my class when a student is draining their energy and patience because of a psychological disability?* Unlike architecture, higher education has no regulations that prescribe tangible solutions like width or height, color or textures that would help to answer these questions. There is counseling and technology available to students and educators—those can be essential means—still, the path to a satisfactory end mostly falls into the instructor's lap.

In 2001, the *"No Child Left Behind"* (NCLB) provisions were enacted. "An Act to close the achievement gap with accountability, flexibility, and choice, so that no child is left behind" (2002, p. 1). More than a decade later a generation of students is entering college with the expectation that a path to success will be accommodated. In their experience a student's failure does reflect negatively on instructors and institutions, regardless of the cause for failure. Diane Ravitch (2010), former assistant secretary of education and former advocate of the NCLB act, spoke out against the act in an National Public Radio (NPR) interview. In her book, *The Death of the Great American School System*, she stated that "the basic strategy is measuring and punishing and it turns out as a result of putting so much emphasis on the test scores, there's a lot of cheating going on, there's a lot of gaming the system. Instead of raising standards it's actually lowered standards because many states have 'dumbed down' their tests or changed the scoring of their tests to say that more kids are passing than actually are" (Morning Edition, 3/2/2010). The failure of NCLB certainly needs to be addressed on a political platform. However, a universal design strategy in curricula development can support students to grow beyond the focus on test scores. It can actively include students in the process of finding the most effective access to their education without lowering outcome standards. It can help students and instructors to transition from accommodation to collaboration to self-reliance.

How do students experience their first professional courses? *Engineering Graphics,* the course chosen for this study, is one of the early professional courses in the engineering and industrial design programs; advanced courses build on students' successful completion of this course. When I first taught a few sections of this course, following traditional methods I found students with poor study skills and students unable to manage their time wisely fell behind quickly and barely made it to the finish line. In essence, I noted a distinct performance gap between course outcome expectation and student achievement. So, I critically analyzed the delivery method that had been established for this course. The workload is substantial and the course objectives define skills and competencies unfamiliar to most students. Students meet twice per week for one hour of lecture and one hour of lab practice. Traditionally, concepts of descriptive geometry, graphic standards and dimensioning methodology were introduced during lecture in sequence with a well-developed but traditional textbook. Graded homework assignments and exams were used to assess students' learning. The lesson plan had no time allowance for reflection or dialogue. Much work was produced but no feedback was solicited to assure that students truly understood the meaning and value of their labor. Students repeatedly commented that the course objectives seem abstract and intangible to them. This seemed to be a key aspect hindering students to experience a sense of progress or accomplishment.

Pre –UDL	Post-UDL
	Students read assigned material and respond to 3 questions online – before class
Instructor collects homework for evaluation	30 minutes at the beginning of class: Students exchange assignments for peer review, students add final touches and submit homework for evaluation by instructor
1 hour lecture: Introduction of new concepts.	30 minutes lecture: Introduction of new concepts – with an emphasis on students' online comments
1 hour lab: Practice of the new concepts.	1 hour lab: Practice of new concepts and introduction of homework assignment. Discussion of strategies to approach the assignment.
Distribute homework assignment focusing on the new concepts, to be completed by the next class period.	

Throughout the initial discussions of the UDL project I realized that introducing an individual assignment that is based on UD principles would not make much difference in students' experience. Consequently, the course delivery was fully revised to maintain the course objectives and rigor of assessment, as well as accommodating time for reflection and self-evaluation. It seemed essential to include strategies that nurture work ethic, study methods and peer respect. Students should be able to experience a variety of activities within all UD categories throughout the semester to broaden their experience and allow for informed choices in upper classes.

Pre-UDL	Post-UDL
Four course objectives listed in the syllabus for students' reference.	First day of the semester devoted to introduction and discussion of the course objectives in their application to students' career choice.
Students are informed about major exam dates in the syllabus.	Students receive a lesson plan including the activities and focus for every day of the semester.

Design & Development

The design and development phase focused on two primary strategies related to the UDL framework: providing options for comprehension and providing options for action and expression. A clear understanding of expectations is allowing students to take charge of their own progress.

Provide UDL options for comprehension. The first major step was to examine the course objectives and translate them into tangible concepts, skills and activities students can embrace, tackle and track. Traditionally, course objectives were listed in the syllabus—short and concise. For example, the first of five objectives listed in the syllabus read:

Pre-UDL
1. Upon completion of this course the student shall develop freehand sketching techniques, to gain an understanding of basic skills to aid and improve one's spatial visualization skills and abilities.

To make the intent more tangible, a form was created that includes skills and abilities leading toward the accomplishment of the objective. This format allows students to track their personal progress by starting with basic recollection before moving toward a level of productive application. This format is revisited during the course intermittently. It is a nice tool for the instructor to gauge what areas need to be emphasized and for students to self-assess and rekindle their commitment to their education.

	Post-UDL			
	Upon completion of this course the student shall...	Remember	Understand	Apply
1	...*develop freehand sketching techniques to gain an understanding of basic skills to aid and improve one's spatial visualization skills and abilities*			
1.1	I can sketch the basic shape of 2D and 3D objects proportionally correct			
1.2	I can communicate a process or idea through a hand sketch			
1.3	I can explain basic drafting tools and media, and can effectively use them			
1.4	I can explain the differences of various projection methods			
1.5	I understand principles of basic geometric construction and related terminology			

All written course material was improved to graphically support quick comprehension and access with screen-reader technology. This material is made available to students in hardcopy and digitally. Written material generated in the engineering field commonly uses a passive voice to support professional and objective communication. A passive voice emphasizes the result of action with no regard to the person acting. A step toward a student's self-reliance is the acknowledgement of personal responsibility to take action, for the instructors and for the students. In a nutshell: "For the duration of this course—this is what I can do, this is what you can do and this is a path we can pursue…" Therefore, the language used in the syllabus was modified to personally address students rather than merely list expectations. For example, the traditional syllabus read:

Pre-UDL
"DESCRIPTION: Fundamentals of engineering graphics…"

The syllabus was adjusted to read:

Post-UDL
"COURSE DESCRIPTION: You did find this brief summary when you signed up for this class: Fundamentals of engineering graphics…"

There were other adjustments made that showed positive results like:
- Course objectives, strategies and resource material are discussed in small groups when the class meets the first time.
- Study techniques and peer-review methods are discussed and intentionally practiced throughout the semester.
- Before each class period students complete reading assignments and give feedback online. This allows students to familiarize themselves with the terminology and the level of complexity they will encounter in the classroom. Based on students' feedback the instructor can focus the lecture on aspects that students find hardest to understand.
- The lesson plan is revised to present content in a more intuitive progression of skill development rather than following the sequence suggested by textbook chapters.

- Activities are included in the delivery of concepts intended to engage students' background knowledge. For instance, objects for sketching and drafting exercises are chosen from students' living environment rather than mechanical parts.
- A research assignment allows students to engage with professionals of their future careers to receive feedback on the relevance of skills and abilities they are studying.
- An online discussion board is established and students are encouraged to reach out to peers and organize study circles.

Provide UDL options for action and expression. The traditional course delivery did not specifically encourage or require note-taking or maintaining reference material. Nevertheless, in my experience information that is noted, sketched or personally documented in other forms is retained more readily than if it is just heard or seen. Since the focus chosen for the UDL implementation is "Self-reliance," students are instructed to organize course resources, assignments, notes and feedback. This collection becomes their study guide and reference. Nevertheless, alternative course material organization is encouraged. Surprisingly none of the students chose another format than collecting material in a binder. I find that physically collecting work and adding a personal touch in embellishing the format to their heart's content seems to be gratifying for students. The self-assessment form discussed earlier does help students to recognize the interrelatedness of course objectives and serves as a "table of contents" for the material collection.

Implementation

During the implementation phase, the different measures are tracked and documented. I strive to make the experience for students tangible and reflective.

Provide UDL options for engagement. I noticed that the most tangible experience for students during early semesters seems to be the feedback they receive when their abilities are tested. Consequently, students' progress is evaluated and discussed through graded in-class and homework assignments, quizzes and exams. Assignments are graded manually or on-line. The use of online feedback can be very effective since it is easy for the instructor to respond quickly and address students personally. Being able to access feedback history throughout the semester allows the instructor and student to recognize patterns in quality and challenge. The evaluation criteria and the assignment emphasis are available to students at the beginning of each task. A grading rubric (Figure 1) is included in all instructions as shown below and assignments are reviewed and critiqued by peers before they are graded by the instructor.

Pts	Content	No	pts/10	Comments
	Drawing			
6	Line quality and accuracy			
3	Title block, layout and lettering			
1	Effective peer review			
10	Total			

Figure 1. Peer evaluation grading rubric.

Historically, the nature of the course allowed little room to consistently offer multiple ways for students to represent their knowledge. Nevertheless, throughout the semester students completed assignments with a variety of delivery formats such as working conceptually, working accurately and data-based, solving problems and applying concepts, and working in groups or individually. Traditionally students' progress was evaluated primarily based on the level a task was accomplished correctly. The UDL format discussed so far encourages a dialogue along the path to accomplishment, it encourages students' active participation in the improvement of their work. Adjustments established in the curriculum include:

Options of engagement	Pre-UDL	Post-UDL
Emphasis given to the practice of peer and self-assessment strategies	no	yes
Engagement of creativity in problem solving strategies	yes	yes
Emphasis given to real-world context	no	yes
Emphasis given to teamwork and peer tutoring	no	yes

What if There is a Sinking Feeling... Where Are the Life-boats?

Despite best intentions students might encounter the sinking feeling of failure. Riding the wave and being buried under it are intrinsically connected sides of the same adventure. We better be prepared with options for support. Information about available options was provided at the beginning of the semester through the syllabus and reminding announcements throughout the semester. Students should be able to identify resources that match their needs, to explore options, to experiment and to discover how they learn most effectively. The following experiences were provided:

- Small class sizes and frequent team assignments, allowing students to get to know their peers, engage in collaboration or study groups.
- Open-lab hours on evenings and weekends encourage students to seek help from teaching assistants and to meet fellow students from other course sections.
- The instructor is available to students through the online discussion board and through daily open-office hours.
- A counseling office on campus is available to support students in managing life and study issues.

Evaluation: Outcome for Students and Instructor

The aspect of UDL that I find challenging and motivating is the balancing act between the desire to nurture and the desire to foster self-reliance.

Self-Reliance

Our society depends on critical, creative minds, able to work hard and to pursue quality outcomes in their work. I have observed students exploring options, discovering their needs and taking charge of their progress. Students' achievements are measured through individual assignments, group projects, drafting and written tests and the acknowledgement of their engaged participation. This course has a long tradition and the delivery methods vary among instructors. Implementing UDL principles into the course has brought instructors together and motivated a shared effort. Discussing measures to engage collaboration and critical and creative thinking for our course curriculum made us aware that we can employ such measures within our own collegial team as well. This collaboration among instructors also had the unintended outcome of producing an ongoing and robust dialogue. The feedback received from students in their self-assessment documents was encouraging, even though it was mostly critical and thoughtful. Some good suggestions were made that will be implemented in the future. These comments provide a refreshing alternative to the traditional course survey, which mostly reflects the spontaneous feelings of like or dislike. A sampling of student comments is listed below:

One practice that supported me when taking this course that I would recommend to other students would be utilizing the knowledge that other classmates provide. I recommend finding a friend to work with because working with a partner or group is a great way to learn. By asking each other questions it not only makes things less stressful when confused on an assignment, but it also assures completeness and quality in one's work. Now that this course is coming to an end, when I reflect back to where I started, I'm really pleased with the progress I have achieved. I wasn't quite sure what to expect when entering this course, but overall found it very informative and interesting. I was always challenged with each new assignment and because of this it allowed me to learn a lot more than I ever expected. (Student comment)

At the beginning of the year I was not too big in to drawing of any sort. This was my first class ever that required me to any sort of drawing or drafting. I did not do too good on some of the drawings and I slowly started getting better at things. As I looked through the assessment sheet that we received at the beginning of the year, I did not know how to really do anything on there except for reading measurements on a scale. When we started drafting, I was really bad at proportions and making my lines look good... Overall through the first part of class I would say I started out below average in my skills and have at least become average in using my new skills. (Student comment)

My thoughts. A course curriculum can be like a delicious meal with many ingredients contributing to the nutritional value. Changing one element can affect the entire flavor. My recommendation to other colleagues is to thoroughly consider the potential consequences of any procedural change, especially related to student assessment. Keep the palette colorful, tasty and nutritious. Don't be shy to experiment and make sure your students feel comfortable to tell you when you fail. It's wise to keep some canned goods at hand as a back-up. Minds are integral parts of our bodies and need to be fed well to work well.

More work ahead. My participation in this yearlong endeavor started with great trepidation mixed with enthusiasm. I wanted to discover the perfect and ultimate recipe for successful teaching. At this point I am convinced there is no easy or perfect solution—no list of regulations that would allow accomplishment by compliance. The instructor and her students need to fully embrace the desire to actively pursue access without sacrificing the quality of the course outcome. The next steps on this journey will include:

- the integration of peer-reviews to improve testing outcome
- the integration of study material, created by students

About the Author

Monika Herrmann is an assistant professor in the Engineering and Technology department at the University of Wisconsin Stout. She holds professional licenses in Architecture and Interior Architecture in Germany and the USA and has been working in the design field for more than two decades. Research interests include sustainability with an emphasis on building performance and on design strategies to accommodate aging in place and independent living. Her academic focus includes quality management in graphic communication in engineering and architecture. Recently, she became the Program Director for the B.S. in Engineering Technology program.

References

Albrecht, D., & Billington, J. H. (1997). *The work of Charles and Ray Eames: A legacy of invention.* New York, NY: Harry N. Abrams Inc.

Americans With Disabilities Act of 1990, Pub. L. No. 101-336, §§ Title 42, Chapter 126, Sec. 12101—12102, 104 Stat. 328 (1990).

Center for Universal Design. (2008). *About UD: Universal design principles.* Raleigh, NC: Carolina State University. Retrieved from http://www.ncsu.edu/ncsu/design/cud/about_ud/udprinciples.htm

Eames, C., quotes. (n.d.). Retrieved October 24, 2017, from https://www.brainyquote.com/quotes/quotes/c/charleseam400733.html

No Child Left Behind (NCLB) Act of 2001, Pub. L. No. 107-110, § Sec.1, Stat. 1425 (2002).

Office of Charles & Ray Eames. (1977). *Powers of ten* [video file]. Retrieved from https://www.youtube.com/watch?v=PbgSVh-gWVc

Ravitch, D. (2010). *The death and life of the great American school system.* New York, NY: Basic Books.

U.S. Environmental Protection Agency. (2009). *Buildings and their impact on the environment: A statistical summary* [PDF file]. Retrieved from http://www.epa.gov/greenbuilding/pubs/gbstats.pdf

10. Providing Academic Choices While Fostering Rigor in Cross-Disciplinary Courses

Glendali Rodriguez, Architect NCARB

Spoon-feeding Students or Improving Learning with UDL?

For architects, "good" design is arguably subjective, yet the amount of research performed for most design proposals involves close examination of a myriad of objective factors including client needs, financial limitations, legislation and context. Collaborative dialogue among stakeholders (owner, builder, designer, inspectors, financial consultants, community, etc.) is critical for a project's success.

During my first three years as a university professor, teaching primarily freshman and sophomore level courses, I received teaching awards and positive recognition amongst peers. While very gratifying, I realized as a member of the 2011-2012 Universal Design for Learning (UDL) project that there was more to learn about creating educational environments that effectively meet the learning needs of the broadest range of students. As part of our preparatory assignment, we read *Universal Design in Higher Education: From Principles to Practice* by Burgstahler and Cory (2008) and engaged in group discussions that challenged our personal definitions regarding good teaching practices. It was agreed that good teaching fostered a healthy learning environment and fueled critical thinking. However, my framework as an instructor was very much in alignment with points provided in the 2004 Minnesota Association for Developmental Education [MNADE] (2011) brochure regarding the academic environment:

- *Teachers assume students have background knowledge and skills.*
- *Teachers expect students to generate questions.*
- *Students are responsible for all material whether or not it is presented in class.*
- *Students must have systems of organization for assignments, notes, handouts.*

As a member of the UDL cohort, I shared that Universal design (UD), as a concept, is well-known in the construction industry. Coined in the United States in 1972, universal design within the built environment is "the design of our environment to be usable by all people, to the greatest extent possible, without the need for adaptations or specialized design" (RL Mace Universal Design Institute, 2013, n.p.). Although comfortable with this particular application of UD, I was new to the scholarship of teaching and learning (SoTL) and decided to formally study student learning in hopes of reaching a broader array of learning styles and enhancing my own continuous professional improvement.

Analysis

As I transitioned from college student to professional designer and licensed architect, and eventually to university associate professor, I realized that I personally preferred service-learning design experiences over theoretical academic design exercises in the classroom. According to the National Service-Learning Clearinghouse (2013), service-learning is a teaching and learning strategy that integrates meaningful community service with instruction and reflection to enrich the learning experience, teach civic responsibility, and strengthen communities. Class projects that had "real clients"—community outreach projects—were effective in providing purpose and objectivity to design problems. Furthermore, a "real client" project gave credibility to constructive feedback provided by both the client and instructor. Currently serving as the Associate Vice Chancellor of Academic and Student Affairs at the University of Wisconsin- Stout, I continue to support the inclusion of service-learning within many of our campus programs because of its inherent value.

As an educator, my instructional style for undergraduate students enrolled in my courses included providing prioritized "real client" investigations in an effort to help them better prepare as future building industry professionals. The students represented very diverse majors including Interior Design, Construction Management, Technology Education, Engineering Technology with Facilities concentration, and more. Within each 15-week term, I structured my courses so that the first half focused on architectural foundation principles, while students during the second half applied their learning to solving "real-world" design issues for a non-profit organization. For each class assignment, I endeavored to make it clear yet rigorous, with the intended result being to foster a quality final product. An essential tool that I presented to all freshman and sophomore students was the MNADE handout (http://docs.wixstatic.com/ugd/f1372d_403d8c9d12364ad28200b2ae38dfd3b5.pdf.) In an effort to promote college success, I began each term emphasizing that open communication between student and instructor was essential for a positive communication experience.

In the spring of 2012, I had the opportunity to co-teach a new course and as I created the course materials, I intentionally integrated the Universal Design for Learning principles that I learned from my UDL cohort experience. The course, "The Built Environment," is a 100-level general education course delivered in a traditional classroom setting. The course is an interdisciplinary study of the built environment, including physical resources and the evolution of human behaviors which inform its design. The course topics include construction and its relationship to resources, materials, and the culture in which it takes place. The student population can be a student in any major, and there are no pre-requisites to the course.

Upon completion of the course, students are able to describe the relationship between examined built structures and the resources/technology available to the society that produced them; describe the relationship between certain built structures and the needs of the society, which produced them; identify contemporary advances regarding built environment regulations; identify ethical issues related to the consumption of resources in the built environment; and identify practices that encourage individual, professional, and civic responsibility regarding resource consumption in the built environment.

UDL's focus on accessibility of information, student freedom of expression, and choice of engagement, initially seemed to contradict students' innate responsibility to invest in the discovery of information and the understanding of structured professional norms. Regarding accessibility: if information is "handed" to the student, will the student not learn research skills? Regarding freedom of expression: if allowances are made on the format of deliverables, will the student not learn industry-respected presentation formats? Was UDL fostering "spoon-feeding"? As educators, we prepare students for a career in the real world and the accommodations championed within UDL principles could be foreign to a number of industry sectors, so is the use of UDL strategies a disservice to our students? By adhering to the UDL principles, was I going to make it too easy to succeed in my courses and underprepare the students? I found resolution to these concerns within the contents of chapter 6 in *Universal Design of Instruction: Reflections of Students* (Burgstahler & Cory, 2008).

Previous Design Approach	UDL Design Approach* Students were provided:	Student Outcomes
For each topic, content is delivered in a single way that is determined by the instructor (e.g. readings, lectures, podcasts). Supportive learning tools and technologies are pre-selected by the instructor and the same for every student (unless they are getting special ADA accommodations).	Multiple Means of Represented Content • Options for Perception (visual, audio, "hands-on") • Options for Comprehension of Content ("novice" to "expert") • Options for Comprehension of Course Expectations (e.g. checklists, video email instructions, student examples, etc.)	Multiple course modes were used to support diverse learning styles, interactive dialogue, group work and documentation of reflective thinking. Rubrics and interactive feedback were used to gauge comprehension.

All students complete the same assignments in the same way to meet the course objectives.	Multiple Means of Action and Expression • Options for Expressive Skills and Fluency (choices for major assignments) • Options for Executive Functions (tools for organizing and prioritizing work such as checklists, overviews, calendars, and planning options)	Expressed strong satisfaction with being allowed to choose research topics and format submission options. Students actively used Content Management System (CMS/D2L) tools to support their learning and to assist in monitoring self-progress.
Students primarily responsible for their own motivation to invest in the course.	Multiple Means of Engagement • Options for Recruiting Interest (pre-survey and multiple surveys throughout course to engage student investment in the course) • Options for Sustaining Effort and Persistence (interactive checklists show % of completed work) • Options for Self-Regulation (modules semi-flexible with hard end-deadlines but opportunities to structure work within those deadlines, timely instructor feedback, options to re-do some assignments, multiple quiz attempts, examples of student work)	Demonstrated growth in critical-thinking skills through a variety of reflective activities. Incorporated instructor and peer feedback along with rubrics to enhance learning. Perceived the ability to choose research topics and presentation modes as unique to former course experiences. Expressed satisfaction with co-teacher model and with the inclusion of industry service learning opportunities.

* Middle column adapted from Center for Applied Science Technology (CAST) (2011). *Universal Design for Learning Guidelines version 2.0*. Wakefield, MA, Author.

Design and Development

For the Built Environment course, I decided to dive in and focus on all three key UDL pedagogical approaches, according to Rose and Meyer (2002):

- Multiple Means of Representation: To represent information in multiple formats and media.
- Multiple Means of Action and Expression: To provide multiple pathways for students' action and expression.

- Multiple Means of Engagement: To provide multiple ways to engage students' interest and motivation.

After reviewing Hitchcock, Meyer, Rose and Jackson (2002), I created a checklist which I used as I prepared each UDL-inspired module for the course (Appendix A). It included a reflection on how the material was presented, the student assignments created and grading rubrics. The checklist was made available to all members of the cohort.

UDL Principles:	Guidelines used to provide options for students:	How guidelines were implemented:
Multiple Means of Representation	Comprehension	Described course content verbally and posted all materials and assignments online. Offered multiple opportunities for assignment feedback, from instructor and/or peers, prior to final submission. Course format supported diverse learning styles, interactive dialogue, group work and documentation of reflective thinking.
	Language, expression & symbols	Taught architectural language and industry codes through course and online formats. Provided course content in a variety of methods: online readings, Power Point slides, guest presentations, YouTube videos, and instructor lectures.
	Perception	Posted course lectures notes, assignments and presentations on D2L.
Multiple Means of Action and Expression	Executive functions	Provided D2L access to assist students in completing course requirements and self-monitoring their progress.
	Expressive skills and fluency	Developed skills through use of technology, interactive dialogue, research methods, project presentation, etc. Students **chose** research topics and ways of demonstrating course knowledge.
	Physical action	Strengthened reflective critical thinking skills through student-research assignments, in-class dialogue, online discussion boards, and team projects.

Multiple Means of Engagement	Self-regulation	Provided detailed grading rubrics suggesting areas of improvement; enabled students to monitor self-progress. Received instructor and peer-based feedback throughout semester. Responded to pre and post surveys and an end-of-term reflection question.
	Sustaining effort and persistence	Provided choices on several assignments, without compromising the ultimate learning objective(s). Provided individual and collaborative assignments to foster mastery of course content.
	Recruiting interest	Used variety of methods including service learning to teach relevant industry content.

To address Multiple Means of Representation, course lecture notes and presentations were posted on the Learning Management System (LMS) with online links to all references. Assignment descriptions and deadlines were explained verbally in-class, as well as posted on the LMS (The LMS used was Learn@UW-Stout, often referred to as D2L). Detailed grading rubrics were provided for each assignment explaining how assignment points were earned and suggested areas of improvement. Multiple opportunities for assignment feedback, from the instructor and/or peers, prior to final submittals were provided. Outside-of-class office hours were held weekly to meet with students, including flexibility of date/time that could be arranged with instructor. Course content was delivered through a combination of online readings, Power Point slides, guest presentations, YouTube videos, and instructor lectures. Course format included highly prioritized engagement through in-class dialogue, online discussion boards, and reflection exercises demanding critical-thinking. The course promoted collaborative group learning through team assignments. In alignment with service-learning, campus buildings and local built environment professionals were woven into the curriculum through site visits, case studies, and guest presentations.

To address Multiple Means of Action and Expression as well as Multiple Means of Engagement, the UDL concept of "choice" was intentionally woven into the course with most student assignments allowing for either choice of topic to be researched and/or the format of the submittal. I repeatedly examined the course learning outcomes and module learning outcomes to create choices on several assignments, without compromising the ultimate learning objective(s). Critical to this process, was to simultaneously create a single grading rubric for each assignment, regardless of the student's chosen submittal format, so that students would not perceive a difference in how they were being assessed. Rubrics were posted at the time the assignments were given, emphasizing clarity of expectation. The timeliness of the rubric fostered grade clarity and permitted time for questions in advance of the assignment due date. Appendices B-D provide examples of assignments and their respective rubrics. Application of these UDL principles and guidelines in my courses allowed me to become more flexible in the ways the information was presented, how students could engage, and how they could demonstrate their acquired knowledge and skills, while maintaining consistent high achievement expectations for all of them. To build their understanding of concepts associated with Universal Design for Learning, students were also provided online UDL links and asked to research its importance, as a course assignment.

Evaluation: Methods of Assessment

To gather evidence about the effectiveness of the targeted UDL principles and guidelines, students were provided multiple formative assessment opportunities throughout the semester including in-class participatory dialogue activities, online discussion boards, reflection exercises, and a final project. Customized rubrics were created to evaluate the reflective exercises and final project. At the end of the semester, pre- and post-course surveys collected student feedback regarding their perceived access to learning in The Built Environment, compared to other courses at the University. In addition, an end-of-term open-ended reflection questionnaire was conducted online that listed all of the UDL strategies used in the course and asked for the students' feedback on each one.

End-of Term open-ended reflection questionnaire. Universal Design for Learning is the design of a course to promote appropriate learning experiences without undermining the challenge of the learning. In the Built Environment, I (the instructor) attempted to foster UDL by:

- Posting course lectures and links to resources on D2L.
- Encouraging a dialogue-format to the course content presented (CMS/D2L discussions or in-class discussions).
- Promoting collaborative group learning assignments (team research activities and presentations)
- Providing grading rubrics showing how points were earned (score sheet based on the assignment descriptions).
- Allowing choice of material to be researched and presentation format (final project and in-class activities).
- Encouraging critical-thinking about the topics presented.

After reviewing the list above, students were asked to share one or two specific examples of course activities that best promoted their access to learning. In other words, which of these instruction methods were most successful for their learning in this course? They were also encouraged to provide one or two specific examples of activities that the particular instructor used to create an environment that promoted their learning. They were thanked for their honest reflections.

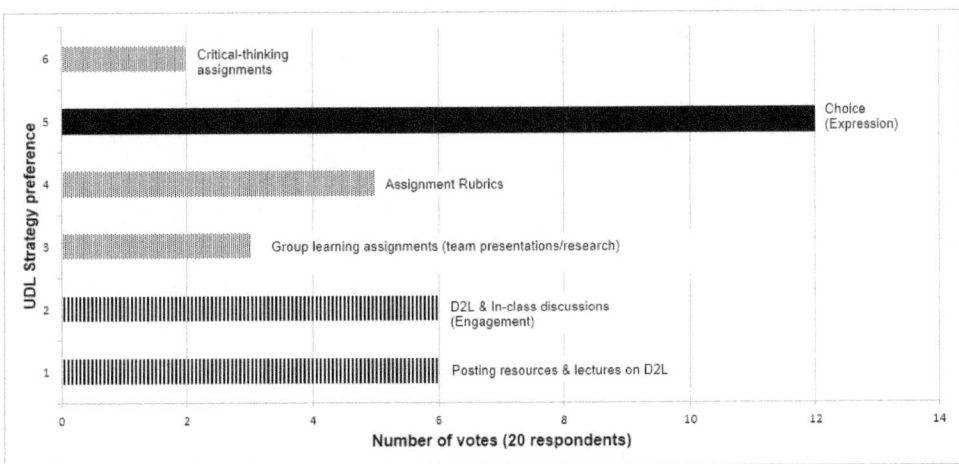

Figure 1. End of term open-ended reflection questionaire results.

Twenty students completed the questionnaire, out of an enrollment of 25. Figure 1 summarizes the student responses. The two-credit course met at 8:00 a.m., twice a week, for 8 weeks. Nine majors were represented: Business Management, Construction, Engineering Technology, Industrial Design, Interior Design, Packaging, Pre-Dietetics, Property Management and Technical Communication. There were eight females and seventeen male students in the class; six freshmen, six sophomores, seven juniors, and six seniors. The responses provided to open-ended questions regarding their learning were detailed and the expanded responses were evaluated using thematic analysis. As a reference, when reading through the responses, "they or instructors" refer to the two faculty who co-taught the course.

Thematic Analysis of Open-ended Question #1
Survey themes, response rate & examples of student reflections:
Question 1: **After reviewing the list above, please share one or two specific examples of course activities that best promoted your access to learning and why. In other words, which of these instruction methods were most successful for your learning in this course?**
Choice of personally interesting course topics (12 responses)
One example of this is that they always allowed a wide variety of topics to choose from when giving projects. They also usually gave us free range on the method we wanted to use for them as well.
I think that the biggest teaching methods that helped my learning were allowing students to choose the topic and style of the final project and the promotion of group activities. I think allowing us to choose our final project was helpful because it gave us the opportunity to work on something that we are actually interested in and in a way that we know works for us. We weren't forced to do something that made us uncomfortable or talk about something that we didn't find any interest in.
Allowing choice on material to be researched and presentation format for the final has been a very great experience for me. Currently I am working on a paper for the final project and I have never been so personally invested in a research project. Because I picked the topic I actually find the project fascinating as I am learning about the massive power that can be harnessed from oceans and waterways.
Allowing choice on material to be researched and presentation format; the way we went about our projects was on our own terms – not the terms of the teacher. It was incredibly thoughtful and helpful to have someone allow you to choose your own path based on one's own skill set.
Interactive student & teacher course discussions/active research component (8 responses)
I also enjoyed in-class discussions. It is good to have contact with a group of real human beings who are living and breathing in the same room as you as opposed to a discussion board. Discussion boards are good for posting ideas but in my opinion there is not actually any real discussion that occurs. I find in class discussions to be stimulating and very educational because of the variety of opinions and the direct input from instructors.
I really liked it when we talked about a subject for the first part of the class then the second part was used for mainly researching that subject/ working towards better understanding it.
Encouraging a dialogue-format to the course content presented; this was evident in every class we had; it allowed me to be more focused in at 8 AM.
D2L discussions and in-class discussion helped a lot. It's kind of easier when students are able to communicate with the teacher. If the teacher talks for the whole class, it tends to get boring and leads the student to lose interest.

Organization and access to D2L course materials (PowerPoints & Grading Rubrics) (7 responses)
I enjoyed pretty much all of the methods listed above. Posting the course lectures allowed me to fill in holes that I miss while taking notes in class and the link reinforced what we were learning. The grading rubrics allowed for me to see exactly where I was losing my points which is always nice to know so I can correct those mistakes on future assignments.
The two that I liked best were posting course lectures and links to resources on D2L and providing grading rubrics showing how points were earned. These helped me because I was able to not worry about missing something during class since I knew it would be online and the grading rubrics because I knew what I had done wrong so I wouldn't make that mistake again and I could improve more over time.
Having the lectures on D2L was the most beneficial aspect of UD for me. Instead of trying to take all of the notes in class I can pay more attention to the lecture and just go to D2L to get the notes. I also enjoyed the fact that I could look at a grading rubric to see where I could improve for future assignments.
Team collaboration/group work (4 responses)
Promoting collaborative group assignments: I felt this was a success because it allowed students to gain experience working at a team, as well as getting a chance to know your peers.
There was usually a critical thinking and collaborative group project as well per class period. This was not always the most enjoyable process but overall it was probably beneficial.
I also thought that the promotion of group activities was helpful because it allowed us to interact with other students and to bounce ideas off of each other.
I also liked when we worked in groups to accomplish something. I feel like in a group you get different points of view you wouldn't normally think of.

These student reflections indicated a strong preference and appreciation for being able to select the topics that they could research. I was pleased to see this response since it supported my efforts to include the Multiple Means of Action & Expression guideline (CAST, 2011) within the course. Eight students commented that they valued the interactive classroom discussions and how they contributed to their learning. Additional reflections acknowledged that making course materials available on D2L and collaborative team coursework often enhances learning. Only one student indicated that he or she did not enjoy doing group projects and would have preferred completing a personal project instead.

Thematic Analysis of Open-ended Questions   *Survey themes, response rate & examples of student responses:*
Question 2: Please share one or two specific examples of techniques or activities that the instructors used to create an environment that promoted your learning.
Research, critical thinking & dialogue (9 responses)
The first example is when we learn something new. The instructors will allow us to do some research on our own and then present it into class later on during class time. This is helpful because you really get a grasp on a concept when you research it on your own, and if you have to present information.
They encouraged discussion in class. Every day we would review and then pair up to discuss/research new topics.
Allowing choice material to be researched and presented and encouraging a dialogue-format to the course content presented.
I really liked the activity when we search through the building codes. I am a construction student and learning more about those regulations will help me in the long run. I really wish that assignment would have been longer because I really enjoyed that.

The encouragement of class discussions was helpful because it allowed for a deeper understanding of the material that was covered in the lecture. I also found that having us do weekly assignments on things similar to what we had learned was helpful too because it forced us to actually think about what we were learning in class and we actually had to pay attention in order to get enough knowledge out of it to be able to do the assignments.

As I have mentioned about doing in class discussion almost every day in class has been really great for my learning and my interest in the class. Also, I liked the in class 10 to 15 min research activities we did where we have a short time to research a product or topic and then presented to the class on it. They were interesting in nature.

When teachers involve the students such as asking us questions or having group presentations, it sort of makes me feel more focused because I have my own input to whatever the discussion is about.

I enjoyed that each assignments presentation was a little bit different because doing a paper or a power point for assignment after assignment gets really old. Having a choice of how we wanted to present the final project was also beneficial because we could pick a method that played to our strengths.

Critical thinking was always a part of their teaching process as well.

Benefit of having two instructors (7 responses)

Having two instructors. Going back and forth between two people helped me to stay focused. Usually if you only have one instructor they tend to get monotone, but with two that doesn't happen.

In all my other 8 AM classes I never was able to pay attention because of how dry the information was and how boring the instructors were. This is not the case for these instructors. They are incredibly helpful and give you passion into the field that you are studying.

Having two teachers teaching this course was really interesting. I've never had a class like this before. I think it's really helpful to be able to learn from two different people with two different backgrounds. It was especially helpful because often the lectures were confusing and having another person rephrase what the first was trying to say made it easier to understand.

I liked that there were two teachers, for a couple reasons, one is that if a lot of people had questions we had two teachers going around helping instead of just one. Also it was nice to hear different points of view. I also liked how nice the teachers were. I felt like I could ask them about anything!

The instructors always seemed very approachable if you ever needed to ask questions or anything. They also encouraged class participation and discussion during each class session which benefits the group.

I did not think I would enjoy the fact that two people were teaching this course, however I ended up preferring it. It helped with keeping people's (at least my) attention this early.

I thought that co-teaching was an interesting concept. This gave two different points of view from two different backgrounds. It also allowed for more student/teacher interaction if you had questions. The instructors pointing out the flaws in the classroom itself, and giving examples of why it was not the best environment to learn in, was helpful. It made me consider the environment of the classroom and compare it to other rooms on campus.

Site visitations (3 responses)

Taking us out of the room and over to the MSC instead of just talking about it.

Another thing I enjoyed was us going on the tour of the Memorial Student Center; instead of the professors talking to us about it we were able to see it firsthand.

Another aspect that I enjoyed were the little field trips, such as the trip to MSC. It allowed us to gain a greater understanding of our surroundings in an environment. In addition to learning about the sustainable product and devices that were utilized throughout the building.

Organization and access to D2L course materials (3 responses)

The lectures on D2L directly helped me with studying for the midterm.

One example of a learning technique that helped me would be having the power points posted on D2L. This was probably the main thing that helped me so I had the chance to study whenever I wanted to.

Power points: I felt the use of power points were a strong aspect to the class. It allowed students to have a visual guide to follow as the professors discussed the material. It was also helpful that it can be accessed easily on D2L.

Student reflections suggest they valued the opportunity to research topics and share what they learned with classmates. In some cases, they recognized how studying a topic and dialoguing about it strengthened their learning. It was also gratifying to see that so many appreciated the input from having two instructors. Several of them also acknowledged that the incorporation of site visits to reinforce course concepts and the organization of materials on D2L supported their learning. In addition, similar to the first question, two students appreciated that they were able to work on group projects, while one student specifically mentioned that providing a variety of presentation materials and assignments made the course more dynamic and interesting. Finally, one student acknowledged that every student was given the same chance to succeed and that efforts had been made to try and accommodate all students enrolled in the course. This reflection was especially meaningful for me, since I always strive to create an equitable learning environment; it also exemplified the intent behind UDL that course experiences should be designed for the broadest range of students.

Overarching survey outcomes specific to course. An overarching survey sent to students in every course that was part of this study (Chapter 3) revealed valuable results, some of which were specific to my course, The Built Environment, AEC-191. The questionnaire attempted to compare students' perception of their experiences with Universal Design concepts in past and current courses. The pre-survey went out at the beginning of the semester and asked students questions about "previous courses" they had taken, while a post-survey was sent out at the end of the semester and reframed the questions to ask about the specific course they were completing. The results of the matched-pairs data analysis are summarized below. There was a total of twenty-five students in this class, and sixteen to seventeen of them took the pre-and post- survey. The difference in their responses was measured and tested for statistical and practical significance.

Table
Course Accessibility Compared to Previous Courses

The Built Environment AEC-191						
Questions:	Cohort	Mean	Standard Deviation	N	Mean Difference	Effect Size (d)
Sensory Abilities In previous courses, the instruction was designed in a way so that essential information was communicated effectively to all students regardless of their sensory abilities (vision, hearing, learning attention, ect.).	Pre	3.47	.94	17	.17**	.71
	Post	4.18	1.07			
Practice Assignments and Feedback Past Instructors routinely divide long-term course assignments into smaller parts or offer "practice" exercises and provide constructive feedback that will help students learn more effectively.	Pre	3.00	1.17	17	.59*	.56
	Post	3.59	.94			
Use of Technology Your past teachers intentionally designed the course assignments/projects to allow for the use of technology and other tools that focused students' attention more on learning and less on requiring physical effort to complete them (ex., use of Internet for text editing versus hand-written editing, ect.).	Pre	3.41	1.23	17	.77**	.61
	Post	4.18	1.29			
Environment Promotes Interaction Your past teachers created a learning environment that promoted interaction and communication among students and between students and instructors.	Pre	3.44	1.21	16	.88**	.68
	Post	4.31	1.35			
Welcoming Environment In previous course, your instructors created a welcome class environment by encouraging students to discuss any special learning needs with them.	Pre	3.59	1.18	17	.77	.65
	Post	4.35	1.17			
Individual Learning Needs Met In the past, previous teachers created a classroom environment and course materials that effectively satisfied my individual learning needs.	Pre	3.44	.89	16	.69**	.67
	Post	4.13	1.15			

Note:**statistical significance at the .01 level; *statistical significance at the .05 level.

Although the sample size (N=17) was small, results from six of the pre- and post-survey questions showed an effect size large enough to indicate practical as well as statistical significance. The mean scores for my course compared to previous courses showed improvement, with student responses ranging between "agree" and "strongly agree" for each statement.

Outcomes. Student feedback gathered from multiple assessment tools, provided credibility, support and encouragement to shift from the misperception of "spoon-feeding" content to the benefits of providing multiple methods of representation, choice of how to achieve the learning outcomes, and the benefits of collaboration. The collected student responses justified that the UDL strategies positively affected learning. Additionally, student comments supported the incorporation of local site visits and guest presentations (that "real" factor) and also revealed benefits of a co-teaching learning environment. In the process, UDL provided me with a different, more critical lens at curriculum development and pedagogy, with a goal to improve student learning at varying levels. At first, I was skeptical about going through extra steps to provide choices for the students, since the "real world" may not be so accommodating. My goal was to prepare students for their next professional experience, and I did not want to compromise this. However, through this journey, I learned that students who are passionate about learning (regardless of their style), benefit from choices for engagement and expression because it stimulates their own investment in the content and deliverable.

Reflections for Practice

After spring of 2012, I continued to implement the UDL strategies from The Built Environment in my other technical architectural face-to-face courses. While teaching, I also used screen-capture technology to provide custom video tutorials for various learning activities. The videos were posted to the LMS and additional videos were created/uploaded upon student request. Overall, the student feedback (formally through course evaluations or informally through class exchanges) continued to support the inclusion of UDL techniques. I was concerned that students would stop coming to class if they could figure out how to complete course assignments from the numerous posted LMS resources. However, the accessibility to information on the LMS did not negatively affect class attendance.

By closely examining the learning objectives, several assignments were generated that met the goals without being confined to a singular type of deliverable (i.e., a paper or a test). The diversity of student submittals promoted dialogue and new opportunities for critical thinking amongst the class participants. Students chose much of their deliverables and they were engaged in their self-selected tasks. As the dissemination occurred amongst the students, the student exchange was professional and insightful.

When given choices on a submittal, I did not see a majority of students choose one format over another. This was encouraging because I did not present one easier alternative over another. Instead, students gravitated towards the option that best fitted and in most cases challenged their learning style. Student-instructor communication was critical each week of the term and the rigor of the courses was continuously sustained.

About the Author

Glendali (Glenda-lee) Rodriguez is a full professor and the Associate Vice Chancellor for Academic and Student Affairs at the University of Wisconsin-Stout. Prior to this, she served as the Construction Department Chair. She is a licensed architect in the state of Wisconsin and Spanish bilingual. She received a Master of Architecture degree from the Georgia Institute of Technology in 2002 and a Bachelor of Fine Arts from Yale University in 1996. Ms. Rodriguez has received teaching awards and prioritizes service-learning experiences for her students. She has taught courses related to architectural technology, architectural design, sustainable design, and sustainable management. Local service-learning clients have included the Eagle Bluff Learning Center, Boys and Girls Club of the Greater Chippewa Valley, Dunn County Historical Society, Arbor Place, Bridge to Hope and the Interfaith Food Pantry. She served as an educational consultant to the Louisville Community Design Center, Louisville, Kentucky prior to moving to Wisconsin in 2004.

An advocate of increasing women in the field of science, technology, engineering and mathematics, Ms. Rodriguez also previously served as Program Director for the Science, Technology Engineering Preview Summer (STEPS) program for 12-year-old girls at the University of

Wisconsin-Stout. The hands-on program celebrated its twenty-second year in the summer of 2018. Participants engage in a variety of workshops that give them hands-on experience with high-tech equipment and processes. Most of the activities during the week focus on analyzing, manufacturing and operating an obstacle-avoiding robot.

References

Burgstahler, S., & Cory, R. (2008). *Universal design in higher education: From principles to practice.* Cambridge, MA: Harvard Education Press.

Center for Applied Science Technology [CAST]. (2011). *Universal design for learning guidelines version 2.0.* Retrieved September 18, 2013, from www.cast.org/udl

Hitchcock, C., Meyer, A., Rose, D., & Jackson, R. (2002). Providing new access to the general curriculum: Universal design for learning. *Teaching Exceptional Children, 35,* (2), 8-17.

Minnesota Association for Developmental Education (MNADE). (2011). *College readiness: Understanding the difference between high school and college.* Retrieved from http://www.mnade.org/readiness.html

National Service-Learning Clearinghouse. (2013). *What is service-learning?* Retrieved from https://gsn.nylc.org/clearinghouse

RL Mace Universal Design Institute. (2013). *What is universal design?* Retrieved from http://udinstitute.org/whatisud.php

Rose, D.H., & Meyer, A. (2002) *Teaching every student in the digital age: Universal design for learning.* Alexandria, VA: ASCD. Retrieved from http://www.ascd.org/publications/books/101042/chapters/What-Is-Universal-Design-for- Learning%C2%A2.aspx

Appendix A: Transfusing Universal Design for Learning (UDL) into the Curriculum

Questions for Instructors Considering Implementing UDL

Definitions:

General curriculum: the overall plan for instruction adopted by a school or school system. Its purpose is to guide instructional activities and provide consistency of expectations, content, methods, and outcomes (Hitchcock, Meyer, Rose, & Jackson 2002).

Background:

Hitchcock et al. (2002) identify four main components of the general curriculum: "(1) goals and milestones for instruction, often in the form of a scope and sequence; (2) media and materials to be used by students; (3) specific instructional methods, often described in a teacher's edition; and (4) means of assessment to measure student progress."

Furthermore, they state that in a Universal Design for Learning (UDL) curriculum: "*Goals* provide an appropriate challenge for all students; *Materials* have a flexible format, supporting transformation between media and multiple representations of content to support all students' learning; *Methods* are flexible and diverse enough to provide appropriate learning experiences, challenges, and supports for all students; *Assessment* is sufficiently flexible to provide accurate, ongoing information that helps teachers adjust instruction and maximize learning."

In response to these criteria, the following checklist has been created to help transfuse UDL into the curriculum. The criteria can apply at varying scales (macro/micro) within the curriculum, depending if UDL is being incorporated at the scale of a particular activity (assignment, lecture, etc.) or through an entire course (or module/unit of a course).

UDL - Goals

Review Course/Module/Lecture and/or Assignment Objectives:	[Yes]	[No]	[Can be argued]
1. Is clear language used to state the learning goals/outcomes? *(These are the instructions that the students get; are they clear?)*			
2. Do the learning goals/outcomes allow for multiple means, media, scaffolds, and supports to help students reach the goal without undermining the challenge and the learning? *(Students will create 2-dimensional drawings-not specifying the medium they will use to create them).*			

UDL - Materials

Review the Course/Module/Lecture and/or Assignment Medium:	[Yes]	[No]	[Can be argued]
3. Are materials presented in a flexible format, supporting transformation between media and multiple representations of content to support all students' learning without undermining the challenge and the learning? *(Provide materials in multiple formats such as pdf, close-caption, transcription, video, mp3)*			
4. Can the content be provided once and displayed in a variety of ways without undermining the challenge and the learning? *(Provide materials in digital format that then can be manipulated by the user)*			

UDL - Methods

Review the Course/Module/Lecture and/or Assignment Methods:	[Yes]	[No]	[Can be argued]
5. Are multiple pathways to achieving goals provided without undermining the challenge and the learning? *(Tic-Tac-Toe Exercise)*			
6. Were multiple examples provided to highlight the critical features that differentiate the concept being taught without undermining the challenge and the learning? *(Good-Not So Good- So So-examples shared with students and explained why)*			
7. Were optional tools/scaffolds provided to the students without undermining the challenge and the learning? *(Additional assistive learning tools-word prediction software, etc.)*			
8. Was the learning context adjusted to emphasize collaboration, rather than competition, as in cooperative learning without undermining the challenge and the learning? *(Peer reviews/sharing).*			

UDL - Assessment

Review the Course/Module/Lecture and/or Assignment Assessments:	[Yes]	[No]	[Can be argued]
9. Was the assessment sufficiently flexible to provide accurate, ongoing information that helps adjust instruction and maximize learning without undermining the challenge and the learning? *(Results/feedback of test allows for adjustments)*			
10. Was the assessment tool effective at measuring the skill or knowledge of the student rather than a specific test media without undermining the challenge and the learning? *(Format of test allows for different ways to demonstrate the learned content)*			
11. Was the assessment able to capture the success of the learning outcome without undermining the challenge and the learning? *(Test clearly assesses desired learning outcomes)*			
12. Was evaluation embedded in the materials with which the students were working throughout the class/project/exercise without undermining the challenge and the learning? *(Throughout the term, class exercises correlated or contributed to the assessment technique implemented)*			

Appendix B: AEC191 The Built Environment Assignment 1

Due in D2L dropbox by stated deadline

Reflecting on class discussions today and your own perceptions, take a moment to answer the following questions in a typed written narrative. Assignment will be graded on depth of answers and grammar. Please include your name, date of submittal, and the course and section number at the top left of the document. Make sure to include any citations if applicable.

1. What is your definition of the built environment? (What does it include and what does it not include)
2. How does this relate to your field of study or career interests?
3. Who are the major players of the built environment?
4. What do you see are "hot topics" or pressing concerns in the area of the built environment?

Grading Rubric:

The Built Environment	Name:		Section:	Date:
Assignment:	HW1-Reflection Narrative			
Pts. Possible	Categories Followed assignment criteria:			Pts. Total
5	Clearly defined the built environment			
5	Clearly described its relation to your field of study or career interests			
5	Mentioned the major players of the built environment			
5	Noted pressing concerns in the area of the built environment			
5	Grammar/presentation			
5	Depth of answers & reflection			
5	Name Section	Date Assignment Title	Citations, as applicable	
35				

Appendix C: AEC191 The Built Environment Assignment Session 9

This assignment will be graded on professionalism of the letter, depth of your thoughts on the subject, grammar and spelling. Please utilize professional letter format.

Draft a professional letter addressed to the University of Wisconsin-Stout Sustainability Steering Committee. Be sure to thank them for their presentation on Thursday Feb. 23, 2012. Include a paragraph on what you took away from this presentation, how it correlates to what you are working on here at UW-Stout, and any professional suggestions you may have for additional items they may consider working on. Utilize the discussion board as a tool to recall discussion topics and answers that were presented during the class period.

The contact information for the Sustainability Coordinator to whom your letter shall be addressed, has been provided.

Grading Rubric:

The Built Environment	Name:	Section:	Date:
Assignment:	HW9- Thank you letter to Environmental Sustainability Steering Committee		

Pts. Possible	Categories	Pts. Total
	Followed assignment criteria:	
5	Professional letter format	
5	Paragraph on what they took away from the presentation 2/23/12	
5	How it correlates to what your interests/efforts	
5	Professional suggestions for additional items	
10	Grammar/presentation/ thoroughness of response	
30		

Appendix D: AEC191 The Built Environment
Final Research Project Spring 2012

Individual Assignment Not a Group Submittal

Select a Topic to Research:

1. **Energy Conservation**
   - What is current legislation/requirements for building energy use?
   - What is accomplished through an energy audit?
   - What does the future of power production look like (globally)?

2. **"Green" Policy**
   - Research policy currently under discussion in US Congress
   - Articulate pros/cons regarding the policy
   - What types of government subsidies are included?

3. **Economics of Sustainability**
   - Comparison of green building to nongreen building from an economic perspective

4. **LEED Certification**
   - Research the full process to achieve building certification
   - Costs, timeframe, players
   - Detail regarding the point structure and a certified project

5. **Water Conservation**
   - What is current legislation for water use?
   - What are best management practices (BMPs) for water conservation?
   - What are advances in plumbing fixtures, for water efficiency?

6. **Cradle to Cradle**
   - Compare and contrast two "common" building products
   - Please compile specific information, including how the products address each of the C2C categories, prices of products compared to their competitors, manufacturer details, etc.
   - Start here: http://www.mbdc.com/detail.aspx?linkid=2&sublink=8

7. **LifeCycle Assessment (LCA)**
    - What is the Athena Sustainable Materials Institute?
    - Review the posted life cycle inventory (LCI) reports on a particular material and provide a summary of the findings
    - What is the Athena EcoCalculator? Discuss a case study with proven LCA information.
    - LCI reports: http://www.athenasmi.org/oursoftwaredata/lcadatabases/availablereports/

8. **Transportation Initiatives**
    - Explain "green" initiatives that are under consideration that relate to the transportation industry
    - Explain the legislation driving it
    - How are successes being measured/quantified
    - Start here: http://www.dot.gov/

9. **Other Topics, as approved by instructor**

Submittal Options (Choose 1)
- ☐ Inclass presentation (limited to first 5 requests) @ 20 minutes.
- ☐ Paper minimum of 1500 words (6 pages)
- ☐ Voice over power point presentation 20 minutes
- ☐ Educational Visual display (poster, materials board, etc. confirm with instructor)
- ☐ Video summary 10 minutes
- ☐ Other format can be approved by instructor

Recommended Guidelines:
- Please review the grading rubric
- Professional quality submittals are expected
- Clearly connect the research material back to your field of study
- Analyze and synthesize the research information; do not just repeat it as a summary
- Cite all resources used to find the information if writing a paper or presentation, use MLA or APA format. All images must be cited.

- Use primary credible resources to acquire the information (.org, .gov, actual client contacts, etc.) If you are not sure about a reference, please confirm it with the instructor.
- Clearly state the impact of the topic on the built environment
- Final submittal should be comprehensive (complete, thorough, appropriate in length/detail)

Remaining Course Timeline:

- Thursday March 1 Identify topic to research and submittal format. Begin research.
- Tuesday March 6 *Inclass lab time to work with instructors and course evaluation
- Thursday March 8 Last day of class presentations and UDL course evaluation

*Work on this project will also require outofclass time

Grading Rubric:

The Built Environment   Name: Section: Date:

Assignment: HW10-Final Project

Pts. Possible	Categories	Pts. Total
20	**Followed assignment criteria:** Cited all resources used to find the information Used primary credible resources to acquire the information (.org, .gov, actual client contacts, etc.)	
20	Clearly ties the research to student's field of study	
20	Clearly states the impact of the topic on the built environment	
20	Individual thought and synthesis of the information- not just a summary of the research findings	
20	Final submittal is comprehensive (complete, thorough, appropriate in length/detail)	
25	**Grammar/presentation quality**	
5	Name Date Section Assignment Title	
130		

11 Final Thoughts

Renee Chandler, Ed.D.

Reflections on Our UDL Journey

We began our exploration of Universal Design for Learning with a look backward to Plato's Academy, where only those males who were recommended as academically elite, wealthy, and generally in the right social circle were admitted. Obviously, higher education has become significantly more inclusive since 387 BC, but are we really as inclusive as we think we are? To a large extent, performance and opportunity gaps persist in educational settings. The facts about diversity in postsecondary classrooms can be overwhelming to those of us who are attempting to lead all students through meaningful learning activities.

During our journey, our authors realized that Universal Design for Learning is not "universal" in higher education today; there has been significantly more research on UDL in K-12 settings. We were encouraged, however, to find evidence of a growing interest in developing ways to meet the needs of the increasingly diverse population on our college campuses. As noted in Chapter 1, the Higher Education Opportunity Act (HEOA) of 2008 includes UDL, an indication of its growing importance. Unfortunately, there is limited research on the implementation of UDL in postsecondary settings. Particularly lacking are studies that describe systemic implementation. In addition, we have learned that most college instructors have little preparation in creating inclusive classrooms that effectively address the needs of a diverse range of students (Ouellet, 2004). All of these realizations suggest future avenues for scholarly inquiry.

The need for research-based approaches that meet diverse student needs spurred the authors of this book to dig deeper. We engaged in classroom-level investigations that inspired us to look at our own teaching differently. We grappled with issues of fairness, social justice, and equity as we made decisions about how to design our courses. It has been (and continues to be) a developmental process.

Lessons Learned

For some reading this book, the ideas may be a little overwhelming. The purpose of it was to provide instructors in higher education settings with a foundational understanding of Universal Design for Learning by including applied examples from instructors across a broad range of disciplines. While we do not purport to be experts on the topic of UDL, we do feel that we gained valuable experiences through the implementation of several of the UDL principles within our own teaching practices. Each of us executed a version of UDL that we were comfortable with at the time of our research. All of us had a primary target of improving learning for all students. One might say we utilized a UDL mindset by individualizing our learning experiences as instructors.

Whether you read this book in its entirety or sample content from chapters that resonate with you, our goal was to "plant a UDL seed." We wanted readers to think about the wide range of student needs they face every day and how they might address some of those challenges. Some of you may choose to implement some aspect of choice into your classes by utilizing multiple means of representation, expression, or engagement. Others may focus on instituting technological changes that make content more readily accessible. Another option might be to start with an entirely new course and build it "from the ground up" using UDL principles. Hopefully, reading this book is the beginning of a UDL journey for you.

As we reflect on our experience, one of the outcomes of our work with UDL is that we continue to find more and more ways to make our courses accessible. Just when we start feeling good about one aspect of our course, we discover strategies that we still have not implemented, but really should. The more we learn, the more we realize that we have a long road ahead of us. We use the term "UDL guilt" to describe our condition. We have each had to come to terms with our own version of UDL guilt and find a balance between designing the "perfect" course and maintaining a level of accessibility that is manageable given our busy schedules.

Many of the authors included "pearls of wisdom" in their individual chapters. In summary, we offer the following advice to anyone who is planning to implement UDL into their classes:

- Begin with a clean, well-organized course with strong learning objectives. Trying to infuse the principles of UDL into a course that is disorganized or unclear has the potential of making it worse rather than better. Keep it simple.
- Give yourself permission to start small. Implementing one aspect of UDL or starting with one unit or module rather than the whole course may be a good option. Again, keep it simple.
- Remember that UDL is not just "good teaching," nor is it a teaching strategy that you can simply add to your repertoire. UDL is intentional and is truly about how you ***design*** your course, not just how you teach it. In order to successfully implement UDL, you need to change how you approach teaching and learning.
- Listen to your students. Ask for feedback and then respond accordingly. You do not need to heed every piece of feedback your students provide, but acknowledge their input and make informed decisions about what you are willing (and not willing) to change.
- Collaborate with colleagues. Having a group of instructors who are working toward similar goals provides support and a range of perspectives. You can share ideas, problem-solve together, and celebrate successes as a group.
- Be kind to yourself. Implementing UDL can be a lot of work for the instructor.
- Celebrate progression, not perfection. Do not succumb to UDL guilt. Strive to make your courses a little bit better each semester.

Ongoing Growth & Positive Outcomes

The University of Wisconsin-Stout continues to grow in the area of UDL. Our Nakatani Teaching and Learning Center recently released a series of Educational Training Content modules, one of which focuses on Universal Design for Learning. This module features one or more content authors from this book and offers instructors a basic introduction to UDL through video, text, interactive activities, and links to additional resources.

Additional campus-wide initiatives include both Chancellor- and Provost-initiated UDL goals and projects. Based on input from the Strategic Planning Group at UW-Stout, Chancellor Robert Meyer has charged a committee with moving forward with "training/credentialing for online instructors." Renee Chandler and Renee Howarton are working with this committee and have encouraged the inclusion of UDL as a critical topic for future training. Provost Patrick Guilfoile has identified UDL as a targeted project for the Academic and Student Affairs division at UW-Stout, with a commitment to provide support so that courses increasingly use Universal Design for Learning principles. Support from the top levels of university administration can be a powerful tool in encouraging faculty and staff to engage in more inclusive practices.

Additionally, UW-Stout is conducting a special project related to accessibility. This pilot project involves working with instructors to make their courses more accessible through research and training opportunities. In the first year, this project facilitated numerous presentations, produced tip sheets, created content and video changes to meet compliance measures, and received grant funding for a virtual reality project. Moving forward, a primary goal is to incorporate UDL into our Instructional Design framework.

The authors of this book decided to embark on a UDL journey to address issues of diversity and inclusivity. We did not anticipate the far-reaching impacts our work would have on our students, our colleagues, and the university community. Higher education is far from fully inclusive, but we have made progress. We continue to seek ways to meet the needs of all students in higher education and hope to encourage others to join us.

REFERENCES

Higher Education Opportunity Act of 2008, 20 U.S.C. § 1001 *et seq.*

Ouellet, M. L. (2004). Faculty development and universal instructional design. *Equity & Excellence in Education, 37*(2), 135-144. doi: 10.1080/10665680490453977.

Index

A
"academic diversity", defined, 4, 133
ADDIE Model, xiii, 19, 21-23, 66, 154
American College Health Association, xii
Americans with Disabilities Act of 1990, 202-03
Applied Research Center (ARC), 53, 60, 121
appropriate placement, 9
Assistive Technology Act (ATA) 1998, 10
Attention Deficit Disorder (ADD), 8, 29

B
Bass, Randy, 27
Beloit College *Mindset List*, xi
Boyer, Ernest, 24

C
Canvas (LMS), 65, 180-83, 199
Carnegie Academy for the Scholarship of Teaching and Learning (CASTL), 24-25, 28
Carnegie Foundation for the Advancement of Teaching,
Center for Applied Special Technology (CAST), 4, 10, 12, 58, 75-76, 131, 134-35, 155-56,
176-78, 225
Center for Universal Design, 29, 202
Center for Universal Design in Education (CUDE), 6
"citizen science", 112
Common Core State Standards (CCSS), 13

D
Daniel RR v. State Board of Education, 9
Desire to Learn (D2L) or Learn@Stout, 65, 83, 169, 180, 221-27
diversity (students), xi-xii, 3-4, 31-33, 46, 239
DO-IT (Disabilities, Opportunities, Internetworking, and Technology) 6

E
Edyburn, Dave, 44-62 passim, 68, 182
environmental education, 109-30 passim
Environmental Education Act of 1990, 111

H
Higher Education Opportunity Act (HEOA) of 2008, 12-13, 239
Hutchings, Pat, 26

I
Individuals with Disabilities Education Act (IDEA), 4, 9-11
Institutional Review Board (IRB) protocols, 47

L
Learning Management System (LMS), 80, 175, 180-82, 185, 197, 221, 229; see also Canvas
Least restrictive environment (LRE), 9-10

M
Minnesota Association for Developmental Education (MNADE), 216-17
Morrill Land-Grant Act of 1862, 2
Multiple means of Expression, Engagement, Representation, 5, 31-32, 45, 81, 83, 85, 115-17, 131, 134, 143, 155-57, 176-78, 184, 205, 208-10, 218-21, 225

N
Nakatani Teaching and Learning Center (NTLC), xvii, 41-42, 57, 69, 168, 242
National Center on Universal Design for Learning, 12, 31
National Instructional Materials Accessibility Standard (NIMAS), 11
National Service-Learning Clearinghouse, 216
No Child Left Behind (NCLB) Act of 2001, 203-04

P
paradigm shift, see UDL paradigm shift
Participatory Action Research (PAR), 78
Plato's Academy, 1-2, 239
Positive Behavioral Interventions and Supports (PBIS), 11

R
Rehabilitation Act of 1973 (Section 504), 9
Response to intervention (RTI), 11
RL Mace Universal Design Institute, 216
rubrics, 7, 81, 86, 90, 98, 106, 134, 143, 209, 218-23, 234-35

S
Sacramento City School District v. Holland Scaffolding (1994), 10
Scholarship of Teaching and Learning (SoTL), 19, defined, 24, 64, 216
Scholarship of Teaching and Learning (SoTL) Research Model, 24-27

Scientific and Natural Areas (SNAs), 114-16, 120, 124
service-learning, 111, 216-17, 221, 230

T
2008 UW System Inclusive Excellence Initiative, 42

U
UDL alignment with Scholarship of Teaching and Learning (SoTL), 27-28
UDL "Choice", 7, 23, 46-47, 51, 63, 74, 81, 85-88, 91, 97, 108, 131-143 passim, 155-66, 176, 180, 222-23, 230, 240
UDL Communities of Practice, 19
"UDL guilt", 166, 241
UDL Overarching Survey, 53-57, 91-93, 121-22, 136-38, 227-28
UDL paradigm shift, 62, 76-77, 125, 129
UDL versus good teaching, xiii, 19-21, 44, 49, 125, 241
United Nations Conference on the Human Environment (UNESCO-UNEP), 111
Universal Course Design, 6
Universal Design (UD), xiii, 3-4, 6, defined, 10,
Universal Design for Instruction, 6-8, 45
Universal Design for Learning (UDL), defined, 4, history, 11-13
Universal Design for Learning (classroom teaching definition), 45
Universal Design in Higher Education: From Principles to Practice, 43
Universal Design of Instruction, 6, 218
Universal Instructional Design, 6
Universally Designed Instruction, 6, 35, 77
U.S. Environmental Protection Agency, 202
United States Distance Learning Association (USDLA), 42
UW-Stout Applied Research Center, see Applied Research Center (ARC)
UW-Stout Counseling Services, 59, 68
UW-Stout Disability Services, 58, 68-67
UW-Stout Office of Research and Sponsored Programs, 47
UW-Stout Online, xvii, 42, 60, 69, 168

www.ingramcontent.com/pod-product-compliance
Lightning Source LLC
Chambersburg PA
CBHW082113230426
43671CB00015B/2691